WILLIAM FAULKNER IN HOLLY SPRINGS

WILLIAM FAULKNER IN HOLLY SPRINGS

Sally Wolff

University Press of Mississippi / Jackson

The University Press of Mississippi is the scholarly publishing agency of the Mississippi Institutions of Higher Learning: Alcorn State University, Delta State University, Jackson State University, Mississippi State University, Mississippi University for Women, Mississippi Valley State University, University of Mississippi, and University of Southern Mississippi.

www.upress.state.ms.us

The University Press of Mississippi is a member of the Association of University Presses.

Copyright © 2025 by University Press of Mississippi
All rights reserved
Manufactured in the United States of America

∞

Photo on title page: William Faulkner seated at his typewriter at his home, Rowan Oak, in Oxford, Mississippi. Courtesy of the Cofield Collection, Special Collections, University of Mississippi Libraries.

Library of Congress Cataloging-in-Publication Data

Names: Wolff, Sally, author.
Title: William Faulkner in Holly Springs / Sally Wolff.
Description: Jackson : University Press of Mississippi, 2025. | Includes bibliographical references and index.
Identifiers: LCCN 2024057938 (print) | LCCN 2024057939 (ebook) | ISBN 9781496856890 (hardback) | ISBN 9781496856906 (trade paperback) | ISBN 9781496856913 (epub) | ISBN 9781496856920 (epub) | ISBN 9781496856937 (pdf) | ISBN 9781496856944 (pdf)
Subjects: LCSH: Faulkner, William, 1897–1962
—Homes and haunts—Mississippi—Holly Springs. | Faulkner, William, 1897–1962—Friends and associates. | Faulkner, William, 1897–1962—Sources. | Holly Springs (Miss.)
—Biography. | LCGFT: Biographies.
Classification: LCC PS3511.A86 Z9859 2025 (print) | LCC PS3511.A86 (ebook) | DDC 813/.52 [B]—dc23/eng/20241202
LC record available at https://lccn.loc.gov/2024057938
LC ebook record available at https://lccn.loc.gov/2024057939

British Library Cataloging-in-Publication Data available

*For the late Elaine and Haskell Wolff,
my beloved parents
For Sam Wolff, my dear brother
For William Dillingham, mentor
extraordinaire and true friend*

CONTENTS

Acknowledgments ix

Introduction: "I Talked, He Listened" 3

Chapter One: Signs of William Faulkner in Holly Springs 17

Chapter Two: "The Fragile and Indelible Signature of Her Meditation":
Ludie's Window as a Source for Faulkner's *Intruder in the Dust*
and *Requiem for a Nun* 78

Chapter Three: "People That I Have Known":
William Faulkner, a Family Who Influenced Him,
and Possible Sources for *The Sound and the Fury*. 100

Chapter Four: Faulkner's *Absalom, Absalom!* and McCarroll Place:
Possible Antecedents. 126

Notes 147

Bibliography 169

Index 175

ACKNOWLEDGMENTS

Profound thanks go to my parents, the late Mr. and Mrs. Haskell and Elaine Wolff, and also to my dear brother, Dr. Sam Wolff, for a lifetime of unwavering support and help. Great thanks go to mentor extraordinaire: Dr. William B. Dillingham, Charles Howard Candler Professor of American Literature, Emeritus, Emory University. Gratitude and heartfelt thanks go to colleagues and friends who assisted in various ways with the preparation of this book: Emory and alumni colleagues Dr. Marie Nitschke, Retired, Robert W. Woodruff Library, Emory University; Mr. Eric Nitschke, Retired, Robert W. Woodruff Library, Emory University; Ms. Mary Ellen Templeton, Retired, Robert W. Woodruff Library, Emory University; and Ms. Erin Mooney, Retired, Robert W. Woodruff Library, Emory University; Dr. Virginia Ross Taylor; Dr. Conrad DeBold; Dr. William Gruber, Professor Emeritus of English, Emory University; Dr. Arthur S. Williams, Executive Director Emeritus, Louisiana School for Math, Science, and the Arts; John Daniel and the late Margie Ann Morris; and Howard Bahr, author.

Thanks go also to Mr. Thomas Todd, Attorney at Law; Dr. Thomas McHaney, Kenneth England Professor of Southern Literature Emeritus at Georgia State University in Atlanta; Independent Scholar, the late Isbell Haynes; George Stewart, colleague and photographer; Keith Gore Wiseman, lawyer and photographer; Peter Greenleaf, colleague and friend; George Nikas, photographer; Dr. Phillip Fry, research consultant; the library staff of the Harry Ransom Center at the University of Texas at Austin; and Hadassah Robbins and Ariel Kaminetzky, research assistants. Numerous current and former citizens of Holly Springs also assisted greatly, including Bobby Mitchell, local historian; Chelius Carter, Historic Preservation Consultant; the late David Person; Phillip Knecht, attorney, historian, photographer, and preservationist; Jim Moore, Director, Marshall County Museum; Harvey Payne, Holly Springs alderman; the Reverend Milton Winter; and the staff of the Marshall County Library System. The help and support of these colleagues and friends contributed significantly to the formation of this book.

Special and heartfelt thanks go to my dear, deceased spouse, Dr. Frederick King, Professor Emeritus, Emory University School of Medicine, and Director Emeritus, Emory National Primate Research Center; and to Dr. Edgar Francisco III and his late wife, Anne, for many reflections and countless hours of talking about William Faulkner.

WILLIAM FAULKNER IN HOLLY SPRINGS

INTRODUCTION

"I Talked, He Listened"

Holly Springs, Mississippi, has at least three attributes that render it important for Faulkner studies: proximity and convenience, family and acquaintances, and historical lore. Full consideration of these topics illustrates the how and why of Faulkner's mingling with its townspeople, the atmosphere, place, and history, and their effects on his writing. Some Faulkner enthusiasts have expressed doubts about Holly Springs as a Faulkner source; indeed, some have asserted that he was never, or rarely, there. Considering the information herein, however, that position seems less and less credible. The people and places that Faulkner encountered in Holly Springs are unique and their circumstances remarkable enough to qualify for literary immortality—because he viewed them as such. The streets he walked, the people he observed there and their characteristics and stories, the vintage architecture of the buildings, and accompanying adornments, receive attention in his novels.

William Faulkner in Holly Springs is a follow-up to *Ledgers of History*, the origin study for my investigation of Holly Springs as a literary source. Faulkner frequently went to Holly Springs, saw, listened, collected, and then remembered. The gold ore of history and literature lies with the folklore of the populace of a town—and Faulkner knew at least some of the people of Holly Springs and successfully mined their recollections. Dr. Edgar Wiggin Francisco III (hereafter Francisco III), for one, has attested to as much. According to him, William Faulkner came to town to visit a friend, Edgar's father, on numerous occasions, to sit on his porch, drink beer or moonshine, and listen to tales recounted by Edgar's father. Scholars have seen that this kind of behavior was common for Faulkner. Professor Don Doyle, for example, has noted Faulkner's habit of sitting and listening to others tell stories "while they passed around a fruit jar full of white corn liquor."[1]

Faulkner also apparently read the Leak family plantation journals, which dated back to the 1800s. Those ledgers are known as the *Leak Diary* and were in the possession of Francisco Jr. at his house called McCarroll Place. This house still sits on Van Dorn Avenue, the main road into town. Leisure time, family time, and socialization in which Faulkner engaged in Holly Springs arguably are the circumstances that bred at least some of the stories found in his great novels.

Upon perusing the *Leak Diary* for the first time in 2008, I turned a few pages and saw names: Sam, Moses, and Isaac, the three main characters in *Go Down, Moses*. After two years of scrutinizing the diary and related materials, I asserted in *Ledgers of History* that Faulkner likely drew from them these names and other important characteristics and information for *Go Down, Moses* and other works. To be clear, I did not propose that this diary was his only source; however, the plethora of interconnections found in that antebellum plantation ledger with Faulkner's works seemed—and still seems—unmistakable.[2]

During the research for *Ledgers of History*, I learned that numerous people in Holly Springs had recollections about Faulkner's presence there and their interactions with him. Numerous citizens and former citizens of Holly Springs remembered Faulkner's visits to their town—and those people were more abundant than Faulkner's biographers previously recorded. I undertook a program of interviews with the senior inhabitants of the town, and they provided me with ample evidence of the veracity of the findings published in my earlier book, as well as new information.

Joseph Blotner and other biographers noted Faulkner's occasional visits to Holly Springs; for the most part, however, this topic has not received a sufficiently thorough examination, even though others have seriously explored different areas of Faulkner country. A close look at why Faulkner and his forebears were familiar with this town, what activities engaged them there, and what effects this singular place had on Faulkner and his works has not previously been available—until now. The present book provides new information identifying and highlighting sources for Faulkner's stories and novels and illustrating that his relationship to Holly Springs and neighboring areas was extended, complex, and significant for him personally and for his work.

That a small town called Holly Springs has received insufficient credit for what effects the place derived from William Faulkner—and the even slimmer recognition of the impact of the place on him—is not surprising. Although Faulkner is no longer a living presence in Mississippi, he nonetheless dominates the literary tradition of his hometown, the region, the state—and indeed, the South and far beyond. Although his influence is wide and deep, and discussed in both popular and scholarly tomes, a place not far away from his home affected him to a degree that deserves scrutiny.

Holly Springs was thirty miles from Faulkner's home in Oxford, Mississippi, and a convenient stop for Faulkner and his family. With a bootlegger, plenty of Civil War history, and people whom Faulkner enjoyed observing and with whom he enjoyed talking, Holly Springs ignited Faulkner's imagination. This small town was close enough to be reached easily by Faulkner and the Faulkner family, beginning in the 1800s by horse and wagon, and later by train and car. In fact, Holly Springs was the next stop on the railroad up from Oxford—and his grandfather was prominent in the railroad business in Mississippi.

Therefore, a reasonable assumption is that Faulkner made that trip numerous times and, as a consequence, met and became acquainted with people in Holly Springs. The town was more than a stop on the northbound railway for Faulkner, however, and evidence suggests that this town provided him—and his relatives, too—a place of respite, conviviality, and friendship. That he drove up to the area of Holly Springs becomes clear from an interviewee who said that Faulkner received not a few tickets for speeding and DUI from a local highway patrol officer and once hitched a ride from that same officer to go to the nearby hospital in Byhalia to dry out.

William Faulkner's relatives also spent time in Holly Springs, both before and during his lifetime. These family visits are unsurprising, given the proximity of the town to their home in Oxford. New and old evidence links the Hindman Doxey family with Faulkner, and Doxey Jr. was a first cousin to Edgar Francisco III, who previously described Faulkner's friendship with his (Francisco's) father.[3] Faulkner's brother John married his fiancée, Dolly, in Holly Springs, and Doxey Sr., who also was one of Faulkner's Holly Springs acquaintances, was a witness at the wedding. Sarah Doxey Tate, a native of Holly Springs, said in a recorded, public lecture at the Holly Springs library that James M. (Jimmy) Faulkner told her that when his parents, John and Dolly Faulkner,[4] decided to marry, they went to Holly Springs, and John quickly recruited Hindman Doxey Sr. to attend the wedding, which took place at the Marshall County courthouse in Holly Springs.[5]

Alabama, whom Faulkner affectionately called "Aunt Bama," attended a ball in Holly Springs, and one of her female friends, Miss Gholson, invited her to spend two weeks with her family (see p. 21, figure 1.1, for a photograph of Alabama Falkner). Faulkner's uncle, John Wesley Thompson Falkner Jr. (known as Judge Falkner), was a circuit court judge and went on the circuit to Holly Springs. Other relatives passed through Holly Springs on their way to Memphis or came to town for social occasions. Faulkner's mother, Maud Falkner, came to town to visit her Butler relatives. Also she was a close friend of the wife of Edgar Francisco Sr., and she brought her young son William with her to Holly Springs for visits—during those times Faulkner bonded with Edgar Jr. and later traveled with him to Memphis on double dates or to hear the music of W. C. Handy.[6]

That Faulkner was a keen observer of Holly Springs and its people becomes even more apparent in my interviews with twenty-seven current and former citizens who provide clear and convincing evidence of having met, seen, and interacted with Faulkner, or having heard about his visits to town. According to their testimony, Faulkner carefully listened to the people and their stories; he visited various places around town; met his lover Joan Williams there; picked up his stepdaughter, Cho Cho, from the Mississippi Synodical College; and attended a variety of social events. He was known to dine with Holly Springs friends, and in turn he invited them to his home in Oxford. Carvel Collins noted that Faulkner dated Louise Caffey Smith (who later became Mrs. Leonard Marbury) and that Louise knew Faulkner from college days.[7]

Faulkner also liked to stop by to chat with the chancery clerk at the Holly Springs courthouse, although apparently he didn't talk much, as was his wont. Faulkner was much more attentive to the clerk's stories. When asked what occurred during Faulkner's visits, the clerk gave a telling reply that reveals Faulkner's fascination with the people around him. The clerk said of his encounter with Faulkner: "I talked. He listened."[8]

Faulkner also established a Boy Scout troop in Oxford with the help of a Holly Springs friend, hunted in Holly Springs, played golf there with L. G. Fant Jr.,[9] changed trains en route elsewhere, and lunched at the Depot Café and Mackie's Café in that town. Reportedly, he visited his bootlegger and attended a horse show and a golf tournament.[10]

Joseph Blotner has noted that on frequent occasions, Faulkner would disappear from home for lengthy periods. "At times, his friend Lowry Simmons remembered, no one in Oxford knew where he was. He would simply leave Oxford."[11] Part of his time away was in Holly Springs, although few knew. He was young and free during some of that time, and trips to Holly Springs, Greenville, and other nearby locations where interviewees recall seeing and talking with him may account for some of his unexplained absences.[12]

Given his regular contact with Holly Springs, and given who Faulkner was, how he created fiction, and what inspired him, the residents, people, events, and scenes from this town and the surrounding area inevitably and frequently found their way into his stories and novels. He references specific places in Holly Springs in his fiction, as well as a host of citizens, along with their sometimes-uncommon names that he places directly in his work with minimal alteration; an example is the name Rittelmeyer, which becomes for Faulkner the character Rittenmeyer in *The Wild Palms*.

Faulkner characters also may have had real-life antecedents in Holly Springs. Caddy Compson, the celebrated heroine of *The Sound and the Fury*, held her wedding at home and, as an older woman, cavorted with a German man—and her story parallels the life of the well-known and theatrically inclined Holly Springs matron Perle Strickland. Another example: real-life sisters Amelia and Sallie McCarroll, embattled but unvanquished Holly Springs survivors of the Civil War, may have served as models for fictional Ellen and Rosa Coldfield in *Absalom, Absalom!* One McCarroll sister died, while the other lived to tell her haunting life story—much as does Rosa, the heroine of that novel. Amelia McCarroll also shares some of the most compelling traits—namely, fearlessness and gumption when confronting face-to-face the armed Union soldiers who appear at her doorstep—that Granny Millard exhibits in *The Unvanquished* and "My Grandmother Millard."[13] The window etching of Louisa Baugh Booth—"Ludie"—who spent the Civil War years at McCarroll Place in Holly Springs, is a likely source for the etched windowpanes that Faulkner describes in two of his novels: *Intruder in the Dust* and *Requiem for a Nun*.

Still other links and resonances of people and places from Holly Springs and the surrounding area appear in Faulkner's works. The house depicted in "A Rose for Emily" is a good example. The Neilson house in Oxford has long been considered the model for Faulkner's famous short story. Faulkner's courtship of Louise Caffey Smith and other physical details in the story also support a link to Holly Springs. The Smith House on Salem Avenue in Holly Springs has a haunting aura appropriate for the focus of Faulkner's macabre story, while the rose-colored glass windows in the nearby mansion, Grey Gables, may have inspired the rose motif that plays through Faulkner's story and its title.

Echoes of Holly Springs places and people appear, too, in *The Reivers*, in which Faulkner's depiction of the fictional Parsham Depot shares characteristics with the real Holly Springs Depot, and in *Absalom, Absalom!* where a man escapes capture by hiding in the turret of a mansion, in an act recalled in the "Garden Pilgrimage to Historical Sites," a brochure sponsored by the Holly Springs Garden Club, April 22–26, 1939: "In a raid of the Federal Troops, the Judge a very small man escaped capture by hiding in the capital of one of the massive Corinthian columns of the portico."[14]

Other references to Holly Springs places and events find their way into Faulkner's novels and establish a further connection between novel and town. For example, references allude to Confederate general Earl Van Dorn's raid of General Grant's supply stockpiles in Holly Springs during the Civil War: "General Grant's stores burning in Jefferson" (*Light in August* 56) and "Van Dorn's cavalry raid to destroy Grant's stores in Jefferson" (451).

McCarroll Place sits on Van Dorn Avenue, named for Earl Van Dorn and his famous raid in Holly Springs. Hubert McAlexander points out that the "street leading to the depot, first called Main Street, then Depot or Church Street, was renamed Van Dorn Avenue in the 1920s."[15] References to the raid appear in several of Faulkner's novels, where the texts link real and imagined places and events. Faulkner clearly was familiar with the details of Van Dorn's raid, although he certainly could have heard about it from sources other than Holly Springs citizens. The specificity of some of his allusions, however, clearly suggests that he had Holly Springs in mind.

Van Dorn Avenue runs a few blocks from town directly in front of McCarroll Place, the multigenerational home of the McCarroll/Francisco family, with whom Faulkner apparently spent significant time visiting. In Faulkner's novel the character Hightower initiates what may be an autobiographical reference for Faulkner. Hightower knows that he could look out onto the street from the window, and he imagines the "house that we will someday own and live in"—which may refer to McCarroll Place, home of Faulkner's childhood friend Edgar. Hightower ruminates about his grandfather's participation in what is clearly Van Dorn's raid (the real raid described in the fictional Jefferson). In a remarkable passage, Hightower says:

> I know the very street that they rode into town upon and then out again.... I know exactly how the house that we will someday own and live in upon the street will look ... where we can look out the window and see the street, maybe even the hoofmarks or their shapes in the air ... setting fire to the store depots of a whole carefully planned campaign. (*Light in August* 457)

This vantage point from which to view and imagine Van Dorn's raid may well be an autobiographical moment for Faulkner. He knew the "very street" because he had sat in a chair on the gallery porch at McCarroll Place and looked right out onto that avenue; here in 1862 the Van Dorn raiders came by on their way from the depot to the town square. A highly creative visitor in the 1930s such as Faulkner easily might have looked out of the front window of McCarroll Place at Van Dorn Avenue and imagined the thunderous sound of the troops as they rode down the street, and he might have seen, too, in his mind's eye, the "hoofmarks" their horses made in the dust.

Near enough to seed his imagination, yet sufficiently distant to shield himself from unwanted exposure, Holly Springs was for Faulkner a lifelong source of characters and events. *William Faulkner in Holly Springs* documents these extensive and accruing correspondences. The peculiar alchemy of the

Holly Springs, Mississippi

Figure 0.1 Nettie Fant Thompson's pen and ink drawing of McCarroll Place. Courtesy of the Fant family.

novelist's gift was to people his fiction with images from his culture. He did so because of the importance he assigned to the stories, the history, and the places, which must—in a favorite word—endure.

》 》 》

To view additional images related to the subject of this book, please visit the author's website at https://educationalconsulting.services/Faulkner.

About Holly Springs

The land around Holly Springs in northwestern Mississippi is known as "rolling highlands,"[16] as distinguished from the low-lying Delta region to the west in areas nearer the Mississippi River, which has flooded those lower-lying regions over adjacent counties over thousands of years and produced startlingly black and famously fertile soil. Hill country land, by contrast, is not as rich in many areas, but pleasant rolling hills and lands are suitable for smaller farms and woodlands.

The town of some seven thousand people straddles the Pontotoc Ridge, which is part of "an elevated and extended range of tablelands in the rolling highlands of North Mississippi. It lies forty miles southeast of Memphis,

Tennessee, and twenty-eight miles north of Oxford."[17] The region was home for centuries to the Chickasaw people of the American southeastern woodlands until the Indian Removal Act of 1830, when settlers in large numbers moved in from the Carolinas, Virginia, and elsewhere. The terrain immediately to the west was named by settlers the Chickasaw Bluffs after the native inhabitants. William Randolph of Virginia is credited with the founding of the town in 1835, three years after the Treaty of Pontotoc Creek; the name Holly Springs, legend has it, derives from a number of small, local springs encircled by holly trees. The Chickasaw had known and used the springs; now only a single, small walking trail recalls the many unrecorded visits to those waters and trees.[18]

The town formerly has been called "The Capital of North Mississippi" and "the cotton kingdom's golden city."[19] Holly Springs flourished significantly for a brief period in the 1850s, prior to the Civil War, during which time townspeople built grand homes, and the elite society thrived. This period has its roots in the cotton wealth of the region, where enslaved people labored in the bottomlands near the Mississippi River and beyond, and landowners built fine homes and prosperity and shipped cotton from Memphis to New Orleans and on to the international market. The Civil War brought an end to slavery, and sharecropping became common. Stories and legends of these times—and the successes as well as the travails associated with them—are, as in Faulkner's works, alive in the oral tradition—passed down through generations in Holly Springs.

During the antebellum years, Marshall County was, as described by *The Mississippi Encyclopedia*, "an economic powerhouse" with "considerable agricultural productivity, and a growing number of commercial and industrial workers. In its first census in 1840, Marshall County had a population of 9,266 free people and 8,260 slaves. Its total population of 17,526 ranked third among Mississippi's counties, and it ranked first in the number of free people."[20] The city became "the center of antebellum culture in north Mississippi."[21] Long and Ridge attribute the "prosperity of Holly Springs" to the "antebellum slave and cotton economics [that] led to the 1850s construction of many larger and grander homes."[22]

In our own time, the town has moved into the modern era while maintaining a vibrant historic district, and many townspeople participate in preserving the history around them. Architectural styles preserved in the area include: simple wood-frame or clapboard structures, log cabins and outbuildings, detached kitchens, Greek Revival mansions, and Queen Anne cottages that "range from modest, single-story and raised-basement cottages to grand mansions with monumental porticos with cast-iron Corinthian columns [in] addition [to] Gothic Revival and Italianate residences."[23] Many of the antebellum homes are still standing and have been renovated, are now bed and breakfast locations, or await renovation. Some of the more well-known homes are Grey Gables, Airliewood (formerly known as Coxe Place), Walter Place, Montrose, McCarroll Place, Burton Place (formerly called Fleur de Lys), Smith House, and the Fort-Daniels House (formerly known as Craft House).[24]

In his various trips to Holly Springs, William Faulkner surely noticed that the town imparts to visitors a feeling of stepping into a bygone era. Antebellum, Civil War, and postbellum history are palpably apparent, as is the educational heritage of the town, and the citizenry always has participated enthusiastically in the oral tradition, an active part of their fascinating history. The Holly Springs National Forest and Wall Doxey State Park are also located nearby,[25] and the Robert Altman movie *Cookie's Fortune* was filmed in Holly Springs in the late 1990s.[26] The art gallery of Holly Springs native Kate Freeman Clark, a local artist of considerable import, is in town and displays her prolific art, over "a thousand paintings."[27] The writer Katharine Sherwood Bonner McDowell (1849–1883), author of works including the novel *Like unto Like*, published under the name Sherwood Bonner, was from Holly Springs.[28]

Since 1936 the Holly Springs Garden Club has sponsored an annual spring Pilgrimage, a tour of historic homes during which tourists may enter the old antebellum mansions and cottages and see examples of the architecture and furnishings of yesteryear. Recently, an organization known as Preserve Marshall County and Holly Springs, Inc. began a new program, titled "Behind the Big House." This tour offers a rare and fascinating look at the dwellings and domiciles behind the antebellum mansions—and the formerly enslaved people who inhabited them. Holly Springs citizenry have done a remarkable amount of research to bring forward the names, identities, and stories of the people who lived in these quarters. The stated goals of the "Behind the Big House" program are to move "beyond the 'Big Houses,' or stately historic homes, to explore surviving slave dwellings and the lives of the enslaved communities who lived and worked in them."[29]

> The Behind the Big House program in Holly Springs, Mississippi, interprets the lives of enslaved persons through the structures in which they lived and worked. The program began in 2012 after Chelius Carter and Jenifer Eggleston, antebellum historic property owners, discovered that one of the structures on their property was a former slave dwelling. To them, it was clear that the personal lives and experiences of those enslaved in Holly Springs [were] missing from

the larger narratives of the city's Annual Pilgrimage Tour of Historic Homes and Churches.[30]

The program has received national attention and won numerous local and state awards.

The prominent and pervasive Civil War history of Holly Springs is further apparent around town. *Britannica* notes that "more than 60 skirmishes were fought there, including a raid by Confederate General Earl Van Dorn (December 1862) that destroyed a Union supply depot and delayed the Union drive to Vicksburg."[31] *The Mississippi Encyclopedia* records: "In 1862 Union forces built a large new supply depot there" and that the General Van Dorn raid "destroyed the depot, captured . . . Union soldiers, and temporarily delayed Gen. Ulysses S. Grant's plans to take Vicksburg."[32] Yankee forces burned much of the town and the Courthouse.[33]

Another important feature for Holly Springs during the war was the railroad. Rev. Milton Winter points to cotton shipping as one of the primary goals: "Holly Springs, in the 1850s, gave itself to building a railroad. As the seat of Mississippi's largest cotton-producing area, Holly Springs was immensely prosperous, and faster transportation was greatly desired. . . . A railroad for the planters' benefit was preached as a boon to the region."[34] In the mid-1850s, Holly Springs was connected to "Grand Junction, Tennessee, by the advancing Mississippi Central Railroad. . . . Toward the end of the century, the Kansas City, Memphis and Birmingham Railroad was constructed to intersect with this line."[35]

Townspeople eagerly regale listeners with the fascinating stories and legends of the Civil War. For example, a docent at Walter Place said that Mrs. Ulysses S. Grant resided at Walter Place while her husband was in the area. Townspeople and Yankees behaved hospitably. In Faulkner's *The Unvanquished*, in the midst of the horrors and ravages of war, several instances occur in which someone behaves in a similarly hospitable manner. According to the legend, Mrs. Grant invited the ladies of the town for tea. They attended her gracious event, and all went well. Then the town ladies decided that the courteous and hospitable next step would be to invite Mrs. Grant to tea, which they did. With the ravages of war bearing down sharply on the town, however, and their supplies severely limited, the townswomen had no tea. They knew how to make tea from sassafras root, however, and so they served Mrs. Grant sassafras tea, and apparently all enjoyed a hospitable occasion.[36] Francisco III said that his great-grandmother told this story with the added detail that the women cut the sassafras out of their yards for the tea.[37] Perhaps the hospitality exhibited by individuals during certain moments of the Civil War, as depicted by Faulkner in *The Unvanquished*, had its root in Holly Springs.

The courthouse is an old and imposing presence on Courthouse Square, in the center of town. The structure has been described as: "the three-story Italianate courthouse which was built in 1870–1872 to replace the original courthouse, burned by Union troops during the Civil War. Regular rows of late-nineteenth-century brick and cast-iron storefronts frame the square. The Marshall County Courthouse, together with the surrounding fifty-nine commercial and institutional buildings, was entered in the National Register of Historic Places in 1980."[38]

The historic old Hill Crest Cemetery, established in the 1830s, is another compelling and unique site. Hill Crest is large and centrally located, with numerous outsized and fascinating monuments. Phillip Knecht noted, "Hill Crest Cemetery is one of [the] great gems of Holly Springs and one of the finest historic cemeteries in north Mississippi":

> Hill Crest Cemetery contains the bodies of many unknown soldiers who died in the Civil War, along with the remains of six Confederate generals. In addition, there are two Confederate monuments in the Cemetery: the Monument to the Confederate Dead, erected in 1874–1876 (the central shaft was not erected until 1901), and a newer monument to the southeast, erected by the Sons of the Confederacy in 1890.
>
> The cemetery also contains a mass burial ground for victims of the Yellow Fever Epidemic of 1878, though this mass grave is currently unmarked. In addition, many of the more notable victims of the Fever are buried in their family plots. There are also two large monuments dedicated to certain victims of the Fever: the Mississippi Press Association monument, dedicated to . . . W. J. L. Holland, Kinloch Falconer and other reporters who died in the Fever, and the monument to Father Oberti and the Catholic nuns who died administering to the sick and dying during the epidemic.[39]

For further information about the yellow fever epidemic that gripped Holly Springs, please see appendix 4-B, "A Note on the Yellow Fever Epidemic of 1878 in Mississippi," on p. 144.

Some of the notable figures buried in the Hill Crest Cemetery include the town "founding fathers, war heroes, local, state and federal politicians and other figures."[40] Numerous generals of the Confederate States Army are buried there, including: "Samuel Benton, Winfield S. Featherston, Daniel Govan, Edward Walthall, and Absolom M. West. Other notable burials include Wall Doxey, Benjamin D. Nabers, Hiram Rhodes Revels, and James F. Trotter. Also buried there are painter Kate Freeman Clark, the wife and son of Alamo defender Micajah Autry, and architect Spires Boling."[41] Confederate soldiers are buried in close proximity to four northern soldiers.

The African American presence in Holly Springs is and has been an important component of the historical, social, educational, and spiritual life of the community. *The Mississippi Encyclopedia* notes, "Postbellum Marshall County became an exciting center of African American educational and religious activity. In 1866 a combination of former slaves and the Freedman's Aid Society of the Methodist Episcopal Church formed Shaw School, which later became Shaw University and then Rust University."[42]

The history of Rust College seems a likely source for Faulkner's abolitionist Burden family in *Light in August*. In the novel the Burdens came from the North to found a school for African Americans. Faulkner's Burdens and their goals match the factual history of the founding of this Holly Springs school: the Freedmen's Aid Society of the Northern Methodist Episcopal Church, according to Long and Ridge, "offered higher education to African Americans."[43] Rust College adds regarding its founding:

> Its founders were missionaries from the North who opened a school in Asbury Methodist Episcopal Church, accepting adults of all ages, as well as children, for instruction in elementary subjects. A year later the first building on the present campus was erected.
>
> In 1870, the school was chartered as Shaw University, honoring the Reverend S. O. Shaw, who made a gift of $10,000 to the new institution. In 1892, the name was changed to Rust University to avoid confusion with another Shaw University. The name was a tribute to Richard S. Rust of Cincinnati, Ohio, Secretary of the Freedman's Aid Society. In 1915, the title was changed to . . . Rust College.[44]

Natalie Doxey founded the famous "Rust College A Cappella Choir, which is still singing today."[45] In addition, other schools that focused on African Americans opened, including the Mississippi State Normal School and the Mississippi Industrial College in Holly Springs.[46]

Noted author and civil rights activist Ida B. Wells (1862–1931) also was a native of Holly Springs. The Ida B. Wells Museum in Holly Springs commemorates her life, accomplishments, and contributions. She "attended Shaw College" in Holly Springs, and as *The Mississippi Encyclopedia* notes, she became a "civil rights activist and a leading opponent of lynching. Wells published a pamphlet, *Southern Horrors*, and a memoir, *Crusade for Justice*."[47]

Marshall County since antebellum days has led in education in other ways as well, especially as home to the Chalmers Institute (later the University of Holly Springs), the Holly Springs Female Collegiate Institute, Franklin Female College,[48] and North Mississippi Presbyterian College (later renamed the Mississippi Synodical College).[49] Long and Ridge add the history of the Mississippi Synodical College, where Faulkner's stepdaughter attended school: "Founded as Fenelon Hall at the close of the Civil War, this school for women became Maury Institute by the 1880s."[50] Later the name changed to Mississippi Synodical College. (See p. 57 for more about the female institutes of Mississippi.) With so many educational choices available, folks came "from near and far" to attend these schools.[51]

For William Faulkner, Holly Springs represented a place away from but in reasonable proximity to his hometown of Oxford. He could travel a short distance and reach Holly Springs to take in the deep and abiding Civil War history, the inclination of the townspeople to preserve their history, enlivening oral tradition, and collective memory of a tragic regional epidemic with particularly negative consequences for the home area. Surely these people and their place nourished and intensified Faulkner's active, colorful, literary imagination.

Chapter One

SIGNS OF WILLIAM FAULKNER IN HOLLY SPRINGS

Faulkner's Presence in Holly Springs

William Faulkner's connection with the town of Holly Springs, Mississippi, and that of his family, was long and significant. Joseph Blotner and other biographers place Faulkner there on numerous occasions. Members of his family visited Holly Springs frequently and often passed through the town en route to other places.[1] Faulkner's brother John had married his fiancée, Dolly, in Holly Springs.[2] Faulkner's presence there is important because he took what he heard, saw, and experienced in that town and wove threads of that material into his fiction. Understanding the correspondences illuminates his fiction and its meaning ever more clearly.

Twenty-seven citizen or former-citizen interviewees from Holly Springs had clear and strong memories either of seeing William Faulkner or hearing about his presence in Holly Springs. He had dinner with friends, started a Boy Scout troop in Oxford with the help of a Holly Springs friend, hunted, changed trains, lunched at Mackie's Café and the Depot Café, visited his bootlegger, and attended a horse show and a golf tournament.[3] Biographers also note that Faulkner played football in Holly Springs.[4] Later he picked up his stepdaughter Cho Cho after classes at the Mississippi Synodical College in Holly Springs.[5] He stopped in to chat with the chancery clerk at the courthouse, received tickets for speeding and DUI from the local highway patrol officer, and had a ride from the same patrol officer to the hospital in nearby Byhalia to dry out.

Dr. Edgar Wiggin Francisco III, who grew up in Holly Springs, presented a detailed account of Faulkner's visiting the McCarroll/Francisco home in Holly Springs, in *Ledgers of History: William Faulkner, an Almost Forgotten Friendship, and an Antebellum Plantation Diary* (LSU Press, 2010). According to Francisco III, his father, Edgar Francisco Jr., visited with Faulkner on numerous occasions at McCarroll Place in Holly Springs, where Faulkner read the *Diary of Francis Terry Leak*, a five-volume set of plantation ledgers of a North Carolinian who moved to Mississippi in the early 1800s and established a plantation.[6] Faulkner also likely read newly recovered personal family letters and papers at McCarroll Place that date back as far as the 1820s.[7] Francisco III did not realize that Faulkner drew from this *Diary* for some of his works, but *Ledgers of History* traces the similarities between the *Leak Diary* and Faulkner's works and suggests that indeed he drew from this text. The book attracted significant approval from numerous senior Faulkner scholars and also criticism from a few. Subsequent interviews support and reinforce some of Francisco's statements. Since the appearance of that book, no evidence has come to light that seriously challenges the basic premises Dr. Francisco made. (See appendix 1-A on p. 64 for Dr. Francisco's rebuttals to some of these challenges.)

Holly Springs townspeople have numerous recollections of Faulkner's presence in town. Jorja Lynn, longtime resident of Holly Springs and prior owner of the antebellum Holly Springs mansion known as Walter Place, says that according to the Walter family, William and Estelle Faulkner dined at the home in the 1930s.

> Well, the house I own[ed] is called the Walter Place. It's on the National Register. It's where General Grant headquartered here with his wife, and his wife talked about living here during the Civil War with her son, Jessie, and her slave, Julia. It's in her book, her memoir. And when I was growing up, and I was fifteen, I would come over to this house and serve at Pilgrimage, and when I bought the house in 1983, Dave Cochran, who was born and raised here in Holly Springs, came over and told me how William Faulkner and his wife, Estelle, would come up here and have dinner because she—when she was Estelle Oldham—was good friends with Anne Walter Fearn, and Anne was born and raised here in Holly Springs, and she had gone to China as a doctor to Shanghai, and she and Estelle were natural friends because they were both expatriates from north Mississippi. And so when she went back to Oxford and married William Faulkner, Anne would invite them to come up here for dinner, and from my

understanding, to use the swimming pool that was in the back. That was a big deal in the thirties.[8]

Ms. Lynn said that one of the Faulkners' dinners at Walter Place:

> probably took place here in 1938, the year Holly Springs first had its first Pilgrimage. It was a really big deal here and the owner of my house, Irene Walter Johnson was born here and . . . restored this house in 1936, and one reason was so her sister Dr. Anne Walter Fearn would have a place to live since her husband and daughter had died in Shanghai, and she had to leave her huge hospital there when the Chinese closed China. Her best friend there was Estelle Oldham. They were both from Mississippi over there in a foreign land and their friendship was a natural. Anne wrote a book here after she returned entitled *My Days of Strength* about her experiences there including the fact that she delivered 6017 babies. (That was in Ripley's *Believe it or Not*.)
>
> Vadah Cochran told me that the Faulkners were frequent visitors, particularly since it was on their way to Memphis, and there was a swimming pool here that they used. He even chastised me when I sold the 1930s dining table and chairs that were in the dining room, saying that it was where Faulkner used to sit and eat! Faulkner was not so famous then and he had married a divorced woman, so it probably was not very important to anyone at the time.[9]

Rev. Milton Winter also describes an occasion in which Faulkner attended a party at Walter Place: "Memorable parties were held, in which Pullman cars full of guests descended upon Holly Springs from St. Louis. During one such gathering, William Faulkner, of Oxford, was seated by a St. Louis socialite. The woman blurted out, 'Tell me, Mr. Faulkner, do you write?'"[10] Howard Hawks recounts a similar story, but in his version, when he asked Faulkner to name his favorite authors, Faulkner's answer illustrates his agility with the quick reply: "'Thomas Mann, Willa Cather, John Dos Passos, Ernest Hemingway, and myself.' And [Clark] Gable looked kinda funny and said, 'Do you write, Mr. Faulkner?' Faulkner says, 'Yes, what do you do, Mr. Gable?'"[11]

Gwen Wyatt, a longtime Holly Springs resident, recalls that her father knew Faulkner and helped Faulkner set up a Boy Scout troop in Oxford: "Our father knew William Faulkner. He was the health officer (coroner) during the time when William Faulkner died. William Faulkner wanted to have a troop of Boy Scouts, and my father helped him make that a reality. They made a raft and floated in it."[12]

Faulkner was characteristically quiet, and he kept a low profile on his visits to Holly Springs. Nonetheless, word of the Faulkner/Francisco friendship leaked out into the community, even though Mrs. Edgar Francisco Jr. (Ruth), a devout churchgoer and daughter of a prominent Presbyterian minister in Holly Springs, believed she had kept secret Faulkner's visits to their home, McCarroll Place, for much of her life because she did not like him. She considered Faulkner sinful and therefore an unfit friend for her husband. Margaret Brown, for example, said, "Everybody knew that Mr. Faulkner visited McCarroll Place."[13]

Other residents, too, recall hearing that Faulkner knew the Franciscos and visited them at McCarroll Place. According to McCarroll Place neighbor and longtime Holly Springs resident Garrie Colhoun, Mrs. Ruth [Bitzer] Francisco in the 1950s ultimately did reveal to Colhoun specific information about Faulkner's visits to see her husband. Mr. Colhoun said in an interview that he knew Dr. Francisco's mother quite well and lived next door to her for many years. He learned directly from her that Faulkner was a frequent visitor to McCarroll Place.[14] Mrs. Francisco not only kept the matter confidential for much of her life because of what she considered to be Faulkner's scandalous behavior and reputation but also had urged her son never to tell anyone that her husband and Faulkner were friends. Until late in his life, her son dutifully obeyed his mother's admonition. Nonetheless, the passing years, and perhaps Faulkner's increasing fame, finally led Ruth to this small but important concession: she told one close acquaintance that Faulkner frequently had visited her home. Garrie Colhoun is now on record as that person.

Faulkner's presence in this town, along with the references to Holly Springs that appear in his texts, increases the understanding of the people and places that he depicted and the meanings he derived from what he saw and apprehended in this and other towns like it in Mississippi. William Faulkner's relatives spent time in Holly Springs, before and during his lifetime. Visits of the Faulkner family to Holly Springs are not surprising, given the proximity of the town to their homes. Since Oxford and the Holly Springs area are approximately only thirty miles apart, social interactions among citizens of prominence occurred frequently. Holly Springs still had many active families and fine homes and a vibrant social life then, even if the heyday of the town was in the past.

Even before Faulkner's day, his elder relatives also were well acquainted with Holly Springs people. The Falkners visited Holly Springs friends, sometimes for extended periods of time; attended dances; married there; heard circuit court cases there; and passed through town when traveling home from elsewhere. Early on, as Joel Williamson has pointed out, William C.

Figure 1.1 This portrait of Alabama Falkner (full name Alabama Leroy Falkner McLean, referred to here as Baby Roy) appeared in the novel *Rapid Ramblings in Europe*, published in 1884 by William C. (Clark) Falkner. Alabama was the beloved great-aunt of William Faulkner. Photo from archive.org/details/rapidramblingsin00falk.

Falkner's uncle Thomas Jefferson Word lived in Holly Springs.[15] These relationships demonstrate long-standing Falkner family ties to Holly Springs that provided a cross-generational foundation for William Faulkner's later connections to the town and its inhabitants. (NB: Jimmy Faulkner explained the reason for the change in the Faulkner name spelling from Falkner to Faulkner in Wolff, *Talking about William Faulkner*, LSU Press, 1996).

Alabama Falkner (figure 1.1), who was Faulkner's "beloved great aunt" and whom Faulkner referred to as "Aunt Bama," also visited Holly Springs.[16] She was a favorite child of William Faulkner's great-grandfather, the Old Colonel. Later, William and Estelle Faulkner would name their first child after Alabama. Miss Gholson of Holly Springs hosted Alabama Falkner there for weeks: "Miss 'Balma [*sic*] Falkner has been the guest of Mrs. S. C. Gholson, Jr., for several weeks."[17] Ms. Gholson lived close to McCarroll Place—another indication of the proximity of and likelihood of friendship among the Falkners and the Franciscos, who were close friends of the Gholsons. Alabama Falkner's connections to Holly Springs, and especially to the Gholsons, do not prove that William Faulkner spent time at McCarroll Place, but the proximity of the two families—and their homes—is difficult to ignore.

Alabama Falkner also traveled to Holly Springs for a "grand ball": "Miss Alabama Falkner of Oxford attended our grand ball on the 27th ult., and while here was the guest of Mrs G W McClain."[18] The Holly Springs newspaper also records that "Miss Falkner, of Oxford, and the Misses Murry, of Ripley, passed through the city Thursday, enroute to Oxford."[19] Also Faulkner's relative Holland Pearce Falkner, who was J. W. T. Falkner's daughter, was, according to Joel Williamson, "a very social young woman. She often entertained friends and relatives from out of town, and she visited friends and relatives elsewhere. It is not surprising that on into the fall of 1896 she had her longtime friend Maud Butler [Faulkner's mother] as a house guest."[20] Also not surprising is that Miss Falkner was married in Holly Springs: "Miss Holland Falkner and Mr. J. P. Wilkins, two prominent young people of Oxford were married at the I. C. Hotel, Tuesday evening by Rev. Mr. Shipman. The young people are well known in Mississippi social circles."[21]

By referring to "Miss Falkner, of Oxford," the Holly Springs newspaper suggests that the editor and likely the townspeople knew her and felt familiar enough with her to omit her first name. The lack of additional identifying information, especially her first name, bespeaks that familiarity. In the same article, several other ladies are identified by both their first and last names. The newspaper writer expected readers to know who "Miss Falkner, of Oxford" was.

Thomas McHaney, who is the Kenneth M. England Professor of Southern Literature emeritus at Georgia State University, adds, "The Murrys from Ripley would be part of the family of John Wesley Thompson Faulkner's wife, and perhaps the 'Miss' in Falkner is simply a mistake, especially since we learned from Edgar [Francisco III] that [Faulkner's mother, Maud] visited Holly Springs to see her friend, etc. William would have been a baby, but all the more reason for a meeting, perhaps."[22] (McHaney's statement reinforces Dr. Francisco's recollection of hearing from his family members that [Francisco's grandmother] Betsy and [Faulkner's mother] Maud visited each other before and after their baby boys were born.)

Train routes were important in taking the Falkners, the Murrys, and later William Faulkner to Holly Springs, Memphis, and beyond. The Falkner family almost certainly came to Holly Springs when traveling by train. The train route to Oxford from Ripley was via the junction at Holly Springs, where passengers changed from the main Memphis-to-Alabama rail line and took a spur line to Oxford. Blotner notes that in the year 1897, "the best way to make the short journey [to Oxford from New Albany] was not in an uncomfortable buggy but by train. One rode the St. Louis-San Francisco Railroad thirty-five miles northwest to Holly Springs and changed there to the Illinois Central for the remaining thirty miles south to Oxford."[23]

Blotner makes clear the powerful impression Oxford made on Faulkner.[24] When Faulkner was three months old, his mother carried him from New Albany to Oxford to visit relatives and changed trains in Holly Springs for the remainder of the journey. Five years later, in September 1902, Faulkner and his mother and brothers followed a similar railroad route from Ripley to Oxford to settle permanently by again switching trains in Holly Springs. Although these early experiences may not have had a deep impact on infant Will Faulkner, he was nonetheless from an early age a traveler on these paths that would one day become familiar and later memorialized in his fictional county. Perhaps Holly Springs had a similar effect.

Faulkner's characters ride and change trains to and from the fictional county seat of Jefferson. In *Sanctuary*, for example, the attorney Horace Benbow, seeking a missing Temple Drake, encounters Sen. Clarence Snopes on the train from a fictional Oxford to Jefferson. "I'll see you at Holly Springs," Snopes calls out, and the characters later disembark and change trains in Holly Springs after pausing for a smoke and refreshment before beginning the final portion of their trip (177).

Some folks used the horse-and-buggy route. Don Doyle notes that since early years, a main road ran from Oxford to Holly Springs.[25] In his book *My Brother Bill*, John Faulkner says: "Dad brought his horses . . . when we came from Ripley. In fact we drove through the country. The sixty miles of road was easier than . . . by train."[26] Perhaps the Falkner and Murry ladies preferred the relative comfort of the train in 1899, instead of bouncing over the dusty roads, like Granny Millard in *The Unvanquished*. The train would have routed them to Holly Springs.

A Holly Springs social crowd, including the Francisco family's cousin Perle, journeyed to Oxford for dances, too: "The following young ladies and gentlemen of Holly Springs went to Oxford Friday evening last to attend the Anniversary ball of the Phi Sigma society: Misses Thornwell Dunlap, Elise Featherston, Mary and Fannie McKie, Perle Strickland and Augusta Finley, Messrs. Lewis Mattison, Kinloch Quiggins, and Lt. Hinton. It was a grand affair and greatly enjoyed."[27]

Business and legal matters too required travel, and the newspaper articles are a good indication that readership avidly followed the comings and goings of travelers to and from their fair city of Holly Springs. Faulkner's uncle, J. W. T. Falkner, a circuit court judge, was well known in Holly Springs, and the newspaper accounts frequently noted his appearances and work in town.

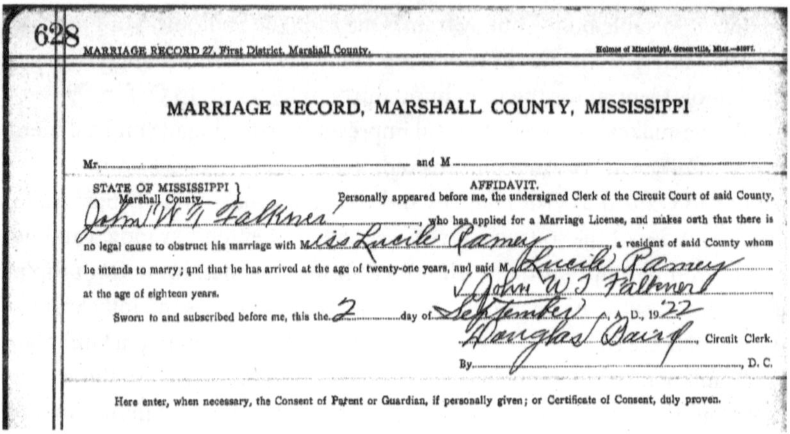

628
MARRIAGE RECORD 27, First District, Marshall County.
Holmes of Mississippi, Greenville, Miss.—81977.

MARRIAGE RECORD, MARSHALL COUNTY, MISSISSIPPI

Mr. .... and M ....

STATE OF MISSISSIPPI }
Marshall County. }

AFFIDAVIT.

Personally appeared before me, the undersigned Clerk of the Circuit Court of said County, John W T Falkner, who has applied for a Marriage License, and makes oath that there is no legal cause to obstruct his marriage with Miss Lucile Ramey, a resident of said County whom he intends to marry; and that he has arrived at the age of twenty-one years, and said M Lucile Ramey at the age of eighteen years.

John W T Falkner

Sworn to and subscribed before me, this the 2 day of September, A. D., 1922

Douglas Baird, Circuit Clerk.

By ...., D. C.

Here enter, when necessary, the Consent of Parent or Guardian, if personally given; or Certificate of Consent, duly proven.

Figure 1.2 John W. T. Fa(u)lkner and Lucille (Dolly) Ramey marriage license, September 2, 1922. Source: Marriage Record 27, First District, Marshall County, Mississippi, p. 628.

He traveled to Holly Springs repeatedly to hear circuit cases. For example: "J. W. Falkner, Esq., of Oxford was in the city a few days ago"[28]; "Col. C. B. Mitchell, of Pontotoc, J. W. Falkner, of Oxford, and W. A. McDonald, of Benton county, are attending the session of Circuit Court."[29]

Newspaper articles also record that numerous people from Holly Springs attended social and other events in Oxford, just as many Oxonians traveled to Holly Springs for similar gatherings. This frequent interaction illustrates the fluid relationship the people from both towns had with each other: "Miss Mary Bonner McDowell is the guest of Mrs. Kyle in Oxford"[30]; "Miss Evelyn Laurance has returned from Oxford, where she was one of the most popular commencement visitors"[31]; "To the regret of their many friends, Misses Jean and Annie Watson have moved from Holly Springs. They will live in Oxford"[32]; "Master Ray Mosby of Oxford is in the city"[33]; "A party of charming schoolgirls came up from Oxford last Friday evening, chaperoned by Mrs. Carrie Smith, who with two of the young ladies, Misses Palmer and Bussey, remained over Sunday with the Misses Pryor"[34]; "Miss Nell Cary went to Oxford last week to be present at the oratorical contest, which resulted in the delegate from Tulane University winning the medal"[35]; "The Oxford ball tomorrow evening will be attended by several young ladies from here."[36] These reports illustrate the frequent interaction among the peoples of Holly Springs and Oxford and the accessibility of one town to the other.

The closeness of the Hindman Doxey family to the Edgar Francisco family, and Hindman's relationship to William Faulkner, supports Francisco III's statement in *Ledgers of History* that Faulkner knew Edgar Francisco Jr. In a recorded talk at the Holly Springs library in 2003, Sarah Doxey Tate, a cousin of Francisco III, said that when Faulkner's brother John decided to marry, he took his fiancée, Lucille (Dolly) Ramey, to Holly Springs, where John quickly recruited Hindman Doxey Sr. to be a witness at their courthouse marriage.[37] (See John and Dolly Faulkner's marriage certificate, figure 1.2.) Hindman Doxey Sr., a Holly Springs native, and Edgar Francisco Jr. became relatives by marriage when Hindman married Mary Bitzer, the half-sister of Ruth Bitzer, who married Edgar Francisco Jr. That John Faulkner enlisted Hindman Doxey Sr. to be a witness at his courthouse wedding in Holly Springs is a gesture attesting to the significant familiarity between Doxey and John Faulkner.

The Doxey and Francisco families were close across generations of time. Francisco III recalls that Hindman Doxey Sr. and his father were childhood friends and members of the same church. They "grew up together in the same small town."[38] He remembers his uncle Hindman as a busy man:

> Uncle Hindman was not casual about finances. He tried very hard through his life to be financially successful and he was. He would never have "dropped out" of any undertaking he started, as he noted that Faulkner had. He stayed so busy that I never saw him at his home. As a child I stopped by the Doxey's [sic] house on my way home from school, since their house was right across the street from the school. Almost every other weekend I was there by invitation to play, snack or have dinner. I don't recall ever seeing him there watching us children at play or participating in the dinner. He was always at work even on weekends. He and his brother, Wall, had started their law office in Holly Springs as partners, but Wall was soon in Washington as Congressman, then Senator and finally as Sergeant-at-Arms, so Uncle Hindman was left to run the law practice by himself.[39]

Francisco III added that his cousin Sarah Doxey Tate "frequently quoted her Dad's negative remarks about Faulkner, including his wonderments about why Edgar tolerated the man in his house. Sarah gave a talk, which she recorded, in which she quoted her Dad's astonishment that Faulkner had gotten a prize."[40]

Evidence from the Francisco family photo album further emphasizes the closeness of the Doxey and Francisco families. In addition to their links through marriage, they spent time together.[41] Francisco III said that Hindman Doxey Jr. and he were close and grew up together. Hindman Jr. was born only two months after Francisco III, and numerous baby pictures of Hindman appear in the Francisco family album. Often they are adjacent to those of Edgar III and other family members. In one photo both very young

Figure 1.3 Edgar Wiggin Francisco III at eleven months old, and Hindman Doxey Jr. at nine months in 1931, both in the arms of their Bitzer grandparents. Photograph taken by Ruth Bitzer Francisco. Photograph copy work by George Nikas, Atlanta, Georgia. Courtesy of Dr. Edgar Wiggin Francisco III.

boys are in the arms of their grandparents, Dr. and Mrs. George Bitzer (see figure 1.3). Personal correspondence, including Christmas and other cards from the Doxeys to the Franciscos, and one from Hindman Doxey Jr. to Francisco III, further attests to close acquaintance. An extant Christmas card from Hindman Doxey Jr. to Edgar Francisco III has the following greeting: "To Eddie, Christmas greetings from man to man. Here's a hearty wish for you on the good old-fashioned plan: A merry Christmas that's your due and nothing less old man! Hindman Jr."[42] Hindman and Edgar III remained close until Hindman's death in 2012. (See figure 1.4.)

Hindman Doxey Sr.'s friendly relationship with Faulkner and close connections with his relatives the Franciscos reinforce Francisco III's claim that Faulkner and Edgar Francisco Jr. were well acquainted. Faulkner and Hindman Sr. were simultaneously at the University of Mississippi, where they shared a theatrical interest. Hindman Doxey acted in one of Will's plays at Ole Miss.[43] The names of Faulkner and Doxey appear on an

Figure 1.4 Dr. Edgar Wiggin Francisco III (left) with Hindman Doxey Jr. at Francisco's lecture about William Faulkner at Millsaps College, February 2011. Photography by Sally Wolff King.

announcement for the theatrical production of *The Marionettes*. Francisco III remembers learning that "as a fellow student at Ole Miss he [Hindman Doxey Sr.] was in at least one of Faulkner's plays," and he was treasurer of Faulkner's theater group. "Sarah Doxey said her Dad was driven crazy by Faulkner's disregard for accountancy."[44]

Memphis citizen Joan Williams had a several-year romantic relationship with William Faulkner in the 1950s.[45] She said in her 1980 article, published in *The Atlantic*, that she met Faulkner frequently in Holly Springs, and he drove with her to nearby Pott's Camp for private picnics of food and beer. Their relationship was not simple. He was an older author, and she was a much younger, aspiring author. She initially sought his guidance, before their relationship became romantic. Holly Springs played a role in their meetings in that it was a place apart where they could be together, albeit briefly, without prying eyes upon them.[46]

Interviews of residents from the area note that at that time, Faulkner's home county, Lafayette County, was dry—alcohol was not available legally there—so many people drove to Holly Springs for liquor, which seems to have been an attraction of Holly Springs for Faulkner and perhaps a contributing reason he and Joan Williams chose Holly Springs as a place to meet.

Faulkner also had a bootleg supplier south of Oxford, and he sometimes depended on at least one bootlegger near Oxford—Motee Daniel—in addition to the noted bootlegger in Holly Springs.[47]

For William Faulkner, the Holly Springs area was familiar territory, as these examples indicate, and furnished him with an important real and figurative gateway into and out of his fictional "postage stamp of native soil"[48] in his home of Oxford, and in his real Lafayette County, and in the fictional Yoknapatawpha County.

Even on Faulkner's final trip in July 1962, to Byhalia, Mississippi, near Holly Springs, again the area became a gateway of sorts, as it had in the past to the world at large—Memphis, New Orleans, New York, California, Europe, and beyond, as well as a familiar transition point for Faulkner as he returned home. He regularly transited but sometimes lingered in Holly Springs, to socialize, hunt, chat, listen carefully to the townspeople—as was his wont—at least when he was not speeding through town on his way elsewhere.

Cleanth Brooks says that Quentin seeks to know more about Thomas Sutpen and "what manner of man he was."[49] Brooks's important conclusion is that the novel "has to do not merely with the meaning of Sutpen's career but with the nature of historical truth and with the problem of how we can 'know' the past."[50] That is one question that Faulkner asks about the people around him whom he depicted. He describes who they are, what their activities are, what is in their minds and hearts, and how those truths apply to others in the world. He delves deeply into the culture around him—considering especially the effects of the Civil War on the communities in his area, for both whites and African Americans—and examines the values and characteristics of these people to determine what manner of men and women they were. Faulkner contemplates the features of theirs that are common, and what truths become self-evident "truths of the heart," as Faulkner said.[51] Answering those questions involves knowing more about people Faulkner describes, and some of them were close to home in Holly Springs. The people and places of Holly Springs have a bearing on Faulkner's depictions and what meanings he derived from them for stories and novels.

Faulkner left traces of his presence in Holly Springs, and that town left an equally undeniable imprint on Faulkner's stories and novels. Exploring more deeply these traces affords a greater understanding of Faulkner, his literature, and his culture. The chapters ahead illustrate some of the ways that Holly Springs appears in Faulkner's fiction and offer a greater understanding of his writings about the people in his area.

William Faulkner's Fiction and Holly Springs

Resonances of Holly Springs people and events find their way into Faulkner's fiction, and better knowing the people, places, and materials that he may have drawn from helps to identify some of the sources Faulkner used and heightens the understanding and meaning of his works. Faulkner invokes Holly Springs people and their activities in numerous works in ways that in some cases call to mind real personages and places. In other cases, Faulkner borrowed and slightly transformed a multitude of big and small signature details from a real environment, including—but not limited to—basic elements such as names of people and places and features of architecture and landscape. As he did in other situations, he used what was in the environments around him, including Holly Springs, to fuel his narratives.

Luella Gibson, a servant in Perle Strickland's home in Holly Springs, is possible inspiration for Faulkner's portrayal of Dilsey Gibson. The name Gibson is a common one in Mississippi and the South more generally, but whether this Gibson is in name and purpose a link to Faulkner's Dilsey Gibson in *The Sound and the Fury* is worthy of open-minded consideration. Many documents from the McCarroll Place papers date from the early 1800s. Some that apparently originated from the Vicksburg area repeatedly mention the family name Gibson. William Faulkner could have seen these papers at McCarroll Place and perhaps took Dilsey's name from a Vicksburg family name. Luella and Dilsey share not only a last name but also similar characteristics.

The older Perle Strickland also may have informed the portrait of Caddy Compson in more specific ways. Perle had an at-home wedding to a German man and traveled to Germany with him. Perle may have inspired these facets of the older Caddy Compson, who similarly was married at home and is last seen in the appendix to *The Sound and the Fury* on the arm of a German staffgeneral (see chapter 3 for further discussion of Perle Strickland and Caddy Compson).

The idea of "host" and "guest" that Faulkner develops in *Requiem for a Nun* may draw upon the role that Edgar Francisco Jr. annually performed as "host" during the Holly Springs Pilgrimage and on Faulkner in an autobiographical representation of himself as a Pilgrimage visitor and "guest"; Memphis native Ludie Baugh seems a likely source for the window etching with a "single name" as described in *Intruder in the Dust*, and Faulkner may have created another self-depiction from his visits to McCarroll Place, when his character walks up onto the gallery porch and views the etching from the outside, looking in, as Faulkner said that he had done there.

"To a Woman You Would Hand a Rose": Faulkner's "A Rose for Emily" and the Smith House in Holly Springs

> Oh, that was an allegorical title: the meaning was, here was a woman who had had a tragedy, an irrevocable tragedy, and nothing could be done about it, and I pitied her and this was a salute: just as if you were to make a gesture, a salute to anyone: to a woman you would hand a rose.
> —WILLIAM FAULKNER, *FAULKNER AT NAGANO*, ED. ROBERT A. JELLIFFE (TOKYO: KENKYUSHA, 1966. FIRST EDITION, 1956), 71

Similarities and correspondences link Holly Springs people and places to Faulkner's works. His famous short story "A Rose for Emily" is an example. Two former Holly Springs citizens suggest connections between this story and Holly Springs. Those who study Faulkner have considered the Neilson house in Oxford, Mississippi, to be a model for Faulkner's story.[52] His courtship of Louise Caffey Smith, a Holly Springs citizen, and other factors support the idea that Louise Caffey Smith's home, the Smith House, in Holly Springs is a possible source for this story. The Smith House has the haunting aura appropriate to the macabre ambiance of the story (see figure 1.5). Interviews with former Holly Springs citizens also point to the rose-colored glass windows in a Holly Springs mansion as having inspired the rose motif that plays through Faulkner's story and its title (see figure 1.6).

Helen Bell Hopkins and Minor Buchanan, both former Holly Springs citizens with long histories there, connect "A Rose for Emily" and Holly Springs. Helen Bell Hopkins links the story to the Smith House on Salem Avenue:

> I was told by someone years ago that the Smith house on Salem Ave. in Holly Springs was used as the setting by Faulkner for his short story A Rose for Emily. He had courted a young lady whose family lived in the house. There may be written documentation for this, but I don't know where. My husband and I owned the house for about 10 years. . . . The house, the last I heard, was owned by some people named Ward, and as far as I know the house has never been on the Pilgrimage as it was built in 1905, a little late for inclusion in the Pilgrimage which mostly focuses on anti-bellum [*sic*] houses.[53]

Some critics will insist that Ms. Hopkins's statement simply seeks to connect her to a famous author. Others will say that she presents only speculative hearsay by an unnamed source, and as such her contribution is unimportant. What cannot be proven immediately does not necessarily disprove it either. Readers who are open to new information will want to consider Ms. Hopkins's recollections. Hopkins is an upstanding and well-regarded member of the community and known for truthfulness and not for seeking personal gain. The Smith House, in which she lived for ten years, was not and is not now on the annual Holly Springs Pilgrimage, so becoming a part of the Pilgrimage was not a reason for her to connect the house with Faulkner's story.

Although Ms. Hopkins's source is unnamed, that source nonetheless could be correct that Faulkner had the Smith House in mind when he wrote "A Rose for Emily." Other sources corroborate that Faulkner once dated Louise Caffey Smith. Carvel Collins notes that Louise knew Faulkner during college years.[54] Faulkner may have employed information about her house in his story. To discount that possibility is perhaps to miss a heretofore unknown potential source for Faulkner's story. Faulkner was well known for listening to people talk and tell stories. He is famous for drawing on the old tales and talking of those people around him. Ms. Hopkins participates in the same oral tradition that appealed to Faulkner and is an integral part of "A Rose for Emily": the townspeople talk and assess information to ascertain and tell the full story of Miss Emily.

Minor Buchanan, a lawyer from Holly Springs now living in Jackson, Mississippi, also recalls a connection between "A Rose for Emily" and Holly Springs. Buchanan said William Faulkner wrote "A Rose for Emily" about the Smith House—the one with the "rose-colored windows."[55] The rose-colored windows are not at the Smith House, however, but they are close by at Grey Gables, another antebellum home built in the 1830s and in the same historic district of Holly Springs.[56] No longer a current resident of Holly Springs, this interviewee perhaps misremembered which house had the rose-colored windows, but both houses are in proximity in Holly Springs. The current owner of Grey Gables notes that the rose-colored windows date to 1870. These rose-tinted windows were in place during Faulkner's day.[57]

Faulkner's awareness of the Smith House is also the focus of a third interviewee who asked not to be identified. This interviewee also knew that William Faulkner dated Louise Caffey Smith, who lived at the Smith House. The 1910 and 1920 US Censuses both indicate that at those times, Louise Caffey Smith was living with her parents in a house on Salem Street (now Salem Avenue) in Holly Springs,[58] the location of the home now known as the Smith House (figure 1.5).

Figure 1.5 Several Holly Springs, Mississippi, native citizens have linked the Smith House, pictured here, to William Faulkner's short story "A Rose for Emily." The architecture is not the same as that described in the story, but the house has an unmistakable aura of mystery, befitting the haunting tale that Faulkner spun. Photo credit: Figure 67, "Smith House, Holly Springs, Mississippi," 91, from Thomas S. Hines, *William Faulkner and the Tangible Past: The Architecture of Yoknapatawpha*, © 1997 by The Regents of the University of California. Published by the University of California Press.

Figure 1.6 The rose-colored glass panes in the front door at Grey Gables in Holly Springs, Mississippi. Courtesy of Scott Faragher, owner of Grey Gables. A color version of this image can be seen at educationalconsulting.services/Faulkner.

In her book titled *Historic Architecture in Mississippi*, Mary Wallace Crocker described the red glass panes at Grey Gables this way: "The front doorway is a thing of beauty with its arched millwork fitted with deeply cut Bohemian glass (photo: the darker panes are the original glass)."[59] Edgar W. Francisco III also commented on the red panes at Grey Gables (figure 1.6):

> I only know what I've read from numerous write-ups. The red Bohemian glass windows [at Grey Gables] and all the hand-carved woodwork and the great staircase were all part of the rebuilding in 1870 when J. J. House, flamboyant and newly rich off the war, made a grand showplace out of James and Maria Nelson's home, often described as a simple two-story cottage, which Nelson built in 1849.
>
> Dad jokingly referred to it as our only example of early 1870 Housian Revival, in a tongue-in-cheek chuckle about the flamboyance of James House. Some call it post-war Italianate. It is clearly post-war Spires Bolling, who greatly enlarged and redesigned for James House the 1849 home of James Henry Nelson and wife, Maria Goodrich. Dad was a friend of the owner when I was a child, and he loved to visit, taking me with him. Dad said he felt a warm welcome from the red glass when he approached the door. I remember that I felt the color even more than seeing it. I don't remember who owned it then. Lois Swaney Shipp has written the most about it and her experiences there. Lois's daughter was frightened when the ghost of the murdered James Nelson crawled through her window and opened her bedroom door. Dr. Hale also was an owner.[60]

In his manuscript "Holly Springs: Architecture of a Small Town," Jack Baum also noted that Mr. L. A. Smith's daughter was "very good friends" with Faulkner:

> This house [the Smith House] was built by Judge and Mrs. L.A. Smith in 1905 because their residence at the time (Oakleigh, which is next door) was not stylish enough.
>
> They got the plan for this house from a mail order catalog published by the architecture firm of Barber and Kluttz, in Knoxville, Tennessee.
>
> Mr. Smith was a Supreme Court justice for the state of Mississippi and had a daughter who at one time was very good friends with William Faulkner.
>
> This house is the best example of Queen Anne architecture in Holly Springs. Some of the Queen Anne elements on this house are the use of different building materials on different floors, the irregular shape

of the massing, the bay windows, the use of gingerbread and ornate fretwork, and the porch and balcony.⁶¹

The implication gleaned from residents around town about the Smith/Faulkner relationship is that William Faulkner and Louise Caffey Smith did not continue as a couple because she chose not to continue seeing him.

Another point of commonality between the Smith household and the short story is that a servant was living in the house, along with Louise Caffey Smith's parents, brother, and grandmother.⁶² At various times in the story, Emily's family members are present, and a butler goes in and out with shopping bags, as he goes to market and brings home food.

The tint of the window does not confirm absolutely that Grey Gables was Emily's house, nor does the lore passed down from citizenry, or similarities in the text, prove that Faulkner had the Smith House in mind as a source. Nonetheless, some arguments are persuasive: word-of-mouth is a strong indicator of southern tradition and memory; the tantalizing hue of the windows, although perhaps not a unique physical determiner, nevertheless is a noteworthy link to the rose theme the writer chose for his story; and, finally, young Will was known to have been stepping out with Louise Smith, and that clue should not be peremptorily discarded, for Faulkner must have been familiar with the street where she lived and the setting and look of her family home. Although no proof is evident at this writing that Faulkner drew from the Smith House and Grey Gables for "A Rose for Emily," what persists is the partially obscured but enduring plausibility—the question whether, given that Faulkner did not always disclose his sources, an allusion to the Smith House is likely and deliberate.

Arsenic "For Rats"

Arsenic is a haunting connection between the poison in Faulkner's story "A Rose for Emily" and that which allegedly caused the death of Holly Springs citizen and Francisco family relative Perle Strickland Badow, who died in 1948. Francisco III remembers that his cousin Ruth LeGrand Strickland Weir named her son William Weir, who became a much-acclaimed MD diagnostician.⁶³ He was named for his great-grandfather William Strickland, the father of Jacob, Frank, and Perle—and his name is an indication of how emotionally attached Ruth was to Strickland Place and her family.

> While going through the house [Strickland Place, where Badow lived with his wife Perle Strickland Badow], their [Dr. Weir's] attention

was caught by the seemingly large amounts of arsenic powder and measuring equipment in the kitchen. They asked Badow about it and were shocked by the violently angry response that it was to kill rats, and if they made any other insinuations, he would sue them for libel. Badow's outburst made them more suspicious. The more they looked around and the more they heard about her [Perle's] last year of illness, the more suspicious they became, leading them to consider calling for an investigation. Dad explained to them that they should not read too much into Badow's response, since it was his usual response. He [Dad] described how he had walked over and knocked several times during Perle's last illness to offer food and help. Badow would yell at him that he needed no help and that he knew what Perle needed and could tend to her. On the last attempt Dad was told not to come back again. The Stricklands did not find this story reassuring, but in the end they decided against an inquiry. We assumed that they forgot about it when they got home, but apparently William did not since his discussions with his wife, Anne, had to have been many years later.[64]

A copy of a book well known in Holly Springs was among William Strickland Weir's papers. The book, *It Happened Here: True Stories of Holly Springs*, by Olga Reed Pruitt (South Reporter Printing Company, 1950), contains an inscription by Weir's mother, Ruth LeGrand Strickland Weir, that makes clear Ruth's belief that Gerard Badow murdered Perle Strickland Badow. Dr. Francisco recalls his father's saying that there was considerable talk about calling for an investigation to resolve the suspicions about Perle's death, one way or another, but no action ultimately occurred.

Faulkner's reaction to the news of Perle's death is clear in Francisco's memory: "Faulkner was ecstatic that others, coming newly into contact, had become as suspicious of Badow as he had been upon first meeting him.[65] Faulkner gleefully boasted to Dad that he had had a premonition of this and had written it up."[66] Francisco III recalls that when asked why he had arsenic in the house, Badow replied that "it was to kill rats."[67]

Similar words and actions relating to arsenic poisoning occur in "A Rose for Emily." Emily turns away visitors to the house, and when the pharmacist asks her why she is buying arsenic, she does not reply, and her silence prompts the pharmacist to label her purchase "For rats."[68] When Faulkner said to Edgar Jr. that he had "had a premonition," and "written it up" he seems to have been referring to "A Rose for Emily" (originally published in 1930), about a woman who poisons the man she loves with arsenic. In the case of Perle Strickland Badow, the genders are switched: the man allegedly poisons the woman with arsenic.

After reading the inscription by Ruth LeGrand Strickland Weir, Francisco III commented further:

> When I told you that a Strickland cousin, Ruth LaGrand Strickland Weir, suspected Badow of poisoning her Aunt Perle, I never imagined that someone I did not know (Ruth's daughter-in-law, Anne Weir) would not only confirm my statement, but produce a copy of the same accusation handwritten by Ruth on the copyright page of a book written about Holly Springs by Olga Pruitt. For Faulkner readers this should be even more sensational given Faulkner's long-standing suspicion of Badow and his [Faulkner's] rarely expressed glee that he had gotten it right but also sadly had predicted a bad outcome for Perle.[69]

Confederate and Northern Soldiers Buried in the Same Cemetery

"A Rose for Emily" and the town of Holly Springs share more in common. Both have Confederate and Northern soldiers buried in the same cemetery. Faulkner's story includes this description of the soldiers: "And now Miss Emily had gone to join the representatives of those august names where they lay in the cedar-bemused cemetery among the ranked and anonymous graves of Union and Confederate soldiers who fell at the battle of Jefferson."[70] Faulkner may have seen these graves or heard their stories in the Holly Springs area and transmuted facts and legends into fiction.

Local Holly Springs historian Bobby Mitchell concluded that four of the soldiers in the Hill Crest Cemetery in Holly Springs were Northern and died after the Civil War. Oral history also plays an important role in their legend. Mitchell recalls that: "it was just one of those things that people would say, that there were Union soldiers. No proof, but word of mouth.... There are 4 other military style monuments in the far southeast part of the cemetery, near where the Confederate soldiers who died in the local hospitals are buried. Purportedly they are Union soldiers."[71]

After further research Mitchell determined that the four Northern soldiers in Hill Crest were privates in Company A, Third US Infantry, and died in 1874–1875. Their tombstones were produced by Sheldon and Sons of West Rutledge, Vermont, a company that provided grave markers for deceased Union Civil War veterans. Mr. Mitchell noted that the markers for what

Figure 1.7 In the center distance in this photo are the grave markers of four Northern soldiers in the Hill Crest Cemetery in Holly Springs, Mississippi. The Northern soldiers are buried separately and at odds with the Confederate grid. Courtesy of Keith Gore Wiseman.

"people here call Union Soldiers . . . do not have a state listed, only a name and 3rd U.S. infantry. The markers are not the traditional size either."[72] (See figure 1.7.) Mitchell later discovered the Northern soldiers' names and death dates: "None died during the war . . . but all were in the mid-1870's, 2 of them on the same date, which makes me think there was perhaps some epidemic or another . . . maybe yellow fever, smallpox, etc."[73]

> Hyson Ramsey, Pvt, Co. A, 3rd US Inf, Died Aug. 18, 1874
> John W. Crosby, Pvt, Co. D, 3rd US Inf, Died Aug. 24, 1874
> Francis McMahon, Pvt, Co. F, 3rd US Inf, Died Sept. 8, 1874
>   (See figure 1.8.)
> Charles A. Kiefer, Pvt, Co. A, 3rd US Inf, Died Sept. 20, 1875

Mitchell concludes: "I still have a suspicion that there was some epidemic at the time, three of them died within 3 weeks. My speculating does not prove anything however."[74]

Additional indications suggest that the burial of the Northern 1870s soldier veterans along with Confederate soldiers in Hill Crest Cemetery may be a source for the presence of both Union and Confederate soldiers in the cemetery in Faulkner's evocative story. Names are one point of similarity.

Figure 1.8 Grave marker of Francis McMahon. Courtesy of Dr. Beth Kruse.

Note that Emily Grierson, the name of the main character in "A Rose for Emily," seems to be an elongation of the Holly Springs name "Grier." One of the Union soldiers buried in Hill Crest Cemetery is named McMahon (see figure 1.8), and Donald Mahon is a character in Faulkner's novel *Soldier's Pay*.

Other Mississippi cemeteries once had burials of both Union and Confederate dead, such as in the Confederate Cemetery at the University of Mississippi in Faulkner's hometown. A University of Mississippi Libraries webpage titled "Contextualization at University of Mississippi: Memorials and Contextualization," states: "The Confederate Cemetery on campus originated from burials during the Civil War when the campus served casualties from both sides as a hospital. Union burials were removed after the conflict to national cemeteries."[75] Dr. April Holm explained that Union soldiers appear to have been moved to the Corinth National Cemetery in January 1867.[76] Removal of these Union soldiers from this cemetery took place long before the birth of William Faulkner.

The Hill Crest Cemetery in Holly Springs, on the other hand, is as old as the campus cemetery at the University of Mississippi. The Northern soldiers at Hill Crest are near some of the Confederate soldiers. The "unknown Confederate soldiers plot" and the proximity of the Northern and Southern graves may be an important link between this cemetery and Faulkner's story.

Mr. Mitchell determined that the northern soldiers "are only a few yards [from] the unknown Confederate soldiers plot" and thirty feet from other Confederate soldiers buried nearby.[77]

Faulkner's including the word "anonymous" in his description of the graves may refer to the "unknown" soldiers' monument at Hill Crest. Carl Rollyson notes that Faulkner's friend Ben Wasson "fondly remembered his friend's [Faulkner] wandering through cemeteries."[78] Faulkner could have stood in Hill Crest Cemetery and simultaneously viewed both Northern and Southern soldier graves, within thirty feet of each other, and substituted his word "anonymous" for the "unknown" Confederate soldiers at this cemetery.

Even if Faulkner did not view for himself those Northern and Southern soldiers in proximity, he may have heard in and around Holly Springs about the Northern and Southern burials. As Mr. Mitchell pointed out, "It was just one of those things that people would say, that there were Union soldiers"[79] buried at Hill Crest. Such folklore and legend had an influential impact on Faulkner's work in general, and this instance is an example. Cemeteries like Hill Crest often are of endless interest to people who visit and become curious about the town and the area. The Hill Crest Cemetery was, like much of what Faulkner found in Holly Springs, lumber in the attic for his works. Making imaginative use of such lumber is entirely consistent with Faulkner's creative process in constructing that striking story "A Rose for Emily."

"Ham So Thin You Can Read the Newspaper through It": The Holly Springs Depot and Faulkner's *The Reivers*

Holly Springs places and events continue to appear in Faulkner's works. For example, the depot in *The Reivers* and the Holly Springs depot share some points of commonality. The reference to the depot and thinly sliced ham in the novel is associated with the Holly Springs depot. This novel contains a reference to thinly sliced ham served at the "depot eating room" (235), and Faulkner's line appears to have a Holly Springs source. An article in *Invitation Oxford* recalls: "The Holly Springs Passenger Station and Hotel was once a bustling hotel and depot, attracting patrons and travelers from all over."[80] (See figure 1.9.) The article specifically notes that "William Faulkner was a visitor and fictionalized its proprietor . . . claiming he sliced meat so thin that he was able to send his family to Chicago on the proceeds of a single ham."[81] In the novel, Mr. McDiarmid serves up the thinly sliced ham so described. The reference to the depot and ham occurs near the final

Figure 1.9 The Holly Springs Depot, June 2023. Courtesy of Keith Gore Wiseman.

horse race, and much of the action in the last hundred pages or so carries a description of the hotel and depot. The Holly Springs depot and hotel are a likely model. References to the train depot appear in other works as well, and it may well have served as a model for some of these waystations in Faulkner's works.[82]

Faulkner's thinly sliced ham reference in *The Reivers* seems to be a line that Faulkner overheard or heard about at the depot café in Holly Springs. James "Tippy" McDermott's father, Robert McDermott, who ran the café at the Holly Springs train depot, apparently originated the line. In one account of the story, McDermott is known for slicing ham for sandwiches so thin he could go to Chicago from the profits from one ham. In another account, he sliced the ham so thin, he could read the newspaper through it. The language in this first version of the story appears in Faulkner's novel *The Reivers* (235), and Faulkner apparently made only a slight change in the spelling of McDermott to the character's name: McDiarmid.

Long-time resident Gwen Wyatt remembers Faulkner's presence in Holly Springs and in connection to her father, who she said once ran the depot: "When the last train would pull in on a Saturday night, a band from Memphis would be on it. They would stay and play all night long and leave on the first train Sunday morning. It was quite an event." She adds that "Mr. Faulkner would come up on the train and listen to bands at the Depot then take the train back to Oxford."[83] In an article published in the Holly Springs newspaper, Tippy McDermott recalled, "William Faulkner even mentioned my father in his book, THE REIVERS," and "Faulkner used to come to Holly Springs a lot. I can remember seeing him walk around outside. He noticed everything, but never talked to anyone. He was real quiet."[84]

Mrs. Wyatt further remembers that her father assisted Faulkner with a Boy Scout troop in Oxford and that Mr. Faulkner "came on the train to visit his daughter and take her home. He walked from the Depot to Synodical College. We know he had friends along Van Dorn Avenue."[85]

Notes taken by Carvel Collins about people in Holly Springs who knew Faulkner include some information from Gertrude McDermott. Her father, Robert, was the man at the depot hotel who sliced the thin ham sandwiches. She also is the sister of Tippy McDermott. Collins's handwritten notes record Gertrude's saying regarding Faulkner that "her father [Robert McDermott] knew him [Faulkner] as an officer in 'RCAF [Royal Canadian Air Force].'" Collins continues that McDermott's "father ran a hotel in early 20's—stopping place at RR on way to Memphis."[86]

In a letter from Gertrude McDermott to Carvel Collins, she elaborates on the times and the setting in which her father met Faulkner:

> My Father ran a Hotel here in the early '20's [sic] and the trains from Oxford brought passengers to Holly Springs who extrained to the Frisco (Holly Springs was the junction) on their way to Memphis. Sometimes the Frisco was late which necessitated passengers to spend a [sic] 20 minutes or so, having a meal etc. This is how my father met Mr. Falkner, in a business though friendly acquaintance.
>
> I was a school-girl in those days myself and I remember seeing Mr. Falkner but I have never met him officially.[87]

Judge J. W. Clapp, the Capital, the Attic, and *Absalom, Absalom!*

Connections between Faulkner's works and Holly Springs continue to accrue and suggest that Faulkner included Holly Springs sources in his works. The brochure "Garden Pilgrimage to Historical Sites," sponsored by the Holly Springs Garden Club (April 22–26, 1939) notes: "In a raid of the Federal Troops, the Judge a very small man escaped capture by hiding in the capital of one of the massive Corinthian columns of the portico."[88] This story is reminiscent of Faulkner's novel *Absalom, Absalom!*, in which a man hides in the attic of a mansion and starves to death rather than "look upon his native land in the throes of repelling an invading army" (*Absalom* 60).

The Holly Springs house called Athenia, built in 1858, also has been known as Oakleigh and the Clapp-West-Fant House.[89] Phillip Knecht records this house as

> one of the great Greek Revival mansions of Holly Springs. The house was built in 1858 by Jeremiah Watkins Clapp (1814–1898), who arrived in Holly Springs in 1841 and opened a law practice. Clapp was an early supporter of the Mississippi Central Railroad, which came to Holly Springs in the early 1850s. Clapp's great Greek Revival mansion is likely one of the first Greek Revival mansions built on Salem Avenue, and was built around the same time as the nearby Airliewood. During the Civil War, Clapp served in the Confederate Congress. A popular local legend states that Clapp hid from Union soldiers inside one of the columns at the front of the house during one Union raid of Holly Springs. After the Civil War, Clapp became a local judge, and was a trustee at the University of Mississippi.[90]

Another rendition of this story is: "The judge, who was quite small in stature, escaped capture by hiding in the far-left Corinthian column. The house passed into the hands of Gen. Absolom M. West, who was twice nominated [as a candidate for] Vice President of the United States. The opulence [of the home] can be seen in the original bronze gasoliers and antique Zuber wallpaper, as well as the extensive art collection of its current owner."[91] Absolom West, a wealthy Holly Springs planter, also may have inspired the name and perhaps some of Faulkner's depiction of Thomas Sutpen in the novel *Absalom, Absalom!*[92]

According to Rev. Milton Winter, "Judge J. W. Clapp, clerk of session in the Holly Springs Church, was a delegate to the Mississippi Secession Convention in January 1861 . . . and elected to the Confederate House of Representatives."[93] Winter quotes Judge Clapp's diary, which describes his hiding in the large cast iron capital of the column of a friend's house to evade capture by the Yankee troops. "I took refuge in the house of a near neighbor, Mr. Nelson, who helped me up into the loft and covered the entrance with a piece of furniture. The day was warm and the heat of my hiding place almost unendurable, but upon reflection I concluded that it was more tolerable than a Yankee prison and submitted to the roasting until the danger was over."[94]

Absalom, Absalom!
"But Not the Ogre: Villain True Enough"

The words "augur" and "ogre" appear on the same page in *Absalom, Absalom!* (*Absalom* 62), and "ogre" recurs at least fourteen additional times in the novel. Those two words occurring simultaneously link to a Francisco family story with fascinating implications for a Faulkner self-portrait. Francisco III recalls his father saying that as a small boy in the 1930s, Francisco III could not pronounce Faulkner's name. When Faulkner came to the house to visit, the young Eddie called him "Augur" instead of "Faulkner." Responding to the child's mispronunciation, Faulkner turned to Eddie and said, "As long as you didn't call me 'Ogre,' it was okay."[95]

Faulkner's association of "augur" and "ogre" reflects the boy Francisco's mispronunciation of Faulkner's name as "augur," and the author's reply distinguishes the word "augur" from "ogre"—a dreaded person.[96] Faulkner's "augur" carries its usual meaning: to foretell, especially from omens.[97] Perhaps this aural cue stimulated Faulkner's imagination. The word most often describes Thomas Sutpen's activities: "not only to beget but to designate the presiding augur of his own disaster" (62).

"Ogre" appears in *Absalom* usually in Miss Rosa's many references to the "ogre-shape" of Thomas Sutpen or his "half-ogre" children: "And what she [Miss Rosa] saw then was just that ogre-face of her childhood seen once and then repeated at intervals and on occasions when she could neither count nor recall" (62). Rosa continues to see Sutpen as an "ogre" until the death of her sister Ellen, at which time Rosa consents, albeit briefly, to marry Sutpen: "Now the period began which ended in the catastrophe which caused a reversal so complete in Miss Rosa as to permit her to agree to marry the man whom she had grown up to look upon as an ogre" (67).

One particular mention of "ogre" from the perspective of a small, "grimly middleclass" house may be another reference to the Francisco-McCarroll home, McCarroll Place, which Faulkner apparently visited and from a window of which he could sit and observe the street "behind the neat picket fence of a small, grimly middleclass yard or lawn, looking out upon the whatever ogre-world of that quiet village street" (21). Perhaps hearing "augur" from Eddie the child and relating it to "ogre" fired Faulkner's imagination in describing McCarroll Place, from which he could view an "ogre-world" from this "quiet village street."

"Mad True Enough" and "Mortal Fallible" --but Not an "Ogre"

Faulkner also apparently creates an autobiographical portrait in his associating the words "ogre," "villain," "mad" (as in madness), and "mortal fallible" (*Absalom* 167). These words purportedly add to the evil depiction of Sutpen, but they also aptly characterize Faulkner's image of himself. The word "villain" appears multiple times in *Absalom* (19, 52, 167, 169). Rosa repeats and links the words "ogre" and "villain" as Faulkner implies that while he, like Sutpen, may be a bad man and a villain, Faulkner nonetheless hopes to be seen as a fallible mortal and as a person less likely "to invoke fear than pity"—rather than as an "ogre" (167):

> . . . but not the ogre; villain true enough, but a mortal fallible one less to invoke fear than pity: but no ogre; mad true enough, but I told myself, Why should not madness be its own victim also? or, Why may it be not even madness but solitary despair in titan conflict with the lonely and foredoomed and indomitable iron spirit: but no ogre, because it was dead, vanished, consumed somewhere in flame and sulphur-reek perhaps among the lonely craggy peaks of my childhood's solitary remembering—or forgetting; I was that sun, who believed . . . (167)

In this moment of self-reflection and self-portraiture, and perhaps alluding to Hamlet's madness, Faulkner depicts himself in "solitary despair" with a "lonely and foredoomed and indomitable iron spirit" (167). He accepts himself as bad, and villainous, and even mad "true enough," but hopes to be thought of, at least in the eyes of innocent children like Eddie Francisco, "not the ogre; villain true enough" (*Absalom* 167). For more on Faulkner's "sense of self disgust," see John Lowe's perceptive analysis.[98]

Faulkner was well known to like children, listen carefully to people talking, and incorporate common speech into his works. Eddie's childhood mispronunciation of Faulkner's name, and the subsequent appearance of "augur" and "ogre" in proximity in *Absalom, Absalom!* illustrates Faulkner's imaginative and creative process and his portrait of himself as a villain or even a madman in solitary despair—but not a vile, hideous, and intolerable "ogre."

Balancing the Books:
Restitution for the Debt of Slavery

Ledger imagery in *Absalom, Absalom!* enhances the conclusion that Faulkner drew from the Leak farm ledger, and that argument was central to *Ledgers of History*. Faulkner turns again in this novel to the metaphor of balancing the books in reference to achieving restitution for the debts for slavery and racial injustice in the South. This theme appears both in *Go Down, Moses* and *Absalom* as Faulkner's financial debt metaphor, illustrating the extent of compensation needed to heal the deep societal injustices of slavery.

After the enormous debt of slavery is paid, then the ledger on the "old sheet" could be burned. Quentin and Shreve discuss: "like what the old Aunt Rosa told you about some things that just have to be whether they are or not, just to balance the books, write *Paid* on the old sheet so that whoever keeps them can take it out of the ledger and burn it, get rid of it" (*Absalom* 325). Faulkner makes clear that the paying of the debt for the wrongs of slavery will not be rectified by people living in his current day, nor by those who committed wrongs, but by the "sons," their "get" (325).

Charles Bon, his mother, and their lawyer tally up the value of property and human lives and revenge on another literal and figurative ledger: "the lawyer behind the desk (and maybe in the secret drawer the ledger where he had just finished adding in the last past year's interest compounded between the intrinsic and the love and pride at two hundred percent)" (337). At the end of the novel, Quentin and Shreve see the death of Sutpen and the destruction of the old house as a figurative clearing of the ledger—"it clears the whole ledger, you can tear all the pages out and burn them" (378)—in a hoped-for return of calm after racial conflict. Sutpen's grandson Jim Bond endures, and his presence is a sad reminder that the effects of racial turmoil and discord are long-lasting, and the figurative, sought-after, balanced ledger is not yet achieved. (See also chapter 4, for a comprehensive assessment of the McCarroll sisters as possible models for *Absalom, Absalom!*)

Holly Springs and Faulkner's *Light in August*

Connections between Holly Springs and Faulkner's *Light in August* are worthy of consideration as sources for Faulkner. One is the history of Rust College and the family name of Burton. Both are relevant to *Light in August*. Rust College, the historically black college in Holly Springs, initially called Shaw University, was founded by the Freedmen's Aid Society of the Northern

Methodist Episcopal Church.[99] This group was a Northern organization that had as its goal the education of African American people. Also Faulkner's great-grandfather, the Old Colonel, William Clark Falkner, is said to have assisted in the development of the school. Fannie Falkner enrolled in Rust College.[100] According to Joel Williamson, family descendants of Emeline Falkner insist that "Colonel Falkner . . . was Fannie's father."[101]

In Faulkner's novel, in a manner similar to the founding of Shaw University, the character Joanna Burden's father is an abolitionist who came down from the Northeast to found a school for African Americans. The Burtons were a prominent family in Holly Springs. Mary Malvina Shields Burton built the antebellum home Burton Place, also known as Fleur de Lys, in 1848 in Holly Springs. Joanna's grandfather's name, Calvin Burden, surely bespeaks the Calvinistic theology that weighs heavily on the souls in this novel and from which most cannot escape. Both the Rust College history and the Burton family name may have provided Faulkner with antecedents for the Burden family's name and religious implications in *Light in August*.

Rev. Gail Hightower's name has attracted general critical attention for what it reveals about Faulkner's negative view of Presbyterianism. Melvin Backman has noted the irony associated with Hightower's name and the "nature of the character."[102] Backman points to the biblical reference in Hightower's name: "my shield, and the horn of my salvation, my high tower and my refuge, my saviour" (II Sam. 22:3),[103] which are attributes that seem to be ironic in Hightower's case. He seems to be one who shields himself—in his high tower—from the pain of the world. Hightower is not a shield, savior, or refuge for his flock, however, but mostly the opposite. Those who come to him for help do not find it.

Presbyterianism in *Light in August* seems to reflect the views of Faulkner toward those Presbyterians he apparently came to know in Holly Springs and elsewhere. Critics have further discussed Presbyterianism in the novel. Robert L. Johnson's "William Faulkner, Calvinism and the Presbyterians" and Elmo Howell's "A Note on Faulkner's Presbyterian Novel" are two examples.[104] Faulkner was married by the minister of the Presbyterian Church in College Hill, a community near his home of Oxford, Mississippi, mostly because the Episcopal priest declined to perform the ceremony, since Faulkner's bride-to-be was a divorcee. Faulkner usually offers criticism of his Presbyterian characters—Doc Hines, MacEachern, and Hightower—as well as the Calvinistic Burdens. The stolid, uncompromising strictness of the Presbyterian approach to life and religion affects them, including the Presbyterian minister, Gail Hightower.

Figure 1.10 First Presbyterian Church of Holly Springs, where Rev. George Bitzer was pastor from 1926 until his death in 1934 (see Winter, *Shadow of a Mighty Rock*, 353). Courtesy of Keith Gore Wiseman.

The Reverend Gail Hightower appears to be modeled on a specific Holly Springs person—the long-standing Presbyterian minister Reverend George L. Bitzer, DD, grandfather to Edgar Francisco III. Bitzer was well known for his religious fervor and was an oppressive force in the lives of those around him. Numerous letters by his daughter, Ruth Bitzer Francisco, reflect his religious fervor and her own, which undoubtedly stemmed from his teachings. Like Bitzer, Hightower becomes warped by Presbyterian dogma. Joe Christmas is a sympathetic person driven to destruction by the hypocritical religious restrictions of his adoptive parents, Doc Hines, and later MacEachern, both of whom try to control and shape him with their fierce, uncompromising Presbyterian standards. Joanna Burden also is deeply affected by these religious principles.

Faulkner did not need the Presbyterian Church in Holly Springs (see figure 1.10) to teach him about the deeply held Christian principles in the culture around him, nor did he need a real-life minister to model the rapture that religion can arouse in both real and fictional people. Nonetheless, close parallels between Faulkner's fictional minister Gail Hightower and the

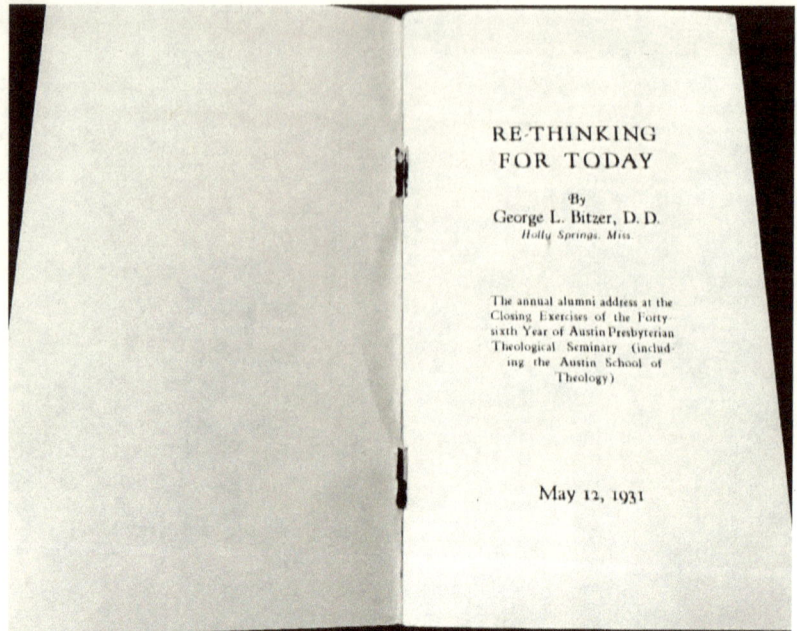

Figure 1.11 The pamphlets announcing sermons by Bitzer clearly specify his divinity degree. These sermons/lectures are among the Reverend George Bitzer Papers, in the McCarroll Place Papers. The McCarroll Place Papers belonged to Dr. Edgar Wiggin Francisco III and his family. Upon the sale of McCarroll Place, the papers transferred to Mr. Harvey Payne, the new owner. Subsequently, Mr. Payne donated the papers to the Department of Archives & Special Collections of the University of Mississippi in 2022 and 2023, and they are currently undergoing processing. Hereinafter these papers will be referred to as the McCarroll Place Papers. Photography by George Nikas, Atlanta, Georgia.

real-life Holly Springs Rev. George Bitzer, suggest that Bitzer provided the novelist a way to satirize an individual in particular and the Presbyterian religion more generally. Some specific indicators suggest that Bitzer, the father-in-law of Faulkner's old friend Edgar Francisco Jr., might have been the target of Faulkner's satire in *Light in August*.

Before her marriage, Mrs. Edgar Francisco Jr. was Ruth Bitzer. Her father, Rev. George Bitzer, held a doctor of divinity degree and was not shy about letting the townspeople know it—he often included the postnominals D.D. on his frequent advertisements. (See figure 1.11.)

Bitzer's publishing his credentials parallels the actions of Faulkner's Reverend Hightower, who, after he is dismissed from his church, posts a sign in his yard announcing both his degree and his commercial artistic talents: "From the window he can also see the sign, which he calls his monument. It is planted in the corner of the yard, low, facing the street. It is three feet long and eighteen inches high—a neat oblong presenting its face to who passes and its back to him" (*Light in August* 52). The sign reads:

REV. GAIL HIGHTOWER, D.D.
Art Lessons
Handpainted Xmas & Anniversary Cards
Photographs Developed (53)

Professionals sometimes append their titles to their names: lawyers use JD, physicians use MD, and professors use PhD or EDD. (Some folks jokingly refer to PhD in derogatory terms.) Nonetheless, a preacher adding postnominals to his sign in his yard or on his mailbox is odd. When Byron Bunch first sees the sign, he does not know what the D.D. stands for: "He asked and they told him it meant Done Damned" (*Light in August* 55). In satirizing Hightower's vanity, Faulkner perhaps was remembering and mocking similar flyers posted by the Reverend George Bitzer of Holly Springs.

Faulkner's depiction of the Reverend Hightower also may reflect the novelist's general dislike of religion or at least Presbyterianism. Faulkner himself was not overtly religious. He did not frequent church: his nephew James M. (Jimmy) Faulkner said William Faulkner went to church only "twice a year—Christmas and Easter."[105] When Faulkner's mother was dying, wrote Joseph Blotner, Faulkner's brother Jack asked, "'What do you reckon happens to you after you die?' [Faulkner said,] 'Well, maybe we'll all come back as radio waves.'"[106]

Scholars have debated the level and extent of Faulkner's Christian faith, but usually they also note a philosophy and natural mysticism that seem to permeate his fiction. The intensity of the characters who believe in salvation and damnation of the Calvinistic, Christian culture are unlike Addie Bundren, who expresses a different view on death as she is getting "ready to stay dead a long time" (*As I Lay Dying* 160). Eternity is not the same as grace that leads to salvation and heaven. Although Faulkner's innermost views of religion are not completely clear, his works suggest that he was capable of naturalistic spirituality. He wrote poignantly with a naturalistic or pantheistic attitude in "The Bear" and other wilderness stories, but also he was steeped in the Christian culture around him, and included it in his works, whatever his personal beliefs may have been.

Presbyterianism was prevalent in the Holly Springs area during his lifetime, but less so in his family. Further motivations for the negative portrayal of Bitzer in the novel may be found in the tense relationship between Faulkner and Edgar's wife, Ruth Bitzer Francisco. The Reverend Bitzer's daughter disliked Faulkner for numerous reasons, including his drinking and cursing, and her views stemmed mostly from her intense religiosity and that of her strict father.[107] Francisco remembers that his mother "did not approve (to put it mildly) of drinking, colorful language, wasting one's time at riding and hunting, and not being 'gainfully employed.'"[108]

Relations between Faulkner and Ruth were fraught. Francisco III says that his mother found Faulkner to be crude, even blasphemous. On one occasion, for example, she made her son wash out his mouth with soap after he mimicked Faulkner's saying "goddamn."[109] Ruth was certain that Faulkner was damned for taking the Lord's name in vain, and she could not abide witnessing her son becoming swept up in Faulkner's blasphemy, which she seriously and fervently believed would lead to damnation. Ruth wanted her son to become deeply religious, as she was, and to remain devoted to God in heart, mind, and language. In his nineties, Francisco III still grapples with his mother's forceful expectations and teachings in this regard.

Faulkner almost certainly was not fond of Ruth, either, since he seemed to engage wittingly in behaviors destined to displease, annoy, and even anger her. At the time of Ruth's marriage to Edgar Jr., Faulkner came to the house with a beer and rabbit and squirrels he had hunted. When the newlyweds returned home during their interrupted honeymoon, Faulkner had sampled the beer, was inebriated, and described Ruth to Edgar Jr., as: "a cute little filly, a spirited little filly, a live one. You're gonna have to break her in."[110] Ruth saw no humor in this situation. Faulkner's taunts and insults were intolerable to her.

As the tension mounted between the two of them over the years, Ruth Bitzer Francisco eventually forbade Faulkner to visit the Francisco house, and that decision relegated all future visits between Faulkner and Edgar Jr. to his downtown office. Perhaps this strenuous, mutual disaffection between Faulkner and the strongly religious Ruth—not to mention her stern, ministerial father—fueled Faulkner's mocking representation of Reverend Hightower. His unflattering portrait of a fictional minister seems likely aimed at the religiosity of Dr. George Bitzer and, by extension, his pious daughter Ruth.

The fictional Hightower and real preacher Bitzer are alike in several important ways: both had similar physical posture, erudite vocabulary, focus on both science and religion, and fervency of religious belief. Both ministers are Presbyterian. They both have "erect," "unbending" postures (*Light in August* 284): for example, Hightower is "sitting a little more than erect" (284). Both he and Bitzer were "tall"—Hightower was "a tall man" (72)—and both he and Bitzer had an erudite vocabulary (Byron Bunch said "he could not think of the word that Hightower would know, would use without having to think of it. 'It's like I not only can't do anything without getting him mixed up in it, I can't even think without him to help me out'" [395–96]). Hightower, like Bitzer, studies and counsels his people who come to him for advice. Dr. Francisco points out that Dr. Bitzer "did see people in his study—people who had issues."[111]

Both real and fictional reverends had a swivel chair in the home office. Hightower is described as having "an ancient swivel chair" (71). According to Edgar Francisco III, Dr. Bitzer had a swivel chair in his church office that he brought to his home office at the Manse:

Dad said Dr. Bitzer would spin around—whirl around—in the chair. Dr. Bitzer was tall and lean. Dad said Bitzer would kick with his feet and spin around in the swivel chair. I never saw the swivel chair, but I heard my parents talk about it. Dad said he didn't think he could spin around in the chair the way Bitzer could. Dad was slow-moving. He said if he were to try to spin around like that, he would put one foot down then put the other one down.[112]

Hightower and Bitzer both preached from the pulpit with religious intensity. Faulkner writes that Hightower used "religion as though it were a dream. Not a nightmare, but something which went faster than the words in the Book; a sort of cyclone that did not even need to touch the actual earth" (56). Bitzer preached in a similarly fervent manner, according to his grandson, Francisco III, and what Faulkner describes in Hightower at the pulpit as "rapt fury" (63) seems applicable to both men.

Both real and fictional ministers also focused on science as well as religion. Hightower "read a great deal . . . books of religion and history and science of whose very existence Byron had never heard" (67–68). George Bitzer's papers, some of which were located at McCarroll Place, reveal an awareness of scientific principles and ideas, general erudition, and the seriousness of his study of religious texts. Edgar Francisco III recalls Bitzer believed that "science was as important as religion, and one should not be discounted to the advantage of the other," and he "gave sermons on science and religion." He emphasized in his sermons that "truth is truth; people should not differentiate between scientific and religious truth. Grandfather was not willing to deny science if it conflicted with religion." Bitzer came out in support of Dr. Diehl, who favored evolution. Bitzer "lectured on evolution, was a supporter of it, and defended Diehl." Later, Francisco III read to the blind Dr. Diehl.[113]

Although Faulkner also could have had other ministers in mind as models for Hightower, and other sources for the "rapt fury" that he depicted, the closeness to hand of the Bitzer connection is worthy of consideration as a source. William Faulkner may have heard from Edgar Jr. of Reverend Bitzer's attitudes and behavior, experienced echoes of them in Edgar's wife Ruth, and suffered from her moral and religious condemnation; that experience, and others like it, may have stimulated Faulkner's anticlerical portraits in *Light in August*.

Religious fanaticism is prevalent thematically in *Light in August* and thus has possible roots, at least in part, in the Reverend Bitzer and his daughter, Ruth. Hightower preaches damnation with "rapt fury"; McEachern's stern and uncompromising manner is extreme; Doc Hines rants about white supremacy to African American congregations; Byron Bunch slips off secretly to lead choir singing; Calvin Burden preaches violent means to abolition; and Joanna Burden insists Joe Christmas pray with her. These characters are among those folks in *Light in August* whose minds and judgment seem warped by religious fanaticism that is deleterious to themselves and others.

As Byron Bunch enters Hightower's home, religious dichotomies become apparent and then manifest themselves in the novel as the tension among goodness, salvation, sin, evil, abomination, and damnation. Hightower, whose name implies a lofty religious and ethical position, nonetheless ironically is less likely to receive salvation than Byron, the humble man who is good of heart. In *Light in August* and *As I Lay Dying*, Faulkner rewards the pure of heart, especially when set in contrast to the hypocrisy of others. Despite their pious, holy, seemingly religious roles, the ministers in Faulkner's novels are not among those most fit for salvation. In fact, the opposite is true. The ministers are the more likely to be sinful, and that fact speaks volumes about Faulkner's opinion of them.

Sin, blasphemy, and abomination also are prevalent themes in the novel, as is a strong motif of devil imagery. McEachern's Presbyterian catechism is an example (*Light in August* 137). Hightower begins discussing evil with Byron Bunch. He assures Byron that he doesn't seem like the kind of person who "could do anything that would be very evil," but Hightower nonetheless cautions Bunch not to "undertake to say just how far evil extends into the appearance of evil . . . just where between doing and appearing evil stops" (289). Hightower says to Byron, "You are already being helped by someone stronger than I am," and when asked to say who, Hightower clarifies: "By the devil" (291). Hightower sees goodness in Byron, however, and continues to describe him as someone who cannot "support even the semblance of evil" (294).

The tension between sin and hope accrues thematic power as the novel progresses. Hightower says that regarding Lena, Byron will have to choose between "sin or marriage" (*Light in August* 298). The fictional minister, like Reverend Bitzer, is a thinker who considers religion, hope, faith, sin, abomination, and evil. Hightower notes that just before church begins, a time when people are gathering and readying for the church service, is "that hour man approaches nearest of all to God, nearer than at any other hour of all the seven days. Then alone, of all church gatherings, is there something of that peace which is the promise and the end of the Church" (346). During this holy time, the mind and the heart are "purged" and "expiated by the stern and formal fury of the morning service" (346), and the "heart quiet now for a little while beneath the cool soft blowing of faith and hope" (347).

The time of faith and hope wanes, in *Light in August*, too, as for Nathaniel Hawthorne's "Young Goodman Brown," as both the Hawthornian and Faulknerian characters alike face the rush of challenges and life difficulties, fall prey to the devil, and plunge into the abyss of sin. Hightower has a premonition of the murder of Joe Christmas:

> the past week has rushed like a torrent and that the week to come, which will begin tomorrow, is the abyss, and that now on the brink of cataract the stream has raised a single blended and sonorous and austere cry, not for justification but as a dying salute before its own plunge, and not to any god but to the doomed man in the barred cell within hearing of them and of the two other churches, and in whose crucifixion they too will raise a cross. "And they will do it gladly," he says, in the dark window.... "They will do it gladly, gladly. That's why it is so terrible, terrible, terrible." (348)

The churchgoers, in ultimate hypocrisy, ostensibly so pure of thought, hope, and faith as they enter the church for the morning services, are among the same citizens who will gladly participate in the execution of Joe Christmas. Their religious beliefs, Hightower concludes, "drive them to crucifixion of themselves and one another" (347).

The devil reappears thematically as Mrs. Hines tells the story of her grandson's birth. During that time, her husband was always fighting. She says: "I told him it was because the devil was in him. And that some day the devil was going to come on him and him not know it until too late, and the devil was going to say 'Eupheus Hines, I have come to collect my toll'" (*Light in August* 352). Later, when Eupheus looks for his pistol with the clear intention of murder, she warns him: "I said, 'Eupheus, it's the devil. It's not Milly's safety that's quicking you now,' and he said, 'Devil or no devil. Devil or no devil,' and he hit me with his hand" (352). Hines is overcome with the power of his temper at the moment, and his violence erupts.

Doc Hines continues to invoke the language of abomination and sin as he realizes his daughter is bearing an illegitimate child of miscegenation: "'It's God's abomination of womanflesh!' the old man cries suddenly" (*Light in August* 353). He says he "had seen the womansign of God's abomination already on her, under her clothes" and that "he should have knowed the walking shape of bitchery and abomination already stinking in God's sight"

(353). He realizes her child is part African American instead of Mexican, as she had told him. He taunts his wife with her warning: "Because you said once that someday the devil would come down on me for his toll. Well, he has. My wife has bore me a whore" (356). The devil seems to have possessed Hines at this point.

War between good and evil rages on in the novel, but faith and hope give way to sin and abomination: "And so sometimes I would think how the devil had conquered God" (*Light in August* 356). As the tension between these two forces mounts, Eupheus allows his daughter Milly to die in childbirth, rather than go for a doctor to help her bear the illegitimate child. Armed with a shotgun, he yells at his wife: "Get back into that house, whore's dam. . . . Let the devil gather his own crop: he was the one that laid it by" (358). Hines sees the devil as victorious. Perhaps Faulkner did too.

Hines reveals further his fanatical religious views: "It's the Lord God's abomination, and I am the instrument of His will" (*Light in August* 360). Although the child, Joe Christmas, is alive, but living elsewhere, to Hines the child "is dead to you and to me and to God and to all God's world forever and ever more" (361). He sees the child as "the devil's walking seed unbeknownst among them, polluting the earth with the working of that word on him" (362). He believes that evil is fully present: "It was in the Lord's good time, for evil to come from evil. And the doctor's Jezebel come running from her lustful bed, still astink with sin and fear" (364). His religious and cultural views are volatile.

For Hines, the war between good and evil culminates as he sees the devil's "face of a ravening beast of the desert" (*Light in August* 364). He quotes God and refers to the ever presence of the devil: "He is still walking My earth" (365). Hines "wrestled" with evil, but "one night he wrestled and he strove and he cried aloud, 'That bastard, Lord! I feel! I feel the teeth and the fangs of evil!' and God said, 'It's that bastard. Your work is not done yet. He's a pollution and a abomination on My earth'" (365). Evil cannot be eradicated, either by the fanatical or the ministerial souls who try in vain to conquer it.

The tension between sin and salvation reaches the crescendo at the cruel murder of Joe Christmas. At the last Joe turns to the minister at least for protection and perhaps comfort, if not salvation from the presence of "that old outcast minister" who was a "sanctuary which would be inviolable not only to officers and mobs, but to the very irrevocable past; to whatever crimes had molded and shaped him and left him at last high and dry in a barred cell with the shape of an incipient executioner everywhere he looked" (*Light in August* 424). Salvation eludes Joe, however, and the ministerial becomes little more than a "chimera, a blind faith in something read in a printed Book" (425). His "hope of salvation" (425) disappears, and the mob of angry men shoot him to death. As is often the case in Faulkner's works, his sympathy lies with the victim, and salvation seems hopeless indeed.

Bitzer and his daughter Ruth were staunch Presbyterians who had strong views and fervent, Presbyterian beliefs in goodness and sin, redemption, and abomination. Abomination, especially the phrase "the Lord God's abomination" appears in *Light in August* (360), and Dr. Francisco says that regarding the phrase "abomination unto the Lord," his "mother used that phrase often."[114] Faulkner depicts in this novel the intense religiosity and fanaticism in the culture around him. He negatively portrays the dangers of religious fanaticism, with a focus on the strict religious minister and those people around him. In doing so, Faulkner appears to enshrine Rev. George L. Bitzer and his daughter Ruth in unflattering literary portraiture.

Additional Bitzer/Francisco Commonalities with Faulkner

Tampico, Mexico, also has a connection to Faulkner and Holly Springs. Bayard sends a postcard from Tampico, Mexico, in *Sartoris*. Francisco III's grandfather attempted to do business in Tampico, Mexico, in the early part of the twentieth century. He traveled there to do land speculation, for possible agricultural sites, and some correspondence and photographs in the McCarroll Place papers document that trip. Faulkner may have viewed that correspondence and photos while visiting McCarroll Place or heard Edgar Jr. describe his father's activities in Tampico.

Other references to Holly Springs places and events that took place there find their way into *Light in August* and establish the connection between novel and town, such as "General Grant's stores burning in Jefferson" (56) and "Van Dorn's cavalry raid to destroy Grant's stores in Jefferson" (451). These quotations appear to refer to Van Dorn's historical raid in Holly Springs and indicate, when added to similar references in other works, such as *The Unvanquished*, that William Faulkner had the Holly Springs context in mind over a long period of time.[115] Another reference to Van Dorn's raid occurs in *Sartoris*. Faulkner gives an account of the raid that is historically accurate. Sometimes Faulkner describes the raid by name, but at other times he includes a description that the raid took place in either the fictional Jefferson or the literal Holly Springs (*Sartoris* 226). (See the introduction, pp. 7–8, for interpretive discussion of Van Dorn's raid.)

Van Dorn's raid was a surprise attack that delayed General Grant's plan to overtake Vicksburg, Mississippi. Historian Ron Chernow describes the "damage" of Earl Van Dorn's raid on "Grant's supply network."[116] On December 20,

1862, Grant learned that "Earl Van Dorn, with 3500 men, had audaciously swooped down at dawn on the Union Supply Depot at Holly Springs, torching millions of rations, dozens of train cars, and hundreds of bales of cotton, while capturing 1,500 Union troops."[117] Shelby Foote adds that "despite an advance warning that a heavy column of graybacks was moving in his direction . . . [Federal commander, Colonel R. C. Murphy] lost not only the stores in his charge but also the soldiers, 1500 of whom were captured."[118] The Confederates were "jubilant" at the "sight of the mountains of food and equipment piled here for Grant's army."[119] They helped themselves and burned the remainder. *The Mississippi Encyclopedia* records that "Van Dorn's men captured supplies worth $1.5 million, according to estimates by the Confederate commander."[120]

The main thrust of Van Dorn's raid occurred from the Holly Springs depot toward the square and down what is now called Van Dorn Avenue. The raiders hit the depot, where the Yankee supplies came in by train. The bulk of the supplies and munitions that were destroyed in the raid were housed in and around the square, with most warehoused in large buildings there. The raiders struck the depot first, then swept into town—by McCarroll Place—and set the great mass of supplies around the square ablaze.

Faulkner's references to this famous raid illustrate that he was keenly aware of the details of the raid and found ways to work facts and creative imaginings about the raid into his work. Hightower's scene of looking out of the window and envisioning the raid is a good example. He vividly reconstructs not only the raid but also a vision of the future home of his friends the McCarrolls and Franciscos and their house overlooking Van Dorn Avenue. He ends with a clear description of the raid on Grant's supplies: "setting fire to the store depots of a whole carefully planned campaign" (*Light in August* 457).

Holly Springs Names and Faulkner's Places and Characters

Holly Springs place names also seem to serve as sources for Faulkner. He refers in *Intruder in the Dust* to a nearby town called "Hollymount" (63, 221), which could be a thinly veiled reference to Holly Springs, or possibly a reference to the old plantation known as Mount Holly near Greenville, in Foote, Mississippi. Shelby Foote's family owned this plantation. Foote grew up in the Delta and met Faulkner in 1937. They became friends. In a C-SPAN interview, Foote recounts details of the friendship, including a joint visit with Faulkner to a bootlegger.[121]

If Faulkner had Mount Holly in mind, perhaps he connected it with a prominent theme in his work: the declining, landowning aristocracy and a decaying mansion. Shelby Foote spent time as a boy at Mount Holly, which his great-grandfather owned. Jean Luckett, a film producer, noted that Mount Holly "figures so prominently in one of Foote's novels," his first novel, *Tournament*, and "was the scene of many of Shelby Foote's boyhood experiences."[122] Mount Holly was, according to Carl McIntire at the *Clarion-Ledger*, "one of the oldest houses of the delta as well as of the state's largest and of unique architecture."[123] The house burned in 2015 and left only the formerly two-feet-thick brick outer walls standing.[124]

Mount Holly and Ammadele, in Oxford, Mississippi, are among the "finest examples of the Italian Villa style in Mississippi."[125] The house also displayed notable architectural features, including gable roofs, round arch windows, bay windows, a balcony, and a veranda, "all of which are common" to the Italian Villa style, and also had a library, a ballroom on the second floor, thirty or more rooms, and fourteen-foot ceilings,[126] as well as "wrought-iron railings, a rosewood staircase, rounded niches for statuary, solid walnut woodwork, and an asymmetrical floor plan."[127] Faulkner may allude to this home in *Intruder in the Dust*. See also Faulkner's reference to "hollyknowe" in *Knight's Gambit*.

In *Requiem for a Nun*, Faulkner mentions a female institute in Jefferson (45) and also refers to a female academy (225). Such female academies and institutes were common in the South, beginning in the nineteenth century. Anne Firor Scott explains, "The first schools for women had appeared in the mid-eighteenth century, and after 1815 female seminaries multiplied," in New England but also in the South as well as other areas.[128] Both Faulkner's mother and wife attended such educational institutions: Estelle attended Mary Baldwin College, which Joel Williamson describes as "a school for young women in the very Presbyterian town of Staunton, Virginia" and adds that "in September, 1889, Maud Butler [Falkner] was an entering student in the Industrial Institute and College for the Education of White Girls of Mississippi in Columbus—now the Mississippi University for Women."[129]

Ralph Lyon sees that these academies and institutes "had a great growth in this region during the Antebellum period," and "'it was by its means and operation that the older Southern life and culture became what it was and remained until' the Civil War" (192).[130] The newspaper in Livingston stated the purpose of the female academy as to "lay a solid firm foundation for female education to secure independence of thought and proper appreciation of the courtesies of life."[131] As a case in point, the Livingston Female Academy "serve[d] as an excellent example of the typical motivations for academies in the South and the nation . . . but it is also the ancestor of a normal school and a state college."[132]

Figure 1.12 Mississippi Synodical College, art class, dated 1895–1896. Courtesy of Special Collections, University of Mississippi Libraries, Chesley Thorne Smith Collection.

Faulkner's stepdaughter attended the Mississippi Synodical College in Holly Springs.[133] Several townspeople attested to Faulkner's picking up Cho Cho after school. The history of Mississippi Synodical College goes back to the immediate post–Civil War period, and the school existed under various names and ownership until it was sold in 1890 and became the North Mississippi Presbyterian College. Shortly after, in 1893, control of the school was passed to the Synod of Mississippi, and it became Mississippi Synodical College.[134] (See figure 1.12.)

Holly Springs Names and Faulkner

A compelling array of Holly Springs people have names that match closely—and in some cases exactly—with the names of Faulkner's fictional characters. Much of the significance of these borrowings/echoes depends on their large number, evidence that Holly Springs was a well Faulkner drew from repeatedly. That Faulkner sourced names for his fictional characters from real-life residents is evidenced by the history of a character called V. K. Surrat/V. K. Ratliff, who appears in multiple works. In his first appearances in texts published up to 1932, the character is named V. K. Surrat. James M. (Jimmy) Faulkner recalled that an Oxford citizen named Surrat called Faulkner and said: "If you don't change that name, the next voice you'll hear will be that of my attorney."¹³⁵ Faulkner transposed V. K. Surrat into V. K. Ratliff, who went on to appear in numerous subsequent fictional works. Obvious borrowings or analogues from Holly Springs are Doxey for Hoxey, Rittelmeyer for Rittenmeyer, and Absalom for the title of Faulkner's novel. Perhaps Faulkner thought that Holly Springs was far enough away that the townsfolk there, both white and African American, would not recognize (or care about) their names in his fiction. In any case these numerous matchings or closely corresponding pairs of names speak to Faulkner's creative process. Indeed, to read or hear the paired names is as if to glimpse Faulkner at work.

A partial list of pairs of Holly Springs names and their fictional counterparts appears in table 1.1. The names from real Holly Springs persons derive from the website Find a Grave (www.findagrave.com) listings of memorials in the Hill Crest Cemetery in Holly Springs, Mississippi, unless otherwise indicated. Names denoted by a single asterisk (*) are from *A Southern Tapestry, Marshall County, Mississippi, 1835–2000* by Hubert H. McAlexander. Names of Faulkner characters stem from lists provided in *William Faulkner A to Z*, by A. Nicholas Fargnoli and Michael Golay and *A Faulkner Glossary* by Harry Runyan. Faulkner character names marked with double asterisk (**) are from the Runyan *Glossary*. The real Holly Springs name appears left, and William Faulkner's character name appears right. Some surnames match with fictional counterparts: for example, Lynwood Hightower and Aaron Birdsong are names once listed on a Holly Springs brochure from Strawberry Fields. The Reverend Gail Hightower is also the name of a prominent minister in *Light in August*, and Birdsong is a white night watchman who runs a crooked dice game in *Go Down, Moses*. Other names align elliptically with real counterparts, such as Compton/Compson; Callicutt/Callicoat; Burton/Burden, Doxey/Hoxey, and McDermott/McDiarmid.

Table 1.1. Holly Springs names and their fictional counterparts

Holly Springs Name	William Faulkner Characters
AMES	Dalton Ames in *The Sound and the Fury*
ARMISTEAD	Henry Armstid and Ida Armstead, poor farmers in *Intruder in the Dust* and other works
Gerard BADOW (known around Holly Springs as "Bad Dough")¹	James Dough, wounded soldier in *Soldier's Pay*
BAIRD	Dr. Baird, physician in *Soldier's Pay* Bayard in *Sartoris*

Holly Springs Name	William Faulkner Characters
BISHOP	Ephraim Bishop, sheriff in *Mansion* "Billy" Bishop, aviator in *A Fable*
BLACK	Mr. Black,** driver, "Death Drag" John Black,** a horse, "Was," in *Go Down, Moses*
BONNER (a prominent Holly Springs family for several generations. See McAlexander 166.)	Charles Bon in *Absalom, Absalom!*
BUFFALOE	Mr. Buffaloe, mechanic in *The Town, The Mansion, The Reivers*
BUFORD	Buford, deputy in *Light in August*
CALLICUTT	David Callicoat, steamboat captain in "A Justice"
Joseph CARUTHERS (The Caruthers family was prominent in Holly Springs and included a founding commissioner. See McAlexander 11.)	Miss Carruthers, organist in Hightower's Church in *Light in August* Carothers McCaslin (Cass) Edmonds in *Go Down, Moses, The Town, The Reivers* Carothers (Roth) Edmonds in *Go Down, Moses, Intruder in the Dust, The Town*
Judge J. W. CLAPP	Walter Clapp, horse trainer in *The Reivers*
COLBERTS* (powerful early family)	David Colbert, chief of Chickasaws in "A Courtship"
COMPTON	Compson in *The Sound and the Fury, Absalom, Absalom!*
WALL DOXEY (a United States Senator.[2] See McAlexander.)	Hoxey, mayor in "Centaur in Brass" Wall Snopes in The Trilogy
DuPRE (DuPre was a prominent Holly Springs family. See McAlexander 120.)	Virginia DuPre in *Sartoris, Unvanquished*, etc.
EDMONDSON	Carothers McCaslin (Cass) Edmonds in *Go Down, Moses, The Town, The Reivers* Carothers (Roth) Edmonds in *Go Down, Moses, Intruder in the Dust, The Town, The Reivers*

FRAZIER	Fraser, hunter in "A Bear Hunt" Fraser moonshiner in *Knight's Gambit* Doyle Fraser and Squire Adam in *Intruder in the Dust* Fraser's Store in *Intruder in the Dust* Judge Frazier in "Tomorrow," *Knight's Gambit*
GATEWOOD	Jabbo and Noon Gatewood in *The Town*
GRIER	Pete Grier, son of Res and Mrs. Grier in "Two Soldiers," "Shall Not Perish" etc. Emily Grierson, spinster in "A Rose for Emily"
HAWKS* (Hawks was a distinguished clergyman who was in Holly Springs for a time. See McAlexander.)	Dennison Hawk in *The Unvanquished* Louisa Hawk and Drusilla Hawk in *The Unvanquished* Hawkhurst in *The Unvanquished* Hawkshaw in "Hair" and "Dry September"
HOUSTON	Jack Houston (aka Zach) in The Trilogy Houston, waiter in *Sartoris* Doris and Mrs. Houston in "Two Dollar Wife" Lucy Pate Houston in *The Hamlet*
Ben INGRAM	Willy Ingrum and Marshall Ingrum in *Intruder in the Dust*
LEGGETT	Will Legate, hunter in *Go Down, Moses*, *Intruder in the Dust*, etc. Bob Legate, hunter in *The Reivers*
LOWE	Julian Lowe, pilot in *Soldiers' Pay*
MAHON	Donald and Joseph Mahon** in *Soldiers' Pay*
McCARROLL (Multiple generations of this family lived at McCarroll Place in Holly Springs.)	Hoake McCarron and relatives in *The Hamlet*, etc.
McDERMOTT (Members of this family are buried in the Hill Crest Cemetery in Holly Springs. See FindAGrave.com.)	McDiarmid, restaurant manager in *The Reivers*
Robert McGOWAN	Skeets McGowan in *As I Lay Dying*, *Intruder in the Dust*, *Town*, *Mansion*, etc.[3]

Holly Springs Name	William Faulkner Characters
McKIE (The McKies were substantial planters before the War. See Hubert McAlexander 38.)	McKie, British officer in "Crevasse"
MOSBY	Mosby, Uncle Hogeye in *Intruder in the Dust*
MOSELEY	Mosely Mottstown, drug store owner in *As I Lay Dying*
Col. ABSALOM MYERS*	Title of *Absalom, Absalom!* Al Myers, pilot in *Pylon*
PARHAM*	Parsham, race location in *The Reivers*
PETTIPOOLES*	Pettigrew, lawyer in "Beyond" T. J. Pettigrew in *Requiem for a Nun* Pettibone, wealthy Virginian in *Absalom Absalom!*
QUINN	Dr. Quinn in *Sanctuary*
VARDAMAN Ray	Vardaman Bundren in *As I Lay Dying*
RITTELMEYER (The Rittelmeyers were Prussian carpenters in Holly Springs. See McAlexander 49.)	Charlotte, Francis, Charlotte II, and Ann Rittenmeyer in *The Wild Palms*
RIVERS	Reba Rivers in *Sanctuary*, etc. Lee Rivers in *Soldiers Pay*
SALES	Sales, airplane inspector in *Pylon*
SNIPES (Several family members are buried at Hill Crest Cemetery in Holly Springs.)	Snopes family in many works
STRIBLING	Henry Stribling in "Hair," etc.
TALIAFERRO* (An early Holly Springs settler. See McAlexander 25.)	Ernest Talliaferro in *Mosquitoes*
WALTHALL	Parson Walthall in *The Sound and the Fury*
ABSOLOM Madden WEST (Brigadier General in the Mississippi Militia. See McAlexander 68.)	Title of *Absalom, Absalom!* David West, steward in *Mosquitoes* Dr. West, druggist in "Smoke" in *Knight's Gambit* Miss West, secretary in "Honor"

Table Notes

1. For further information, see endnote 10 in chapter 3.
2. James L. Harrison, comp., *Biographical Directory of the American Congress, 1774–1949: The Continental Congress, September 5, 1774, to October 21, 1788, and the Congress of the United States from the First to the Eightieth Congress, March 4, 1789 to January 3, 1949, Inclusive* (US Government Printing Office, 1950), 1101.
3. Francisco III points out that Holly Springs men Mr. McCrosky, McCarroll, and McGowan all were fellow Scotsmen and good friends. They had their photos taken together. Francisco III, telephone communication with author, December 2018.

Some people in Holly Springs knew Faulkner; others remember meeting or seeing him. Some who knew him did not care for or about him. "Who cares about some damn writer?" one citizen said in an interview about Faulkner.[136] Some were embarrassed by his writings; others enjoyed his company and went hunting with him but simply did not read his works. Two additional examples illustrate some of the views Holly Springs townspeople held of Faulkner. When he died, the Holly Springs newspaper did not carry the obituary. Also, legend has it that when Faulkner's novel *Sanctuary* came out, the Holly Springs librarian literally sat on the book, so that patrons could not read it.

Holly Springs—quite near home yet just far enough away—provided Faulkner with a space apart. There he felt free to listen to stories; study the ample history of the area; find more tales and information about the Civil War, which deeply affected Holly Springs because of its direct contact with the Yankee troops of Ulysses S. Grant; and hear cherished, collective remembrances. In some cases the recollections of Holly Springs citizens came to Faulkner via oral tradition, but sometimes they included the hard evidence of war—the Confederate sword found boarded up in the wall at McCarroll Place or the constant and modestly productive Geiger counters search for buried Civil War era coinage. These memories and artifacts are the fabric of his stories.

The people of Holly Springs seemed ready and willing to share with Faulkner their stories and evidence of war casualty, such as the legends that arose about the fallen Northern soldiers whose markers remain in the town cemetery. The townspeople were quick to include descriptions of the personal struggles of their ancestors during the Northern invasion, and they readily aired their residual feelings of hurt, guilt, and pride, so characteristic of both the rational, irrational, prejudicial, and self-protective responses of the South to the war and its aftermath. Such stories and evidence were prevalent then and persist even now in Holly Springs. The tales Faulkner heard and reminders he saw of a time gone by weave their way into some of his most compelling fiction.

Appendix 1-A: Dr. Edgar Francisco's Rebuttal to the Article "Confabulations of History"

Dr. Edgar Francisco III provided the following essay as a rebuttal to Jack D. Elliott Jr.'s "Confabulations of History: William Faulkner, Edgar Francisco, and a Friendship That Never Was," which appeared in the *Journal of Mississippi History* 74, no. 2 (January 2012): 309–48. Francisco III composed the essay in October 2023. Printed by permission.

INTRODUCTION

When I first saw a copy of Jack Elliott's article "Confabulations of History," I thought it was a collection of absurdities, and people would just laugh at it. I read only bits of it and dismissed it. Now that Dr. Wolff has convinced me that some people have been deceived by his misinformation, I decided to read the full article and have determined that I must respond. I don't see a correct conclusion in his entire article, which is full of false accusations based on either false information, no understanding of what he is citing, or just his opinion. He seems to criticize me with insufficient and inaccurate information. Lately I have reviewed again what Dr. Wolff quoted from me in her book, *Ledgers of History*. With the exception of two minor errors, which I shall enumerate here, all is exactly as I remembered it or remember being told, despite the candid-camera interview method she used.

Before I discuss and correct a representative sample of Elliott's false conclusions, it is most important to note that Dr. Wolff primarily focuses a lot of her attention on our family's two (the only two) desperately kept secrets—one of them kept for three generations. If I had written about the family, I would never have mentioned either secret, Faulkner, or the *Leak Diary*. I was committed to keeping secret our three-generational mission to destroy the *Diary*, or at least hide our connection to it. Also, I had sworn with hand on Mother's Bible never to admit that I had met Faulkner (Dad had to do the same), but Dr. Wolff was so enthusiastic about Faulkner that I impulsively thought it would be safe after more than 70 years keeping Mother's secret to admit I knew Faulkner.

If I had remembered the horrible reason why Mother had made me promise to keep Faulkner a secret, however, I would not have even talked to Dr. Wolff. This is not at all a criticism of Dr. Wolff. On the contrary, I need to congratulate her. Because of her lifelong study of Faulkner's writings, her extensive research and persistent questing, she uncovered our family's two secrets, both contributing to Faulkner research, and both of which otherwise would never have been revealed. I need to take time to explain why the secrets were so important, however.

Each of my parents had a traumatic secret that obsessed them until death. Each thought the other's secret was absurd. From childhood I was caught up in both, and into adulthood I honored each and tried my best to be supportive.

DAD'S SECRET

Dad's secret was the three-generational struggle to destroy or get rid of the original handwritten *Leak Diary* and its resident curse and keep secret the long, destructive battle waged at McCarroll Place between the family and the curse. A more complete description of the "resident curse" is that Grandmother, Betsy Leak, believed that an angry spirit would place a curse upon anyone who used the *Diary* for personal gain. She believed it had placed a curse on her grandfather, causing his death for writing it and describing his use of slaves on his plantation. She believed her father had been killed by the curse for using the *Diary* to guide him after he was in charge, and probably it killed her baby brother as further punishment, leaving her mother without a male heir. Her fears extended to the belief that the very presence of the journals in the house implied an appreciation of the *Diary* and therefore was a danger to all who lived there.

Betsy's mother, Amelia McCarroll Leak, had brought Betsy and the *Diary* back to McCarroll Place, after her husband died, in thinking the *Diary* would provide evidence of assets she was entitled to receive. When that failed Amelia wrapped each ledger separately in a linen cloth, numbered the packages, and stored them in the bottom drawer of her chest. Dad said that Betsy had told him that she wore gloves each time she planned to burn them but always lost the courage to touch them.

Dad thought the diaries were untouched until many years later when he mentioned them to Faulkner, who wanted to see them. I remember one time I saw Faulkner looking at one of the journals, and I remember being very scared. Faulkner must have said something to Dad, because Dad left the sunroom and returned with gloves. He went up to the front bedroom and returned carrying a package in gloved hands stretched at arm's length and placed the package on a side table by Faulkner, who unwrapped it, pulled out his little notebook, turned through the ledger, read a bit, and then wrote in his notebook. He had cursed as he read, not in anger or fear, but seemingly in surprise or interest, but I took my cues from Dad's expression which I perceived to be fear. I was so preoccupied with my fear that I think I missed some conversation between the two men because the next thing I noticed was Faulkner wrapping back up the ledger, leaving it on the table and walking out the garden door right next to his rocking chair. Crashing over me was the discovery that something very dangerous was in my house. For a year after that I didn't want to go in the house after coming home from school unless Mother was back from her afternoon activities. I would ride my bike around until I saw her car back home.

As a child I fully bought into the mission to destroy the volumes of the *Diary* and the curse along with it. Grandmother, Betsy, died still lamenting that each time she tried she lost the courage to burn the diaries quickly before the curse killed her. When I asked, Dad said he was planning to bury them. That sounded most unsatisfying. So, I was determined to prove I could burn them, and fantasized I would be acclaimed a hero. I was almost 13, and in the rapture of building a huge fall Saturday bonfire down the hill at the dry creek, when I realized this was the perfect opportunity to burn the journals. Nobody was home; I could get in the front guest bedroom (off-limits to me) where the diaries were—but Mother came home unexpectedly.

Elsewhere I have told the rest of this story with all its ups and downs. After hearing my boast that I would finish the mission, Dad decided the safer option was to give in to his cousin Perle's repeated pleas to allow her to handle the donation in Dad's name to the University of Mississippi. She had shifted to this plea after she gave up on ever getting him to loan her a ledger for her to display. Her husband, Gerard Badow, would come to pick them up so Dad wouldn't need to do anything. Perle understood the importance of her offer to "handle" the donation for him. Betsy had told her son, Edgar, that she and Perle had met every day when teenagers, walking through the gate connecting their homes, to share their day's experiences and thoughts. Betsy would have shared her fears and failed attempts to destroy the *Diary*. Dad agreed to Perle's offer upon her promise to include a letter of donation in which he would express his strong disapproval of the *Diary*. A long time later Perle told him she thought he should donate the *Diary* to Chapel Hill. Dad didn't care and didn't ask why. His only interest was to get rid of it quickly. A long-time later Dad caught a glimpse of Badow walking away from our house. He had been on our property only once before when he was sent by Perle to pick up the ledgers for Dad's donation. Looking to see what he left Dad spotted a book in the rocking chair on our porch. It was a copy of one typed volume of the *Diary*. He looked for his letter of donation, which contained a blistering denunciation of the diary's contents and the activities of its author. He believed his letter was essential to prove his donation did not mean he admired its contents, and he was shocked to not find it, but when he noticed that Perle had listed her name, not his, he was overjoyed. He was off the hook, but why did she do it? We talked about that a lot, and the only reason we could think of for Perle to shift the donation to Chapel Hill, then list her name and omit Dad's letter, must have been that she was offered money for it, which necessitated the deletion of his letter and his name.

Before Badow started delivering the typed volumes of the *Diary*, Dad had knocked on Strickland Place door a number of times to inquire about Perle's health. Usually no one answered, but when Badow did he said Perle was too ill to be disturbed. The last time Edgar inquired, Badow threw open the door in a rage and said he was tending to Perle and Edgar was interfering, and if Edgar came again, he would take legal action. Dad's only comment at the time was if his mother was alive, she would be certain that Perle was at high risk of death by the curse for admiring the *Diary* and what it described and profiting from it. Perle died shortly thereafter, and her forensic physician cousin came to offer condolements. He noticed in the kitchen a container of rat poison, a scale for measuring minute amounts of power [powder], and other equipment that made him suspicious. He asked questions and concluded that it was most likely that Badow had slowly killed Perle with small amounts of rat poison. [See further discussion of this point on pp. 34–36.]

Dad never knew the details of how the change in donation status came about, but for the rest of his life Dad believed that Perle's need for money and her resulting deception had totally hidden forever the fact that the original hand-written copy of the *Diary* had been hidden at McCarroll Place, while we obsessed with keeping it all a secret. I believed that also, until Dr. Wolff discovered it because I had delayed destroying it until I got up the nerve to read a bit first. Dr. Wolff's research would uncover the donation records, which showed that the University had produced two typescript copies of the *Diary*; one for Perle and one for Edgar Francisco. I continued to believe that the receipt of cash was the only explanation for Perle's changes, but wondered why she said her 2nd copy was for Dad, and why did Badow deliver them when Perle could not? Very recently an alternative explanation has occurred to me. Perle knew that Dad had hesitated to donate the *Diary*, because that would take it out of hiding, so what if Perle saw a win-win opportunity for her to take credit for the donation and Edgar would be thrilled that his secret was secure, and he and McCarroll Place were free of the *Diary* and the curse forever. This seems like classic Perle. She delighted in deception as theater art. She worked on perfecting her skill at lying as part of her performance.

Dad, with Perle's help, accomplished his mission, and then I blew it. Once the secret was uncovered, I tried to accept it and act as if it was acceptable for people to know. But it was not alright. While I don't blame myself for failing to burn the *Diary* when I was 13, it is my fault that I did not destroy the unwanted typed copy. I betrayed Dad's trust, and I cannot forgive myself for that.

MOTHER'S SECRET

Mother's secret was Faulkner's association with Dad. More specifically, she made Dad and me promise to keep the friendship secret because of her belief that blasphemy was the greatest sin. Mother believed that "taking the name of the Lord in vain" was the only unforgivable sin, based on the unique wording of the 3rd commandment, and the punishment would be burning in hell forever. My earliest childhood memories are of her talking about blasphemy a lot, but I had no idea what "taking the Lord's name" was. I found out when I got a mouth-washing for practicing saying "God damn," the new expression I had just heard Faulkner use. A day or two after my mouth-washing, Mother informed Dad and me that she had petitioned God to forgive me if we all promised never to mention Faulkner again and deny we knew him if asked. I continued to keep my promise until late in my life, even though I must have repressed the reason within a day or two. The horror of my situation must have been more than a child could process.

If Dr. Wolff had not repeatedly asked about any other reasons for secrecy then [sic] Mother's embarrassment over Faulkner drinking and cursing in her house, I might never have recalled the actual reason, and I didn't until after my interviews with her were finished. As final editing of *Ledgers of History* was wrapping up, my repressed memory of childhood terror and horror came flooding back, and it seemed related to Faulkner. When I told Dr. Wolff, she asked me to tell her about it, and she could add an afterword. On page 177 I am quoted as saying: "I feel that I should try, although I do not fully understand it yet." What an understatement that turned out to be. The best I could do at that time was to relate that memory of terror to my discovery that the writer of the *Diary* whom Faulkner seemed so angry with was my ancestor, so Faulkner would probably not speak to me again. Dr. Wolff and I were trying to tell an important story with no knowledge of why it had been so necessary to keep it a secret. Long after publication, more, perhaps all, of the repressed memory surfaced. It was all due to Mother's obsession with blasphemy and her belief that she needed to tell me my fate to impress upon me the necessity of keeping Faulkner a secret. I totally believed she was right about hell and my fate. The terror of it had to have been repressed that day, probably within hours. Dr. Wolff wrote about this after the memory emerged and I told her, but it's worth repeating here. Thanks to Dr. Wolff's persistent questioning, once the memory came back, I could process Mother's false belief and dismiss it, and then the nightmares I had since childhood stopped.

I think readers have no idea how unlikely it was that anyone could discover the secrets that Dr. Wolff uncovered or have the persistence to document them. Since Dr. Wolff never pointed this out, I need to give her credit. While I had decided it was alright for me to break my promise to Mother to never tell anyone about Faulkner's visits to McCarroll Place, surely there wasn't one chance in a million for discovery of the secret that the Leak diary was hidden at McCarroll Place for over 70 years or the trauma it caused.

As a Faulkner scholar, Dr. Wolff was there [at my home with my wife Anne and me] to do an interview about Faulkner's time spent at McCarroll Place [my family home in Holly Springs, Mississippi]. In her lap was a typed copy of the original diary she now knew he had read, and she had spotted material that she recognized as almost identical to material in one of his books [*Go Down, Moses*]. This connection could never have been made any other way or by anybody else. Prerequisite to the living room event was the extremely unlikely survival of the original ledgers to make possible the donation of them, and my possession of the typed copy. The volumes were still in the house because I had not gotten around to destroying them. I had not explained to Anne that the diary was a family secret, and I planned to destroy it, so she blurted out would Dr. Wolff like to see an old diary. I couldn't think fast enough of how to avoid bringing down a volume, hoping she wouldn't be interested, but she asked, and I had to admit that Faulkner had read some original ledgers.

Then, Dr. Wolff's discovery was just the beginning. Incredible perseverance and many months of research were required to piece the story together and document it for publication [in *Ledgers of History*]. While I will probably always harbor some guilt over betrayal of Dad's lifetime success of keeping the diary a secret, except for his showing it to Faulkner, I have the highest respect and regard for Dr. Wolff's scholarship and literary achievements.

THE McCARROLL PLACE DEED

In the course of his diggings, [Jack D.] Elliott discovered a gap in the deed book about the ownership of McCarroll Place, my family home of five generations. Many people at the time of the "gap" knew about it and giggled, but Elliott knew nothing of that history and didn't check with me to find out. He sets the stage with some facts to lend creditability to his attack, in this case noting that John B. and Delilah Love Moore were the first individual owners of lots 362 and 363, which were part of a section allotted to them by the federal government in 1839. They had sold to Kyle and Mitchel, who sold to Lewellen and Alderson, and then Elliott highlights his suspicious gap. But there was nothing suspicious about this gap—merely amusing events.

McCarroll had been a friend of Delilah for over a decade, and he had told her he wasn't interested in buying the lots because he was looking to buy NW of town. Just to persuade his wife to move the family there from Tennessee, so he could run for sheriff for the 1840 to 1844 term, John McCarroll in 1836 had moved his house up from the spring, located down the hill from where McCarroll Place now sits on Van Dorn Avenue. Until the government allocated land to individual Chickasaws in 1839, tribal leaders who were friends of McCarroll seemed not [to] mind that he was hunting each fall and building on tribal land. When Delilah received and was ready to sell the lots McCarroll had built on, Elizabeth Eddins McCarroll, wife of John R. McCarroll, and Louisa Eddins Hill, wife of Byrd Hill panicked and persuaded Hill to purchase the lots. McCarroll said rather than buy the lots from Hill, he would give his current house to him when he built his new home, but finally he gave in and reimbursed Hill. I was told that when McCarroll asked Hill for the deed so he could file it, Hill told him to get the deed from Lewellen and Alderson, since Hill had only been an agent for McCarroll. When McCarroll went to Lewellen and Alderson, they said that they had sold the lots to Hill, who never mentioned McCarroll, and they did not want to be accused of selling the lots twice. McCarroll concluded that it was correct to record his purchase from Hill and tell Hill to record his from Lewellen and Alderson. Hill never did record his purchase, leaving this gap. Local historian Bobby Mitchell confirms that in these early times in the Holly Springs area, "Some people never recorded their deeds."[137]

Well, time goes by, and 150 years later Mr. Elliott spots this gap about which he has no clue but seems to have recognized that he could use it as a weapon. Then he adds yet another misinformed assumption. He seems to have misread the recording clerk's handwriting and concluded that the lot McCarroll purchased from Hill was "302." Apparently he did not see that this clerk's "6" always looked like a "0." Mr. Elliott seems to have spent an enormous amount of time on what surely seemed trivial in 1840, especially considering the volume of land sales immediately after 1839, and the loss of early records in the courthouse fire of 1864. Elliott's purpose seems to be to imply that my family still didn't own the lots the house was on, despite our having been charged and having paid taxes on 363 and 362 (not 302) for over 150 years. In my opinion Elliott's article is of this nature and quality. Nothing there. Smoke and mirrors.

McCARROLL PLACE HOUSE HISTORY

Mr. Elliott begins one of his many attempts to discredit my family and me in his article, "Confabulations of History," by saying that he "will first examine the standard historical narrative of McCarroll Place that has appeared in newspaper and Pilgrimage brochures for decades since the 1930s. Presumably these accounts would reflect the story that Edgar told" (325). This introductory statement set the stage for Elliott to select an article that included statements differing from what I said. Many articles written about McCarroll Place were substantially correct, but he didn't select them. Elliott picked an article that contains misinformation supporting his attempt to prove I didn't know my own family history. Elliott claims this account forms the "standard" narrative, but the article he chose is one of the most outrageously false articles ever written about McCarroll Place and written by a person with insufficient knowledge of the family. Elliott proposes that my mother possibly wrote the article [as it appeared in the newspaper article "Family in Same Residence for Ninety-two Years," in the Holly Springs *South Reporter*, December 15, 1932]. She did not. Elliott's claim that the historical narrative of McCarroll Place, as reflected in this article, has appeared for decades since the 1930s, also is, to the best of my knowledge, false.

The 1932 *South Reporter* article Elliott cites notes correctly that McCarroll Place has the record for the longest continuous occupancy by the same family.[138] My parents were surprised to see the article, however, since no one had contacted them for information. If the article author had contacted my parents, she would have learned the full and more interesting story. The staff writer was correct about the land being bought from Byrd Hill in 1840, but her assumption that McCarroll built the house after purchasing the land was wrong. McCarroll built a three-room house in 1833, down the hill by the spring below where McCarroll Place now sits, and he moved those rooms up to the current location of the house in 1836 and attached those rooms to another two rooms he had built earlier that same year.

The writer of the *South Reporter* article also didn't know that McCarroll had first come down into Mississippi to explore and hunt in 1824 at age 20, after having moved the first of his aunts and her family from North Carolina to an area east of Memphis and north of what would become Holly Springs. His mother was one of six Ramsey daughters. She had died the year he was born, and he was raised by the remaining five aunts. Between about 1822 and 1836 he lived in Tennessee as he helped move, one by one, four of the families to that area. The fifth moved to Memphis. He lived with one or another of the families as he built the house for the next one. McCarroll would come down to Holly Springs each fall to his hunting shack at the spring to hunt for a couple of weeks. Beginning in 1832 he started constructing the permanent three-room home by the spring.

The *South Reporter* writer's false assumption in her article appears to be the total of Elliott's "adequate material" for calling a lie our family story about the building of the house. He states, with no evidence, to my knowledge, that Ruth Francisco wrote the *South Reporter* article. The paper did not credit her as having sent in the story. It seems to me that everyone would assume the article was staff written. Surely, that would be the normal assumption unless otherwise stated. Elliott thus seems to be trying to discredit Mother as well as our family story.

A decade later I saw the 1932 *South Reporter* article in a scrapbook, and I asked Dad if he ever tried to correct the article, and he said he didn't. His explanation was that the staff writer was a sweet lady, and she was very proud of her article. He said he never would have embarrassed her by asking for corrections in print. That was an important lesson in empathy that my teen-age brain had difficulty embracing at the time.

If the writer of the 1932 *South Reporter* article had checked her story with my parents, she would have had the correct and much more interesting story of McCarroll constructing hunting shacks and hunting on his Chickasaw friends' land, and then finishing the south three rooms in 1833 down the hill at the spring. To get his wife to move down from Tennessee he had to pull the three rooms up to their present location in 1836 to join a new two-room addition on the north end. McCarroll apparently built the earlier three rooms mostly by himself. His Chickasaw friend, Sam, is alleged to have occasionally watched but offered little help. My parents were horrified by erroneous information about the house history that appeared in writings about the house over the years. I will in a separate venue attempt to correct for the sake of history these and other factual misrepresentations about the fascinating history of the antebellum McCarroll Place.

VIEW FROM LUDIE'S WINDOW

Dad's favorite Pilgrimage activity was leading visitors through McCarroll Place to the sunroom to view Ludie's name etched on a windowpane of what had become an interior window when the open gallery had been enclosed as a sunroom. Dad would add that his grandmother, Amelia McCarroll Leak, told him that Ludie was watching soldiers that were marching on the section of the road to the Depot, and that she could see them from the window as she etched her name.

Dad had confirmed that he could see the street from where Ludie had stood, but in the fall of 1929, his bride, Ruth Bitzer Francisco, enclosed the open gallery to form a sunroom. After that, the view from Ludie's now-interior window was the sunroom. Then Mother added a bathroom north of the sunroom, which extended so far east that the view from the sunroom door was only the south wall of the bathroom.

In 1932, Mother added outside a raised, wrought-iron fence, separating the front yard from the garden. Now standing outside the house in the garden, you could not see the front yard. Thousands of visitors over decades have noted that the thick interior wall with Ludie's window had to have been an exterior wall before the sunroom was enclosed.

Elliott, in his attempt to debunk the Ludie story, wrote that the street couldn't be seen from Ludie's window. He perhaps did not know about or at least did not mention the structural changes that had occurred inside McCarroll Place that blocked the view of the street from Ludie's window.

Several stories make Ludie important to our family. [Please see the extended accountings of these stories in chapter 2, pp. 81–85.]

Faulkner was much drawn to the story of Ludie's short and tragic life, including the fact that both Ludie and her mother had died as a result of pregnancy. I watched Faulkner staring at Ludie's etching in her glass windowpane and walking over close to view her name in reverse. Dad told him he could go into the bedroom to see her name from the right side, but Faulkner said he didn't want to disturb Ludie. When Dad appeared to be either nervous or skeptical, Faulkner said Ludie had been there so long that Dad had become insensitive, but he knew Ludie was there. That room had become my parents' bedroom, and I never went in when they were there, but when no one was around I would peep through the window. For a while I thought I saw Ludie, but when I was about ten she seemed to disappear. Everyone I knew who had an opinion believed in ghosts.

MY PARENTS' WEDDING

On page 84 of her book *Ledgers of History*, Dr. Wolff asks when my mother first met William Faulkner. I apologize for giving Mother's birthday instead of my parents wedding date, but the rest of the story is exactly as Dad told it. The interview method achieves authentic spontaneity, but at the cost of an occasional error, especially in dates, since the candid-camera, off-the-cuff responses to many questions leave little time for thought, and no time for research. However, I believe this is the only serious error in the book. (One minor error is one event that I dated a year earlier than it happened, because with no time to think about it, I underestimated my age.) I had asked Dad the same question, and he told me that they had interrupted their honeymoon after the first night to return to Holly Springs for the weekend to handle a business crisis, and there was Faulkner sitting on the gallery with a beer, a rabbit, and squirrels, talking about roasting up the game and having a celebration. Mother was offended by what he said to her that he apparently intended to be a compliment—that Edgar had found himself a "cute little filly" and that he would "have to break her in," and she was shocked by the game.[139] I believe that neither Faulkner nor Mother had ever met anyone like the other. Dad usually ended his stories without adding the "what happened next." This kept the story lingering in one's imagination. I never asked so I have wondered for over 80 years. I guess the men had a couple of quick beers, and the party was over. Dad would have given the game to one of the people he knew would love to have it, since he would never have thrown it out. The story reminds me of how precious are my memories of Dad teaching me to skin and prep game and roasting it together. I doubt either of us thought much about it at the time. We were just having fun, but later I realized that these repeated rituals were bonding between father and son.

I had Dad all to myself sitting side by side in the "deep woods" watching the fire, listening to the sizzle of the meat, and talking of manly things.

If I had been writing this story of Mother's first encounter with Faulkner I might have thought to explain why my parents had interrupted their honeymoon, or, more likely, I would have just described the event without dating it, since the date really didn't matter. The encounter is interesting and revealing, but the circumstances under which it occurred are irrelevant in my opinion. However, because Elliott noticed the wrong date, and because the newspaper announcement Elliott cited did not know (and therefore could not report) that the couple had interrupted their honeymoon for a brief return to Holly Springs, Mr. Elliott took another opportunity to discredit me, and that opportunity would have been lost if he simply had checked with me.[140]

On page 324 of his article, Elliott uses the technique of asking the reader instead of me. Dr. Wolff told me she offered Mr. Elliott the opportunity to meet and talk with me, which he declined. Instead he poses questions to which I readily could have supplied the answers: "Why such a short honeymoon?" "How would Faulkner have been able to coordinate with the newlyweds—?" I would think that a reporter who had questions about a story he was critiquing would ask the author of the story, but he did not ask me. Instead, he asked the readers of his critique. Perhaps most readers recognized Elliott's unethical journalistic style, but now I must provide the details, in spite of how irrelevant they are to the story.

During the week leading up to my parents' wedding at Montreat, North Carolina, someone from the Montreat Association office delivered a message to Dad, that his dad needed to talk to him immediately. Bitzer Cottage had no phone and wouldn't have one for over 20 years, so Dad made a collect call, probably from the Association office. Grandfather had a business issue that couldn't wait two weeks. Handling it over the phone was not even considered. (All the way till at least 1950, Dad received one 3-minute-long distance call each year at Christmas from his sister in California, and that was because her husband worked for the phone company and got free minutes.) Dad couldn't drive and return before the wedding on Thursday, so he agreed that after only the first night of their honeymoon they would arrive back home late afternoon the next day, which was a Friday, giving them all day Saturday to work in Holly Springs. They then returned to North Carolina on Sunday to resume their honeymoon. When I was grown up, Mother confided in me that while she eventually understood the seriousness of the crisis, at the time she was hurt by the interrupted honeymoon, but she kept it all to herself because if she told a soul, she would be humiliated by the gossip.

Of course, the newspaper did not know about the interruption at the beginning of the honeymoon. Therefore, on page 324 of his article, Elliott asked how Faulkner was the only one who knew these details. Elliott assumes that simply posing this question would be devastating to my credibility. If he had first asked me, however, he much more readily would have received the facts. Sometime that week Faulkner was in Holly Springs, as he frequently was. He climbed the steps to Dad's office as he usually did to say hello, and was surprised to hear about the wedding from Grandfather. He asked when Edgar would be back. Grandfather spoke so directly and firmly that Dad often thought he was rude. So, Grandfather told Faulkner the couple would be back Friday evening, but only for the weekend on a business matter and would not have time to visit. Edgar and his father would spend all day Saturday behind locked doors at the office with a sign which read "Closed for the day." Later, Grandfather told Dad that he had said he was sure Edgar would enjoy seeing Faulkner when back in September. Dad thought this dismissal was rude, but Grandfather thought he had simply made it clear that for the whole weekend, Edgar Jr. would be unavailable. Faulkner, however, saw Friday night as open for a party, and he made considerable effort to make it memorable.

Elliott's comment to my noting that Faulkner brought with him the beer, a rabbit, and a couple of squirrels, was that "this story with all its elaborate details raises questions." Here is my question to him: what is so elaborate about "beer, a rabbit, and a couple of squirrels"?

I deeply resent that I had to spend so much time on a detail so trivial, but I realize that doing so was necessary. I do not have sufficient space to rebut each point, or even the majority of Elliott's attacks, but that should not be necessary because the attacks are all the same, beginning with a "fact," then introducing a false premise or misinformation, then building a faulty narrative on that to discredit me. I have so far identified five characteristics of his strategy:

(1) Choose a printed article full of errors, and then claim that since my story differs from the printed word, I am discredited. The articles he quotes were known to contain errors at the time of publication, but Elliot had no knowledge of that.

(2) Falsely claim that Mother wrote an erroneous article, which either discredits her, or discredits me. She didn't write the article he cited as written by her. In the tangle of questions and doubts, the reader has no way to unpack and label his nonsense.

(3) Report doing exhaustive search of newspapers over decades leading the reader to believe that if our stories were true, they would be in print,

and failing to find them proves them false. Surely he knows that not all facts land in the newspaper. He should not get away with this supposition, and hopefully he did not.

(4) If the story is complex, as most interesting stories are, dismiss it as contrived, when the converse is true: his arguments for the most part are what is contrived.

(5) If a gap occurs anywhere in the narrative, or if how something happened that is not fully explained, he fills in with fiction to meet his purpose and claim his version is more likely to be the true story.

Quoting from what he has learned second-hand about Holly Springs from the newspaper, Mr. Elliott tries to establish himself as knowledgeable about Holly Springs. In my opinion, with regard to individual family histories, such as mine, he knows little to nothing. A lifetime living in Holly Springs is necessary to begin to know fully some of the stories, and that is from word of mouth from longtime, trusted friends. "Family business" never reaches the paper. Ask any longtime resident how much family history ever got in print, and they will say: "Very little, thank God."

Elliott's attacks largely are based on misinformation. He depends upon repeating words like "confabulation" and his erroneous claim that "the story falls apart." I have not found a single conclusion in his entire article that I believe to be true.

Chapter Two

"THE FRAGILE AND INDELIBLE SIGNATURE OF HER MEDITATION"

Ludie's Window as a Source for Faulkner's *Intruder in the Dust* and *Requiem for a Nun*

> The aim of every artist is to arrest motion, which is life, by artificial means and hold it fixed so that 100 years later when a stranger looks at it, it moves again since it is life.
> —WILLIAM FAULKNER, IN JEAN STEIN, "THE ART OF FICTION XII"

A full consideration of Faulkner's Holly Springs sources must include a discussion of the inscribed windowpane at McCarroll Place. Faulkner's descriptions of windowpane etchings, which appear in several of his novels, have stimulated inquiry for many years—and interest in them continues.[1] Further research, textual evidence, and witness statements suggest that the windowpane etching of Mary Louisa Baugh Booth—"Ludie"—at McCarroll Place is a likely source for the etched windowpanes that Faulkner describes in two of his novels. Other etchings in and near Faulkner's home in Oxford, Mississippi, and the surrounding area also may have served as prototypes for Faulkner's window etching images, especially in the novel *The Unvanquished*. Accruing information, suggests, however, that Ludie's glass inscription is a likely source—although perhaps not the only one—for Faulkner's novels *Intruder in the Dust* and *Requiem for a Nun* and may include self-portraits of the novelist in both works. (See figure 2.1 on p. 86.)

Mary Louisa Baugh, nicknamed "Ludie," was a young woman whose romantic love story and early, tragic death bear the unmistakable hallmarks of high fiction. Indeed, her dramatic story is so tender and sad that few will wonder why William Faulkner seems to have written of her beauty, frailty, and early death, set against the backdrop of the Civil War. The McCarroll/Francisco family story about her is that in the years leading up to the Civil War, Richard Baugh, who was mayor of Memphis, Tennessee, at that time, sent his beautiful and fragile daughter, Mary Louisa Baugh, to live at McCarroll Place, the McCarroll family home in Holly Springs, Mississippi. Ludie's condition was frail, and her health problems prevented her from even light work inside the home. In his Civil War story "My Grandmother Millard," Faulkner seems to describe Ludie's move from Memphis to Holly Springs: "Cousin Melisandre finally got out of Memphis and came to live with us" (Faulkner, "My Grandmother Millard," in *Collected Stories*, 667). Later, Bayard Sartoris describes her as "our cousin. From Memphis" (678). Faulkner's description of Melisandre's departure from Memphis during the Civil War matches Ludie's move to her aunt and uncle's home, McCarroll Place, in Holly Springs during the war. At the advent of the Civil War, Ludie Baugh was "standing in the sitting room looking east, out the open gallery and watching the troops move back and forth on the road to the depot. . . . [With her diamond ring,] she inscribed her name on the window pane."[2] She etched her single name—"Ludie"—on the glass windowpane.[3]

Ludie's courtship and marriage to her Civil War soldier, Henry Booth, her haunting etching in glass, and her early death are captivating and romantic moments in her sad story. Small wonder she attracted the attention of novelist William Faulkner. The survival of her story, down through the generations, also exemplifies the vibrant oral tradition in the South, in Mississippi, and in Holly Springs, and its powerful effect on this family. Ludie's courtship and marriage to a soldier also may be a model for what J. B. Carothers and K. J. Sheldon see as the courtship and wedding of Philip and Melisandre in "My Grandmother Millard" (672).[4] As in Ludie's story, Melisandre catches the eye of her soldier who comes back to marry her. Against the backdrop of the chaos and turmoil of war, Faulkner ends the story with a touching, romantic, and realistic moment of romance as he imagines and depicts a hurriedly wrought, at-home, wartime wedding like Ludie's.

Faulkner's brushstrokes provide the details: Philip and Melisandre celebrated their wedding with family amid newly polished silver successfully spared from Yankee pillaging, and dogwood and redbud branches and cut flowers carried in baskets, "until the house was so full that Ringo and I would believe we smelled them even across the pasture each time we came up" (697–98). The food furnished as a result of Rosa and Louvinia's efforts at cooking is so delicious that the boys reminisce about it long afterward. In a story replete with soldiers, uniforms, braids, swords, and the smell of horses, Faulkner depicts a stolen moment of romance and floral splendor for one soldier and his "beautiful, tender girl" (678).

After their marriage, Ludie and her soldier husband left town. Dr. Francisco recalls: "Immediately after the war, they left. No one ever saw either of them again, much to the distress of everyone in town."[5] Communications after the Civil War were poor in their area of the country, and the townspeople did not know where the young couple had gone.

About two years later, the townsfolk heard that Ludie had died. Her Holly Springs community collectively mourned her death. A touching eulogy to the beloved Ludie appeared in the area newspapers.[6] Subsequent research revealed that after the war, Ludie and Henry Booth had returned to Memphis, where her father lived. Ludie's health had been poor before her marriage, and extant records suggest—sadly—that Ludie bore a stillborn child. Matters worsened: Ludie, too, died a few days later, most likely from the effects of the childbirth.[7]

Dr. Edgar Francisco III recalls Ludie's story with compassion:

I feel I know Ludie because of how Dad recounted Amelia's emotional telling of Ludie's story. The events in her life are so compelling for me that I have no doubt Faulkner had to be drawn back to her story time and again. . . . Now you [Dr. Wolff] have the opportunity to enable your readers to feel they really know Ludie by experiencing the emotion of the storyteller as Amelia recounts all four of the tragic periods in sequence and thru her tears and rage feel the accumulating impact of it on Amelia's life as well as Ludie's. [I hope your chapter will reveal her] as someone you feel you know and for whom you have such compassion that you understand why Faulkner would be so drawn to her story.[8]

Dr. Francisco's four-part retelling of Ludie's story gives a clear sense of her importance in the family, the grief his great-grandmother Amelia felt at Ludie's death and why the impassioned story may have been a compelling narrative for Faulkner.

Ludie's Story

My family knows the story of Ludie through the emotional telling of it by her cousin, Amelia McCarroll Leak, my great grandmother, who told the story many times to my Dad. Her sister, Sallie, confirmed everything many times after Amelia died, except for the first events, which occurred before Sallie could remember them. Amelia told the story as four tragic episodes with one happy interlude in the middle, and I think that is how it should be retold.

I

Amelia always began with when she heard the terrible news. She was rocking one year old Ludie as she had for most every waking hour since Ludie had been left with Amelia's parents (Ludie's Aunt Elizabeth and Uncle John McCarroll) while her mother, Emily Baugh, was giving birth to her second child. Amelia started screaming. Her mother told her to hush because she was scaring the baby, but Amelia wouldn't hush—she was seven. The expectant mother and her sister, Louisa Hill, wife of Byrd Hill, had gathered at the home of their mother, Mary Eddins (Amelia's grandmother) for the birth. Now Aunt Elizabeth was telling Amelia that the tornado a couple of days before had killed them all. Ludie was named Mary Louise Baugh for her grandmother and aunt. The three Eddins sisters and their mother, who had thought and moved as one were down to one, Elizabeth McCarroll. When Amelia finally stopped screaming, she stopped rocking, held Ludie tightly and promised Ludie over and over "I'll take care of you, I'll protect you, I'll never let anything happen to you."

II

Ludie was soon taken from Amelia when her Uncle Richard Baugh moved to Memphis to make a better living, taking "Amelia's baby" with him. Amelia went into a decade and a half rage over her inability to keep her promise, and her awareness that in this situation she could not be in control, a desire that seems to have defined her life. They came back for visits, which rekindled Amelia's fury as she perceived her baby growing sadder, frailer and lonelier. Baugh had financially provided well for Ludie with a governess and maid, and when old enough he sent her to a good girl's boarding school, but that was perceived by

Amelia as a very poor substitute for Amelia, and her sisters and mother at McCarroll Place. The most frustrating part was that Ludie seemed resigned. She didn't scream and fight her way back home as Amelia knew she would. Ludie seemed too frail to fight.

Family legend has it that in 1860 Baugh decided that with war looming and occupation of Memphis possible the daughter of the mayor might be in danger, so he arranged to hide her out in Holly Springs with her Aunt Elizabeth and Uncle John, who just happened to be the Sherriff [sic], then in his 21st year in office. I think it more likely that Baugh noticed that Ludie was sixteen and in need of instruction and additional care. The belief that Memphis would be occupied had to have come from John McCarroll, who was certain that Memphis and all river ports would be captured by Union forces to block river transportation by the Confederacy. For years he had been publicly deriding the notion that southern gentlemen plantation owners on horses could successfully lead the repelling of an industrialized force. I think he could say this and continue to be re-elected because the vast majority of voters were not slave owners and had no stake in preserving the institution, which by 1845 McCarroll had recognized as intolerable for slave and soul diminishing for owner. However, only a few trusted friends knew the degree of his opposition, or the charade he had worked out with his people.

Ludie is alleged to have been watching through the sitting room window as troops marched down what later would be named Van Dorn Avenue when she scratched her name on a pane of the window glass. She would have had a good view of the street then as she looked northeast across our open gallery to the street, because that was before the street was graded down beginning at Maury and extending to the Strickland Place, so that it became below eye level in front of McCarroll Place. These two homes had been built at the edge of the hill on which Holly Springs was located and just before a steep decline to the railroad. However, the primary obstruction of view was added in 1929 when the north end of the gallery was enclosed to make a bathroom for my newlywed parents. The remainder of the gallery was also enclosed to make a sunroom and enclosed walkway from the north rooms down to the dining room and kitchen. So, today looking out through Ludie's window you can't see the front yard, much less the street.

Amelia told about the times she and Ludie would hand out pecan tarts to the soldiers assembled in the street, and she figured that's how Ludie met John [Henry] Booth.

When Gen. Grant selected Holly Springs for the staging of his campaign against Vicksburg, he took over the top floor of the Walter Place for his family and set up his headquarters at another mansion though he was rarely there. However, another general was located full time in Holly Springs. He selected McCarroll Place for his headquarters and took his lodging and meals next door at the Strickland Place. It has been alleged that Col. Strickland's wife, Mildred, became even more unpopular when it was revealed that she had written to her Confederate officer husband praising the Union general as a fine man and gentleman.[9] The general was not that well received at McCarroll Place, where according to Amelia's story, he ran into Amelia. His staff had demanded occupancy of the entire house. Amelia stood in the doorway and declared that they would have to kill her first.[10] They settled for three rooms. The family remained, crowded into the two rooms at the south end. Perhaps Amelia benefited from having a father who was already called the "unbeatable" Sherriff, and who would remain Sherriff through the occupation and reconstruction till his death in his 37th year in office. The irony is that if Baugh thought Ludie would be further from the action in Holly Springs, she ended up living in the room next to a union general's headquarters.

III

After the war Henry Booth came for Ludie. She promised to write about where she was and what she was doing. The first word they got was she was dead. All they ever learned of this period was that she died at her father's home. Amelia raged and cried at length about the other periods, but whenever anyone wondered about this brief time Amelia looked away.

IV

Finding Ludie and bringing her home became a hundred year preoccupation. The day the notice was received stating that Ludie was to be buried in Holly Springs[,] Elizabeth McCarroll marched the three blocks to the cemetery to find out when and vent about not being told. She was assured that they knew nothing about it, but when they heard something they would contact her as next of kin in Holly Springs. She went back for several days to vent again, and then John and Elizabeth McCarroll went to Memphis. Richard Baugh was family, and visibly torn between loyalties. Baugh explained that he had written the obituary assuming Ludie would be buried in Holly Springs, which was home to all the Eddins and McCarrolls, but he hadn't known that John Booth was totally opposed, and Booth was after all her husband. When John McCarroll said they wanted to visit Ludie's grave Baugh said the location was being kept secret. When asked about Ludie's pregnancy Baugh claimed to know nothing about it. At that point McCarroll said that the secrecy raised suspicion, which if not relieved would cause him to request a court order to exhume and examine the bodies. Baugh tried to convince McCarroll that perhaps there had been poor judgment from lack of knowledge or sufficient attention to their situation, and perhaps not the best of medical care, but that further investigation would prove nothing more and only add to the grief. John McCarroll explained all this to Amelia when she came storming in upon her 1872 return to McCarroll Place. Also, he told her that he had continued to investigate, calling on additional resources and interviewing several people until he concluded there was no value in further investigation. He and Elizabeth died within a year. Amelia continued, retracing his steps herself, but finally gave up with nothing left to do except place a suitable tombstone in the family plot, but with no remains to bury she decided to place a better stone for Ludie's mother, Emily, in the midst of the hastily placed stones from the tornado. On this stone she could add that Emily was wife of the Memphis mayor even though she died years before he was mayor, and she would note that Emily was mother of Ludie—she would have Ludie's full name on the stone. Apparently, she was crushed when she realized there was not enough money for it—not for the line with Ludie's full name; not even just Ludie. She was still lamenting to Dad when he was a child that she couldn't even have a remembrance of Ludie in the cemetery. That would remind her of the tragic outcomes at the Leak plantation. Years later when Dad and Faulkner heard her sister, Sallie, still lamenting the tragic outcomes at the Leak Place they would wonder if something happened that no one was telling. They never knew that Amelia was burdened by her guilt that she had lost the McCarrolls' life savings, which they had lent her to help restore the Leak plantation after she married John Leak in 1866. After he died in 1872 Amelia came home bringing daughter, Betsy, and the Leak diary, which disappointingly did not help her get the loaned money back from his estate. This loan was discovered by Dr. Sally Wolff during her research. The family story is that Elizabeth wanted a mansion like her friends had and John agreed to build it but showed little interest in owning anything or displaying it, so he had kept delaying the building, and now had the money to loan to Amelia. With McCarroll's death Amelia's loss of all the money put the family in unfamiliar financial limitations.

Faulkner was fascinated by the story and would ask Edgar to tell it all again and Dad would begin with the tornado and end with his own enduring sadness that they were never able to bring Ludie home. That's when Faulkner said "She found her own way home. She is standing there looking out the window." That's why he [Faulkner] never went into that room—because he did not want to disturb her. He always stood on the outside looking in and seeing her name in reverse.

Edgar Wiggin Francisco III
June 8, 2017

》 》 》

In these reminiscences Faulkner is rocking in a chair near Ludie's sitting room window, talking with Edgar Jr. about her, considering the import of the old etching in glass, and asking Edgar to tell again and again the compelling story of Cousin Ludie. "Tell me again, Edgar," William Faulkner said to his friend. Francisco III recalls, "Dad was quite willing to tell the story."[11] Upon hearing Edgar tell the story of Ludie's beauty and her unfortunate, short life, Faulkner said he believed that Ludie was still standing in her sitting room, looking out the window: "She's still standing there," Faulkner would say to Edgar. "Ludie is not there," the more down-to-earth Edgar would retort. "Edgar, you may be immune," Faulkner would insist, "but I know Ludie is still standing there."[12]

Faulkner's belief in the spirit world seems clear at this point. In another example, his delight in regaling children at Rowan Oak with haunting ghost stories may relate to his awareness of Ludie's spirit at McCarroll Place.[13] The presence of spirits seems to be an integral part of Faulkner's understanding of the world. Certainly his view is clear that the past is alive in the present. Jay Parini points out that "the intermingling of the past and present" is a "trademark" of Faulkner's style.[14] Those views are apparent in his response to Ludie Baugh and her window etching.

Ludie's Civil War life and premature death live on in these family memories and the novels of William Faulkner, who had a rare gift for hearing in the "old tales and talking" around him stories from which he would establish compelling characters and narrative lines. Ludie Baugh Booth and her Confederate soldier husband seem to have stirred Faulkner's imagination and compassion as he captures anew her bittersweet story.

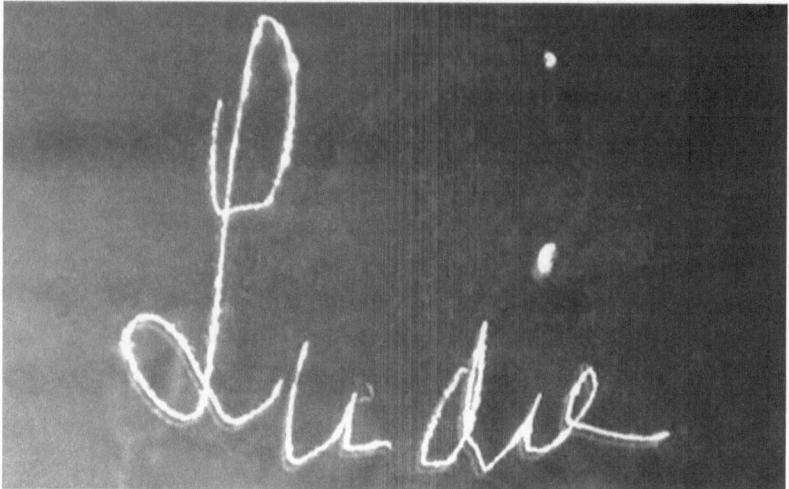

Figure 2.1 Photograph of Ludie's etching on the gallery window at McCarroll Place. Photography by George Nikas, Atlanta, Georgia.

"A Young Girl's Single Name": Ludie Baugh Booth and Faulkner's *Intruder in the Dust*

Ludie Baugh Booth's poor health and dark fate link her insignia on the old windowpane at McCarroll Place with Faulkner's novels. According to Francisco III, who was a boy in the 1930s, Faulkner was well acquainted with Ludie's window etching and her story. Numerous inscriptions were present in and around the Oxford area, and tales about them circulated, as did many stories of buried treasure on the old plantations, and apparently Faulkner found an inspiration in Ludie. Ludie's inscription may have inspired Faulkner's depiction of a window etching in *Intruder in the Dust*.

Discussion of the windowpane etchings in Faulkner's work must include Jane Isbell Haynes's article "Another Source for Faulkner's Inscribed Window Panes," in which she proposed that Ludie's etching at McCarroll Place in Holly Springs, Mississippi, is a likely source for at least one of Faulkner's window etching images.[15] Haynes points out that in *The Unvanquished*, "the fictional young girl gazes out the window at General Nathan Bedford Forrest riding down the street on his horse while she writes her name on the glass: Celia Cook." Haynes concludes, "Here Faulkner is closer to the Cook legend."[16]

In her article Haynes speculated but could not establish conclusively that Faulkner had seen the name Ludie etched on a windowpane at McCarroll Place. Nonetheless, Haynes theorized that Faulkner could have seen this etching during the annual Holly Springs Pilgrimage tour of homes. The

McCarroll/Francisco family owned McCarroll Place for almost two hundred years, across five generations, and into the sixth, and for many years they opened their home for the Pilgrimage tours. In her article Haynes argued that in *Intruder in the Dust*, "Faulkner's description is closer to the Ludie single-name signature than to the Jane T. Cook full signature."[17] She quotes the relevant passage from Faulkner's novel: "a young girl's *single* name, written by her own hand into the glass with a diamond" (emphasis added).[18] Faulkner's description in *Intruder in the Dust* closely approximates the McCarroll Place etching with its "single," one-word name—Ludie. (See figure 2.1.)

Other window etchings in the Oxford, Mississippi, and surrounding area, including that of Jane T. Cook, also could be models for Faulkner's window etchings. Faulkner apparently lived at the Cook-Tate house in Oxford, Mississippi, from his ninth through fifteenth years, during which time he must have seen daily the Jane T. Cook window etching in that home.[19] The Cook etching could be a model for Faulkner's etchings, especially in *The Unvanquished*, but Haynes's point about Ludie's single-name etching may more closely link her to the etching that Faulkner described in *Intruder in the Dust*.

Textual similarities link *Intruder in the Dust* to the Francisco family story of Ludie's life details, including her illness, inability to work, marriage, and early death. Faulkner's seeing Ludie's name "in reverse" is a good example (*Intruder in the Dust* 50). This short phrase is a verbatim match between the novel and the family story. According to Francisco III, Faulkner liked to sit with Edgar Jr. outside McCarroll Place on the gallery,[20] look into the window at Ludie's etching, and ponder its meaning. About Ludie's etching, Faulkner would say, "I always see her name in reverse, Edgar."[21] Faulkner was viewing the etching "in reverse," or backward, because he was seeing it from the outside looking in.

In *Intruder in the Dust*, Faulkner appears to include a portrait of himself in connection with Ludie's window etching. In this description, he chooses the same wording—"in reverse." Faulkner depicts his own actions in approaching the gallery several times a year to visit and each time seeing the etching on the window. He is outside the house looking in the window. He sees the "single name" etched "in reverse," and the etching prompts him to consider its meaning:

> Because scratched into one of the panes of the fanlight beside the door was a young girl's single name, written by her own hand into the glass with a diamond in that same year and sometimes two or three times a year he would go up onto the gallery to look at it, it cryptic now *in reverse*, not for a sense of the past but to realise again the

eternality, the deathlessness and changelessness of youth. (*Intruder in the Dust* 50; emphasis added)

The reasonable assumption is that Faulkner describes himself in approaching the gallery at McCarroll Place several times a year, when he came there for visits, viewing the "single" name etching "in reverse," and pondering its "cryptic" significance. In his novel *Intruder in the Dust*, Faulkner considers the resonant meaning of the glass inscription across the generations. His story matches three components of the Francisco family story: the "single" name of Ludie's etching on the windowpane; how often he viewed the etching, in accord with his visits several times a year; and how he viewed the etching—"in reverse"—from outside the house, looking in.

"Her Frail and Workless Hand": Ludie and Faulkner's *Requiem for a Nun*

In *Requiem for a Nun*, other verbatim descriptions further connect Faulkner's fictional girl, who is "frail," and her "fragile" etching, with the Francisco family story. Cousin Ludie was "frail" and "fragile." She was known in the family to be unwell, housebound, and too weak even to do housework.[22] In the novel Faulkner's young girl similarly is "a frail anemic girl with narrow workless hands" (*Requiem for a Nun* 229).[23] She has too much time in which to think and ponder: she "mused hour after hour and day and month and year." Faulkner's fictional girl, like Ludie, and also Melisandre in "My Grandmother Millard," is too unwell to perform ordinary household chores—even cooking and drying the dishes. Faulkner describes her sitting near the

> window in which mused hour after hour and day and month and year, the frail blonde girl not only incapable of (or at least excused from) helping her mother cook, but even of drying the dishes after her mother (or father perhaps) washed them—musing, not even waiting for anyone or anything, as far as the town knew, not even pensive, as far as the town knew: just musing amid her blonde hair in the window facing the country town street, day after day and month after month and—as the town remembered it—year after year for what must have been three or four of them, inscribing at some moment the fragile and indelible signature of her meditation in one of the panes of it (the window): her frail and workless name, scratched by a diamond ring in her frail and workless hand. (229)

In "My Grandmother Millard," Melisandre similarly is often in ill health and bedridden. Helpers bring her food and tea on a tray. She is so weak that even her attempts to polish the silver are ineffective, and it has to be polished again. Louvinia "could pick out the ones she polished without hardly looking and hand them to Philadelphia to polish again" (*Collected Stories*, 698). Melisandre's inability to work is clear in this story too.

With no work to do, Faulkner's anemic girl has plenty of time, like Ludie and Melisandre, to muse and meditate. In both family story and novel, Ludie etches her name in the glass window with her diamond ring. In both real and fictional stories, the townspeople collectively remember her—"as the town remembered it"—and they grieve her death communally.

Ludie's particular infirmity and inability contribute to narrative and imagistic presentation in *Requiem for a Nun*. For Faulkner, his fictional girl's "meditation" becomes "indelible" when she etches her name on the glass, "inscribing at some moment the fragile and indelible signature of her meditation in one of the panes of it (the window)" (229). In describing the poor health of his fictional girl, Faulkner describes her as "frail" and "workless," apparently draws the details of her specific illness and disability from the Francisco story, and transmutes them into worklessness: neither real nor fictional girl is well enough to work, even inside the home. Faulkner focuses on his fictional girl's "workless" condition: "her frail and workless name, scratched by a diamond ring in her frail and workless hand" (229).

In *Requiem for a Nun*, "the young dead bride" (259) may well allude to Ludie's life story and also to John Keats's famed newlywed: "bride of quietness." In his novel Faulkner's couple leaves town together, just as the war begins. In life, Ludie's soldier-husband Henry Booth came back for her, and they left town. Faulkner seems to commemorate Ludie's youth and early death in his fictional, Keatsian girl. Faulkner's "young dead bride" (*Requiem for a Nun* 259) alludes to Keats's "Ode on a Grecian Urn," in which the poet depicts a "bride of quietness," who is still and silent but whose legend nevertheless carries her into immortality via her carved image on the urn.[24]

The stranger, peering in at an etching in age-old glass, and apprehending its life and meaning for the present day, may be another portrait of the artist. Ludie's image is enshrined in a glass window that was during Faulkner's day almost a hundred years old. Faulkner may allude to himself in his interview with Jean Stein, in which he mentions both the hundred-year time span and a stranger looking at the object:

> The aim of every artist is to arrest motion, which is life, by artificial means and hold it fixed so that 100 years later when a stranger

looks at it, it moves again since it is life. Since man is mortal, the only immortality possible for him is to leave something behind him that is immortal since it will always move. This is the artist's way of scribbling "Kilroy was here" on the wall of the final and irrevocable oblivion through which he must someday pass.[25]

That stranger looking at the hundred-year-old object indeed may have been William Faulkner.

The Holly Springs Pilgrimage and William Faulkner's *Requiem for a Nun*

The Holly Springs, Mississippi, Pilgrimage began in 1936.[26] Francisco III recalls:

> Ruth and Edgar Francisco finally got down to the Natchez Tour either in 1934 or 1935 after having wanted to since it started, I think, in 1932. They were disappointed. They had almost forgotten that Natchez had largely been burned to the ground. These homes were beautiful, but new reproductions, supposedly based on pictures of some originals. The builders could not replicate either the way materials had been produced or the original construction methods. They concluded that anyone who really wanted to experience the look and feel of antebellum homes needed to visit Holly Springs. Compared to Holly Springs, they thought Natchez looked like a Hollywood movie set. Ruth started talking about it with her good friend Marjorie McCrosky before church. Marjorie's husband's great grandfather [Levi McCrosky, who was elected the first sheriff of Marshall County in 1836][27] had been John R. McCarroll's best friend. The three women knew they needed approval from the city Board of Aldermen, so Ruth went to a meeting of the Board and got the approval. Her enthusiasm was contagious and her husband, Edgar, who was the Alderman for the 3rd Ward had pitched the event before she came in. Also, the three women decided the Garden Club's support was essential, so they recruited Mrs. Cochran who took on the task of getting the Garden Club to sponsor the event. The Garden Club created and staffed the many needed planning committees and provided the needed sustaining enthusiasm.[28]

Ruth Francisco, Marjorie McCrosky, Miss Nina Craft, and Mrs. Vadah Cochran, were the primary planners of the first Pilgrimage, along with Mrs.

Egbert Jones, Gladys Harris, Katherine Mattison, Mrs. George Buchanan, Mrs. Jim Tucker, and other members of a newly formed Garden Club. The first Pilgrimage events began on October 22, 1936, and included tours of homes, a horse show, historical skits, a jousting tournament, a Confederate Ball, historical programs in churches, a pilgrimage to Hill Crest Cemetery, and a concert by the Rust College Singers, under the direction of the director, Natalie Doxey. The Holly Springs homes that opened for tours in 1936 were: Coxe-Dean Place, known as Airliewood; Grey Gables; Freeman Place; the McCarroll Place; the Crump Place; the Polk Place; Featherston Place; Walter Place; Bonner-Belk House, now known as Cedarhurst; Box Hill; The Pines; Maplewood; Summer Trees; and the Cochran House.[29]

That first Holly Springs Pilgrimage was not guaranteed to succeed. Mrs. Vadah Cochran, a member of that first group of planners, pointed out that people were skeptical: "Holly Springs would never attract people like Natchez. We didn't have the big estates. We didn't have the Deep South setting, the azaleas, the moss-covered live oaks. We didn't have 'Old Man River' flowing by our door."[30] Nonetheless, the group persisted, and when the Pilgrimage opened, throngs of people attended from around the South, including from "Memphis, from the Delta, from the hills, from the prairies, from Tennessee, from Arkansas, from far-away places, on they came!"[31]

Since that first year, the Holly Springs Pilgrimage has enjoyed decades of visitors who came to town by the thousands to participate in the tour of homes and other events. Mrs. Jack Wittjen, a later Pilgrimage chairperson, noted that "crowds numbering 2,500 to 3,000 each year tour 10 of the 60 antebellum homes in Holly Springs."[32] Recently the numbers were much lower—in the seven hundreds. Other similar festivals take place around the state. With the inclusion of the "Behind the Big House" tours, the Holly Springs Pilgrimage has entered a new phase, with more emphasis on uncovering and highlighting details of the slave culture that supported the antebellum homes and owners, and appreciation not just for the homes but also for those who built them.

Now, in the days when Confederate statues are coming down and relocating to museums, some African American people in Holly Springs say nonetheless they want to preserve the antebellum homes, because their ancestors built them and because the work of those ancestors on the homes has lasted for so many decades. They take great pride in the fine accomplishments of their ancestors. Others say it is time for the houses to disappear into the far corners of history. That Faulkner sought historical accuracy in his depictions and sought the same for the Holly Springs Pilgrimage attire was a good step, but more than simply the historical accuracy of attire is at stake in representing accurately the complex struggles of the dark Southern past.

He took head-on these issues of race and class across numerous novels and did so in an era when writing about those issues was unpopular.

Textual evidence connects *Requiem for a Nun*, Edgar Francisco Jr., and Ludie, in Faulkner's fictional characters of the "host" and "stranger," both of whom come under the enchanting spell of the old glass etching. Both unnamed, the "host" and "stranger" are important characters in the novel and link to Ludie's window at the 184-year-old McCarroll Place. The annual Holly Springs Pilgrimage sponsored "hosts" at the various antebellum homes, which each spring are open to visitors. These "hosts" would greet visitors at each home on tour; Edgar Francisco Jr. annually was host at his home, McCarroll Place. He would sit and talk with the many folks who came through to see the home, tell them the story of Cousin Ludie, and show her etching on the glass window to his Pilgrimage guests.

The "stranger" again may be an autobiographical depiction of William Faulkner, and Faulkner may have depicted his childhood friend Edgar Francisco Jr. in his role as "host" at McCarroll Place during Pilgrimage, a time when visitors come from away to view the antebellum homes and evidence of the past. Faulkner's "host" sits near the window and tells the story of the glass etching to an out-of-town "stranger." Both host and traveler view the glass together and ponder its meaning.[33]

Faulkner also may describe himself as an artist who makes such impressive moments "indelible." The etching—a sign of Ludie's "meditation"—is "indelible" in glass. For Faulkner, this indelibility is a role of an artist. Faulkner reiterates verbatim wording from his interview with Jean Stein. Ludie's etching mesmerizes a "stranger," who "100 years later," will look at it anew and for whom the etching, like an artist's creations, will "move again." The etching now joins together the host and stranger in the act of viewing and appreciating the etching and remembering its significance:

> drawing the two of you from almost a hundred years away in your turn—yourself the stranger, the outlander with a B.A. or (perhaps even) M.A. from Harvard or Northwestern or Stanford, passing through Jefferson by chance or accident on the way to somewhere else, and the host who in three generations has never been out of Yoknapatawpha further than a few prolonged Saturday nights in Memphis or New Orleans . . . and (all you had to do was look at it [the etching] a while; all you have to do now is remember it.) (*Requiem for a Nun* 260–62)

The haunting etching in old glass reaches through the generations and unites both out-of-town guest—the stranger away from home—and his

Figure 2.2 Host and hostess tags worn at the Holly Springs Pilgrimage. Courtesy of Jorja Lynn, who was a hostess at and later the owner of Walter Place, Holly Springs, Mississippi.

host, who like Edgar Francisco Jr. did not stray often from his ancestral home but steadfastly remained at the home place, except for occasional forays to Memphis. Newspaper records reveal those trips and their infrequency. Each year Edgar showed to his Pilgrimage and other guests Ludie's signature in the glass and retold her story. The reasonable conclusion is that Faulkner saw Ludie's etching, heard her painful story, depicted her indelible creation in his own writing, described himself in viewing her work, and preserved in his artistry important meaning derived from her life and handiwork.

The old, surviving glass, fragile with age yet imperishable to time, elucidates Faulkner's perspective on the past, in which time is a boundless continuum: "The past is never dead. It's not even past" (92). At the time of Faulkner's writing, the etching had survived "almost a hundred years" (and now almost 184 years), including the years of the Civil War. The etching holds the observers rapt until its meaning clarifies in the imagination. This single-name signature from a lost time, like the Grecian urn, instructs those who stop and consider. The etching teaches that "there is no time: no space: no distance" (*Requiem for a Nun* 261). Past and present coexist.

In *Requiem for a Nun*, these images coalesce as stranger and host view together the delicate but enduring glass signature. Faulkner focuses on the "fragile and workless" hand who carved it: "a fragile and workless scratching almost depthless in a sheet of old barely transparent glass" (261). Although utterly vulnerable, the thin, and "almost depthless," "indelible" etching in the old glass nonetheless survives for generations. Faulkner's girl's "workless scratching" in this novel may be another clear reference to the particular physical frailty and inability of Ludie Baugh Booth, and also in her etching, which is fragile and without adornment.

Numerous Holly Springs citizens came forward after the publication of *Ledgers of History* and contributed corroborating statements and recollections that Faulkner saw Ludie's window at McCarroll Place.[34] They offered their clear recollection that Faulkner visited McCarroll Place and viewed Ludie's etching there. These people reinforce the statements of Edgar Francisco III in *Ledgers of History* that Faulkner visited McCarroll Place, knew Edgar Francisco Jr., and viewed Ludie's etching in glass. Mr. Frank Hurdle, formerly of Holly Springs, as well as Bobby Mitchell, Jane Callicutt, Scarlett Hurdle, and others who currently are citizens of Holly Springs, recall that Faulkner saw Ludie's etching there. Hurdle is a lawyer in Mississippi who served as a Pilgrimage guide in the 1970s. He recollects hearing that Faulkner visited Edgar at McCarroll Place and viewed the etching there.

> I remember seeing the etched glass back in the 1970s and being told of the Francisco-Faulkner connection. I called my high school history teacher [Bobby Mitchell] this morning and he said he had been aware of that story all his life (he's 75). . . . Many of us have heard of the etched glass/Faulkner/Francisco connection all our lives. I don't know that it was described as a great friendship, but remember being told that he [Faulkner] had seen and was fascinated by the window when he was a visitor in their home.[35]

Pilgrimage hosts and hostesses wore ribboned tags (figure 2.2), so the guests could easily identify who was hosting in the various houses open to visitors. Hurdle also explained the different roles of the hosts, hostesses, and guides at the Holly Springs Pilgrimage. Mr. Hurdle recalls these host tags:

> I really think these were around for a few years; some Pilgrimage chairman no doubt thought they would be a good idea and ordered them. I remember seeing that my older brother had one and wanting one

for myself. I may have worn the "host" tag only one year, but probably more. The young people who served in houses were considered "hosts," and people who served in morning houses would often spend the afternoon visiting their friends in the other houses. . . . The "host" (or "hostess") ribbon was just a 1.5" wide vertical ribbon with the word "host" or "hostess" printed on it that I think was pinned to the front of one's jacket. But I think for at least one year I wore one as a guide.[36]

Bobby Mitchell, retired history teacher and local historian in Holly Springs, said that he heard Faulkner visited in town and saw the etching at McCarroll Place.[37] Scarlett Hurdle and Jane Callicutt also remember hearing that Faulkner visited McCarroll Place. Scarlett Hurdle recalls that "everyone knew that William Faulkner visited McCarroll Place."[38] Ms. Callicutt said, "I've always been told that," and she had known about it since she was a teenager: "He wrote about the window pane in the Franciscos' house."[39] These statements reinforce the claims of Francisco III that Faulkner visited Holly Springs and specifically McCarroll Place and its etching.

Faulkner's depiction of "host" and "stranger," who together view the glass etching and meditate on its resonant meaning for history, time, and eternality, reaches narrative and imagistic power in *Requiem for a Nun*. Faulkner's likely viewing of the etching at McCarroll Place and his presence during the Holly Springs Pilgrimage may well have inspired the creation of his host and stranger characters in *Requiem for a Nun*. Although unnamed, these fictional personages logically represent Faulkner's friend Edgar Francisco Jr. in his role as host to thousands of out-of-town strangers who came to town annually to visit McCarroll Place and other homes during the Holly Springs Pilgrimages. William Faulkner apparently was one of the guests whom Edgar Jr. hosted at the Holly Springs Pilgrimage.

Host and guest in *Requiem for a Nun* previously received critical attention. In his article E. O. Hawkins noticed, "The story is related as if a townsman were showing a visitor the historic sights, telling him of local legends."[40] Indeed, Hawkins continues, the story "seems to be almost legendary to the townsman."[41] Hawkins's views now seem especially perceptive in light of these recent new connections. Although Hawkins did not link Faulkner's host and guest characters with any particular person, or even with the annual Pilgrimage, he noted Faulkner's depiction of an "anemic only child,"[42] which now seems a clear match with Ludie's personal details, especially her precarious health.

Noel Polk also discusses Faulkner's window etchings and points to the penchant in the area for engraving names in panes and notes the idea expressed in "Kilroy was here"— that such writings and etchings preserve the identity of the person who is penning or etching them.[43] Michael Millgate equates the etchings with the artist's yearnings to be remembered: "No one was more sensitive to the survival into the present of witnesses to the fact that individual human beings *were* in the past, that they lived, moved, and left permanent records of that life and movement in the form of letters, tombstones, scratches on windowpanes, entries in commissary books—just as the artist, in Faulkner's favorite phrase, seeks through the legacy of his work to write 'Kilroy was here' on the walls of the world."[44]

Jay Watson cogently asserts that the "girl's dated signature, scratched into the glass of a jailhouse window ninety years ago" is one "conquering time and distance" and is a "kind of linguistic self-assertion.... The signature, that is, represents Cecilia's refusal to be objectified, her insistence on speaking as a subject, on naming and thereby asserting herself."[45] Catalina Montes focuses on the presence of host and guest in her article "'Listen, Stranger: This Was Myself; This Was I': *Requiem for a Nun*."[46] She notices "the narrator, the host, and a second person, *you*, the guest whom both the voice and the author-narrator address" and sees the host as "the voice of a historic consciousness":

> The voice, on the other hand, states in the past "this *was* I"; the past as opposed to the present; a past that is heard in the present, that speaks to the present *you* and *now*. In other words, the voice of a historic consciousness. From historical truth it addresses the stranger from the North—the one who lives in the South has the dream, the legend, the heritage.[47]

The host, the "one who lives in the South," may well refer to Faulkner's friend Edgar Francisco Jr., who readily possesses "the dream, the legend, the heritage." Edgar's heritage includes the long, complex struggle of the Civil War, slavery and its aftermath, the history of the antebellum homes on display during the Pilgrimage tour, and the oral traditions—the family legend, recounted annually to thousands of guests, of beloved Ludie and her sad fate. These components coalesce in a way that seems especially compelling for a fiction writer: a more-than-one-hundred-year-old antebellum house, in which resides the beautiful but frail bride of a Civil War soldier—but her fate is death and loss. Faulkner thus seems to create from the compelling details of Ludie's life story imagistic and emotional power and narrative line, significant components of *Requiem for a Nun*.

Faulkner also encountered or engendered discord with the wife of Edgar Francisco Jr., Ruth Bitzer Francisco, with whom he disagreed about the appropriateness of historical detail in period costumes common at the

Figure 2.3 Ruth Bitzer Francisco, in dark blue hoop skirts, ready for Pilgrimage, in 1949. Francisco recalls that the photo was "taken by Dad after Pilgrimage hours, 1949. Mother designed the dress and was struggling with it while I was home for Christmas, 1948. I think she got some help finishing it. The dark material is deep blue velvet. The white crouched [sic] sashes were made by Dad's great aunt Sallie, he thought. Certainly not his grandmother, Amelia, who was the warrior. All the dresses, crouched [sic], and embroidery, were done by her sisters. Note that the cedar shown in the house picture taken in 1948 is missing. We think it was struck by lightning in fall, 1948. Dad and I examined it at Christmas, 1948 and agreed it had to go. The south side had already rotted out, which didn't show in the 1948 picture of the house. The stomp [sic] sanded to ground level, is hidden I think by where Mother is standing." Dr. Edgar Wiggin Francisco III, email correspondence, May 24, 2023. Photograph taken by Edgar Francisco Jr. Photograph copy work by George Nikas, Atlanta, Georgia. Courtesy of Dr. Edgar Wiggin Francisco III.

annual Holly Springs Pilgrimage. His view was that the Pilgrimage costumes should commemorate accurately the history of the area.[48] Ruth's view was that hoop skirts were appropriate. Faulkner objected. Ruth and a few of her Garden Club friends had initiated the Holly Springs Pilgrimage in the mid-1930s. Ruth wanted the hostesses at Pilgrimage to dress in period costume—and for her a central feature was hoop skirts. Faulkner, as Edgar III recalls, argued that inaccurate period costume was "beautifying history" and "dressing up the past that lived in most people's imaginations and had not really occurred."⁴⁹ A woman of indomitable will, Ruth prevailed, in that the tradition of wearing hoop skirts at Pilgrimage has continued through the decades even into the twenty-first century. (See figure 2.3 for a photo of Ruth Bitzer Francisco, in hoop skirts and ready for Pilgrimage.)

Faulkner seems to have won this debate with Ruth Francisco, however, in the terms he knew best: in writing. In a letter to his publisher Harrison Smith, he wrote to "keep the hoop skirts and plug hats out."⁵⁰ Joel Williamson establishes a context for this statement. Faulkner was:

> acutely conscious of the tendency of Southern writers "to draw a savage indictment of the . . . magnolias and mockingbirds which perhaps never existed anywhere." . . . There were no hoop skirts in *Light in August*, and the writer would view hoop skirts—that is, pretentions to gentility in the ante-bellum mode—in *Absalom, Absalom!* with a very jaundiced eye.⁵¹

Faulkner's conflict with Ruth Bitzer Francisco about the historical accuracy of attire at the Holly Springs Pilgrimage may have been the backdrop—or the foreground—for his letter to Harrison Smith. Faulkner clearly preferred, in *Absalom, Absalom!* at least, the accurate representation of historical attire, which for him did not include the elaborate hoop skirts, reminiscent of the attire worn in *Gone with the Wind*. He sought to preserve truth and authenticity about the old days instead of "beautifying history" and "dressing up the past."

In *Intruder in the Dust* and *Requiem for a Nun*, the signature in old glass instructs through time and history. As Faulkner approaches the glass etching, from the outside looking in, he reaches thematic power in the "eternality, the deathlessness and changelessness of youth" in the first of those novels (*Intruder in the Dust* 50). In the second novel, both stranger and host view the etching, contemplate its haunting meaning, and invoke the bygone days of the Civil War, when a young girl, infirm and unwed, with too much time on her hands, inscribes her name in the windowpane with her diamond ring, meets her soldier, marries him—but all too rapidly becomes a "young dead bride" (*Requiem for a Nun* 259).

Faulkner's window etchings in these two novels share the hallmark details of Ludie Baugh Booth's life, more so perhaps than other window etchings in the area, such as that of Jane T. Cook, who also etched her name in windowpanes and died young. Ludie's "single-name" etching may distinguish her from Jane T. Cook's multiple names. Faulkner's fictional girl links more closely to

Ludie's personal life details—her anemia, fragile condition, worklessness—the same health-related issues that surely contributed to her early demise.

In creating the "host" and "stranger," Faulkner seems clearly to allude to Edgar Francisco Jr., the hometown man rooted in strong heritage, who regales his out-of-town guests with legendary, Civil War family stories—and to Faulkner as one such out-of-towner, listener, and onlooker. Faulkner's pairing of the unnamed host and guest in this novel seems to refer not just to any randomly-thought-of host and guest or solely to an overarching "historical consciousness" but to a particular man hosting the annual Holly Springs Pilgrimage. Year after year the host recounts her sad story and shows her etching to traveling strangers—and to one such man in particular. Faulkner likely depicts himself as that particular visitor from out of town, viewer of the etched window at McCarroll Place, and deeply moved by the story and image, as Faulkner may well have been.

Close textual analysis, eyewitness testimony, communal memory, autobiographical portraits of the artist, and ephemera link Ludie's signature in glass to Faulkner's novels. Faulkner incorporates her etching, the "indelible signature of her meditation" into his ruminations on youth, eternity, and time and history in *Intruder in the Dust* and *Requiem for a Nun*. The old etching traverses time and space: "across the vast instantaneous intervention, from the long long time ago" (*Requiem for a Nun* 262). Faulkner concludes that "all you had to do was look at it a while; all you have to do now is remember it" (261–62). The "fragile," "cryptic," and "indelible" glass inscription beckons through time for all to consider and remember—as indeed William Faulkner did.

Chapter Three

"PEOPLE THAT I HAVE KNOWN"

William Faulkner, a Family Who
Influenced Him, and Possible Sources
for *The Sound and the Fury*

> They are the people that I have known all my life
> in the country I was born in....
> —WILLIAM FAULKNER, IN JOSEPH L. FANT III AND ROBERT ASHLEY, EDS.,
> *FAULKNER AT WEST POINT*, 96

William Faulkner's celebrated heroine of *The Sound and the Fury*—Caddy Compson—may have had real-life antecedents. That is a theory put forward in my 2010 study, *Ledgers of History*.[1] More support for that argument has become evident since then. New research and analyses of information suggest that Perle Strickland Badow (see figure 3.1) and Ruth LeGrand Strickland (see figure 3.5 on p. 111), both descendants of Francis Terry Leak and cousins of the Franciscos, may have inspired important characteristics—as well as the home and wedding—of Caddy Compson, Faulkner's compelling heroine. Additional research contributes to the case that the Leak/McCarroll/Francisco family informed some of Faulkner's most famous novels, including *The Sound and the Fury*, *Go Down, Moses*, and *Absalom, Absalom!*

Figure 3.1 Perle Strickland as a young woman. Photograph copy work by George Nikas, Atlanta, Georgia. Courtesy of Dr. Edgar Wiggin Francisco III and Anne Weir.

Perle Strickland Badow, Her Three Brothers, Niece, Servant, German Lover and Husband, and *The Sound and the Fury*

In family configuration, a mammy surnamed Gibson, a beautiful girl in a swing who becomes an alluring woman, wedding details, a German lover, the layout of the house and grounds, and the fictional Compson family depicted in *The Sound and the Fury* resemble that of Perle Strickland, her home—Strickland Place—and her family, who were cousins of Francisco III.[2] They and he were descendants of Francis Terry Leak; Perle Strickland and Francisco's grandmother, Betsy Leak, were first cousins and granddaughters of Francis Terry Leak.[3] The Stricklands lived next door to their Francisco cousins in Holly Springs. (See figure 3.2.)

Figure 3.2 Left to right: Perle Strickland Badow, Edgar Wiggin Francisco III, and Edgar Wiggin Francisco Jr. Strickland Place appears in the background. Photograph taken by Ruth Bitzer Francisco. Photograph copy work by George Nikas, Atlanta, Georgia. Courtesy of Dr. Edgar Wiggin Francisco III.

When young William Faulkner visited Edgar Francisco Jr., according to Francisco III, the two boys heard many stories from the family elders about the Strickland relatives, and they frequently visited Perle Strickland and family.[4] In December of 1926, near the time when Faulkner began writing *The Sound and the Fury*,[5] this small, conservative Mississippi town experienced an unexpected social event: Perle Strickland married an immigrant, newly relocated in Holly Springs. He was a German national named Gerard Badow. Apparently, the family and some townsfolk had already been surprised to hear the unmarried Perle say that she had traveled abroad with Herr Badow.[6] After all, she was a single woman of middle years, and such behavior was no doubt untraditional. Francisco III remembers being told that when Perle planned to wear a white wedding gown for her nuptial attire, his family members raised their eyebrows at that and the newspaper's description of her as a "blushing bride."⁷

Francisco III recalls that Perle said she traveled with Badow:

> Then and through my time there the people relished [the] risqué and bragged of their naughty citizens. Any expression of surprise would have been tongue-in-cheek. Perle was always acting on the stage she created as if she was a New York star. So, when she returned from a trip to New York and dramatically whispered to receptive ears that she had been abroad with him [Badow] that spread as fun, titillating gossip. The talk was— "did she really, or is this another play she is writing?" She loved to be mysterious, and she was a good enough actress for people to enjoy it. She kept the story going awhile by saying in regard to a planned trip after the wedding that this time they would travel as husband and wife (always in a whisper, of course).
>
> Her story travelled through family, relatives and neighbors, but it may not have made much traction through the town which was accustomed to her theatrics. First I heard of it was when Pauline [a family friend] visited when I was home from college in 1951 and asked Dad if he knew what really happened.⁸ She was still entertained by it. So, later Dad told me the whole story. He was amused that Pauline was still wondering about it, but he did say that at the time there was a buzz over it, and he and Faulkner talked about it. Will was reading the *Diary*, was aware of the whole family story—Janie [Leak] coming to [Holly Springs] to marry Strickland and the rest. Will seemed very interested in the entire Strickland bunch.⁹

Perle's behavior continually seemed fascinating and risqué to her cousins next door.

Caddy Compson's Wedding and Perle Strickland's

Caddy Compson and Perle Strickland share characteristics, and their weddings were similar. Faulkner was aware of the Strickland-Badow wedding, according to Francisco III, and like many in the local community, Faulkner had not taken a liking to Gerard Badow: "Immediately on meeting Badow, Will said: 'I don't trust this man. What is he doing with a middle-aged

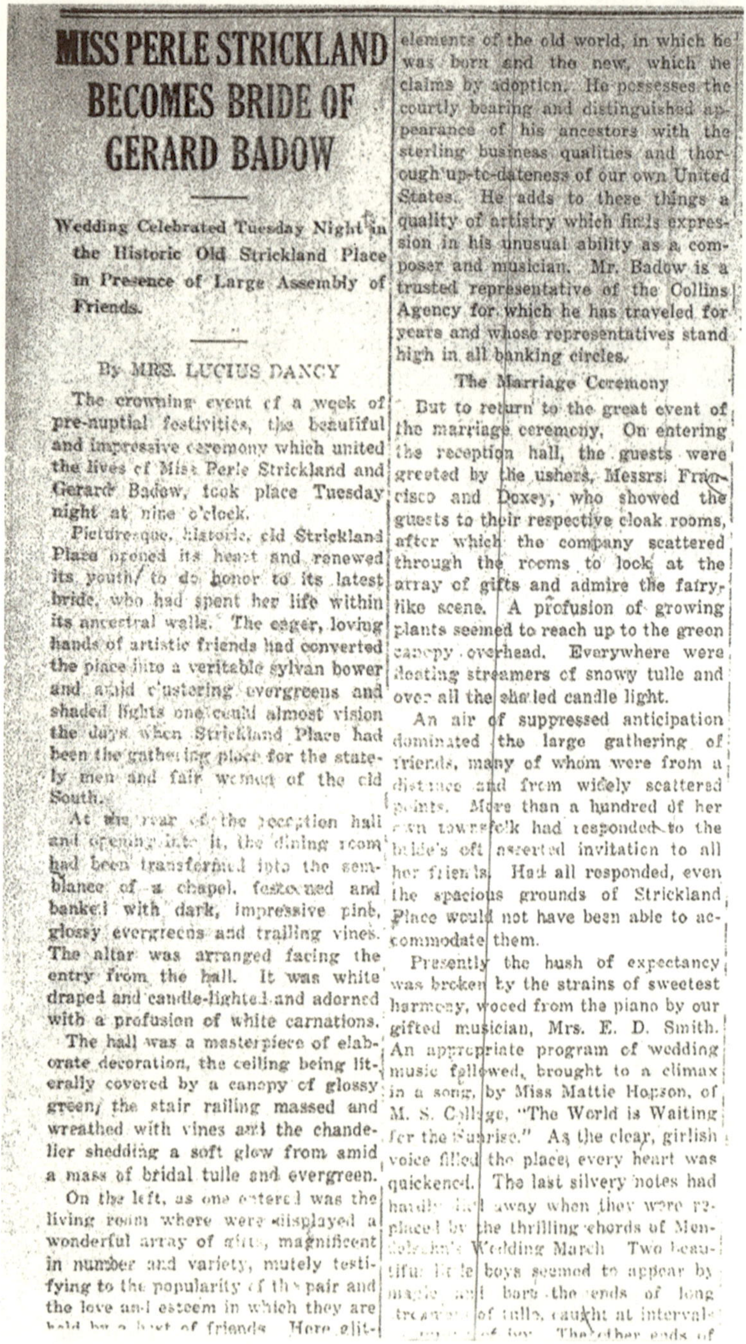

MISS PERLE STRICKLAND BECOMES BRIDE OF GERARD BADOW

Wedding Celebrated Tuesday Night in the Historic Old Strickland Place in Presence of Large Assembly of Friends.

By MRS. LUCIUS DANCY

The crowning event of a week of pre-nuptial festivities, the beautiful and impressive ceremony which united the lives of Miss Perle Strickland and Gerard Badow, took place Tuesday night at nine o'clock.

Picturesque, historic, old Strickland Place opened its heart and renewed its youth to do honor to its latest bride, who had spent her life within its ancestral walls. The eager, loving hands of artistic friends had converted the place into a veritable sylvan bower and amid clustering evergreens and shaded lights one could almost vision the days when Strickland Place had been the gathering place for the stately men and fair women of the old South.

At the rear of the reception hall and opening into it, the dining room had been transformed into the semblance of a chapel, festooned and banked with dark, impressive pine, glossy evergreens and trailing vines. The altar was arranged facing the entry from the hall. It was white draped and candle-lighted and adorned with a profusion of white carnations.

The hall was a masterpiece of elaborate decoration, the ceiling being literally covered by a canopy of glossy green; the stair railing massed and wreathed with vines and the chandelier shedding a soft glow from amid a mass of bridal tulle and evergreen.

On the left, as one entered was the living room where were displayed a wonderful array of gifts, magnificent in number and variety, mutely testifying to the popularity of the pair and the love and esteem in which they are held by a host of friends. Here glit-

elements of the old world, in which he was born and the new, which he claims by adoption. He possesses the courtly bearing and distinguished appearance of his ancestors with the sterling business qualities and thorough up-to-dateness of our own United States. He adds to these things a quality of artistry which finds expression in his unusual ability as a composer and musician. Mr. Badow is a trusted representative of the Collins Agency for which he has traveled for years and whose representatives stand high in all banking circles.

The Marriage Ceremony

But to return to the great event of the marriage ceremony. On entering the reception hall, the guests were greeted by the ushers, Messrs. Francisco and Doxey, who showed the guests to their respective cloak rooms, after which the company scattered through the rooms to look at the array of gifts and admire the fairy-like scene. A profusion of growing plants seemed to reach up to the green canopy overhead. Everywhere were floating streamers of snowy tulle and over all the shaded candle light.

An air of suppressed anticipation dominated the large gathering of friends, many of whom were from a distance and from widely scattered points. More than a hundred of her own townsfolk had responded to the bride's oft asserted invitation to all her friends. Had all responded, even the spacious grounds of Strickland Place would not have been able to accommodate them.

Presently the hush of expectancy was broken by the strains of sweetest harmony, voiced from the piano by our gifted musician, Mrs. E. D. Smith. An appropriate program of wedding music followed, brought to a climax in a song, by Miss Mattie Hopson, of M. S. College, "The World is Waiting for the Sunrise." As the clear, girlish voice filled the place, every heart was quickened. The last silvery notes had hardly died away when they were replaced by the thrilling chords of Mendelssohn's Wedding March. Two beautiful little boys seemed to appear by magic and bore the ends of long streamers of tulle, caught at intervals

Figure 3.3 Mrs. Lucius Dancy, "Miss Perle Strickland Becomes Bride of Gerard Badow": wedding announcement of Perle Strickland and Gerard Badow, from the *South Reporter*, December 2, 1926. Reprinted with permission of The South Reporter, Inc.

woman? He wants the house, probably." Faulkner was suspicious of Germans. That may have colored his attitude toward Badow. Dad was very much aware that Will had animosity toward Badow."[10]

The Holly Springs newspaper, the *South Reporter*, published extensive coverage of Perle's wedding. Faulkner likely may have seen these articles and/or known firsthand of Perle's behavior with the German and her marriage plans. The engagement announcement appeared on November 18, 1926: "Frank Leake [*sic*] Strickland of Holly Springs and Jacob Leonidas Strickland of Louisville, Ky., announce the engagement of their sister, Perle, to Gerard Badow of Philadelphia, Pa. The marriage will be solemnized on the evening of Tuesday, November 30, at Strickland Place."[11] The *South Reporter* prominently announced the details of Perle's wedding on the front page (figure 3.3). The large-print type in the newspaper article headline was an indication of how dramatic the news of Perle Strickland's wedding was for the community:

MISS PERLE STRICKLAND BECOMES BRIDE OF GERARD BADOW[12]

Perhaps William Faulkner found in this nuptial some raw ingredients for fiction. The newspaper included elaborate details of Perle's wedding, which occurred at home: "The crowning event of a week of pre-nuptial festivities, the beautiful and impressive ceremony which united the lives of Miss Perle Strickland and Gerard Badow, took place Tuesday night at nine o'clock."[13] The narrative continues: "The eager, loving hands of artistic friends had converted the place into a veritable sylvan bower and amid clustering evergreens and shaded lights one could almost vision the days when Strickland Place had been the gathering place for the stately men and fair women of the old South." The article depicts in fanciful terms a bygone southern scene in which this wedding occurs.

Perle's wedding attire—a long gown, train, and veil—also received prominent attention in the article and carries numerous likenesses to Faulkner's rendition of Caddy's marriage in his famous novel. Hubert McAlexander, a native of Holly Springs, includes a compelling description of Perle's marriage to the German, and a photograph of Perle in her later years, in his study of the Holly Springs area of Mississippi. The photograph caption reads: "A serpentine walk led to the mouldering, but charming old house, where 'Miss Perle' entertained visitors with dramatic tales. In her fifties, she came down the staircase at Strickland Place gowned and veiled in white to marry a German (much younger) recently arrived in Holly Springs."[14] Rev. Milton Winter includes the same photograph of Perle Strickland and Strickland Place in his book *Civil War Women*.[15]

Such vivid headlines and wedding details would be difficult for anyone in town to miss, especially for the bride's cousin Edgar, living right next door, and his good friend William Faulkner, a frequent visitor. The "dramatic tales" with which Perle regaled her listeners at Strickland Place may well have reached Will Faulkner's ears, highly attuned for southern lore; he was busy already next door gaining familiarity with the Leak plantation ledgers at the Franciscos' house. Edgar Francisco Jr. and Hindman Doxey Sr., who later would become brothers-in-law, participated in Perle's wedding ceremony: "On entering the reception hall, the guests were greeted by the ushers, Messrs. Francisco and Doxey."[16] The Reverend George Bitzer, who would soon become Edgar Jr.'s father-in-law, performed the ceremony.[17] Hindman Doxey Sr., according to Sarah Doxey Tate, was present at the wedding of John Faulkner, William Faulkner's brother.[18] At the time of Perle's 1926 wedding, Edgar Francisco Jr., Hindman Doxey Sr., and William Faulkner were all still single.[19]

Perle's high-spirited actions in bragging about traveling with a German male companion may have captivated Will Faulkner: this mischief, after all, was plot line. In her home—the "mouldering" Strickland Place—the novelist also would have noted the suggestive atmosphere and authentic setting. Her family story contained themes that he amplifies in *The Sound and the Fury*: children coming of age, self-discovery, and sexuality, all of which propel them toward an inevitable fall. Caddy's high-spirited actions and tone resemble Perle's, especially in the later-life dalliances with a German man. In the last photograph of Caddy Compson, she is on the arm of "a German staffgeneral."[20] Caddy's story eventually leads her to catastrophic flight and deceit, portrayed symbolically by William Faulkner in terms of personal, and even foreboding of political, treason.

Similarities between Perle and the adult Caddy are noteworthy. Caddy's older age at the time of her German dalliance; her at-home wedding, traditional gown, veil and train, and an abundance of roses; and her mammy and three brothers all are evocative of the familial configuration, attire, and ambiance of Perle Strickland's family and her highly publicized, at-home wedding. Both Perle and Caddy's wedding ceremonies take place at home. Perle's wedding, "Celebrated Tuesday Night in the Historic Old Strickland Place in Presence of Large Assembly of Friends,"[21] seems an even closer connection with Caddy Compson's nuptial location than does the first wedding of Estelle Oldham, Faulkner's childhood sweetheart and later his wife, who (it has been theorized) also could have served as a model for Caddy. Estelle and her first husband, Cornell Franklin, were not married at home, however—they were married at church.[22] Faulkner's wedding to Estelle also occurred at church. Caddy's at-home wedding location more closely parallels that of Perle Strickland.

From here the wedding parallels multiply rapidly and suggest a convergence. Caddy's bridal dress, especially her veil, and flowers, notably roses, resemble Perle's:

> The costumes of the bridal party were of unusual beauty and richness, that of the bride being a sleeveless, semi-decollete model of ivory satin crepe draped with priceless old rose point lace and crowned with a floating veil caught to her dark, wavy hair with sprays of lilies of the valley. Her arm bouquet was of Bride roses, lilies of the valley, and ferns with streamers of satin ribbons.[23]

The floating veil "caught" in Perle's hair is particularly noteworthy. Faulkner's verbatim "caught" describes the position of Caddy's wedding dress train, and in the same sentence with her veil: "her train caught up over her arm . . . her veil swirling in long glints" (52). Faulkner was observing or reading closely, perhaps. Benjy notices that Caddy, like Perle, has "flowers in her hair," and "a long veil like shining wind" (25). That Caddy runs across the porch *"fast clutching her dress onto her shoulder"* (52) may be Faulkner's allusion to the décolleté dress—strapless or with a low neckline—worn by Perle Strickland. An abundance of roses accentuates both Perle's and Caddy's wedding. Faulkner emphasizes them in his repetition: *"out of the banked scent. Roses. . . . Roses"* (49). Mrs. Jacob Strickland, wife of Perle's brother, also participated in the nuptial activities, and her name is not far removed from that of Caddy's mother—Mrs. Jason Compson.

Perle Strickland's German Lover --and Caddy Compson

Age at the time of a German escapade closely connects Caddy Compson with Perle Strickland's age at the time of her wedding to Badow. According to Faulkner's 1945 appendix to *The Sound and the Fury*, Caddy is forty-eight in 1940 when she "vanished in Paris with the German occupation" (208). When she appears in the photo with the German staffgeneral, it is 1943, and Caddy is fifty-one. The date of the photograph remains unclear, however, so

Figure 3.4 Gerard Badow. Photo from his 1921 Form for Naturalized Citizen immigration documents. "NARA Series: Passport Applications, January 2, 1906–March 31, 1925; Roll #1767," database with images, Ancestry (www.ancestry.com/discoveryui-content/view/55980:1174: downloaded 25 May 2023), imaged certificate 94484, Gerard Martin Johannes Badow passport application 31 Oct 1921; cited by Ancestry as "National Archives and Records Administration (NARA); Washington D.C."

although she was forty-eight in 1940, she may have been even older when she is last seen with the German.

Perle Badow in reality was over fifty years old at the time of her marriage, but research suggests that her stated age was lower. She was born about 1869, according to the 1870 and 1880 United States Census records,[24] but by the time she and Gerard appear in the 1930 census as a married couple,[25] she claims to be the same age as he, which is fifty in 1930. In 1926 she probably would have been admitting to about forty-six or seven but was in fact fifty-seven. In any case, the age she stated corresponds closely with Caddy's age when she vanishes in Paris: forty-eight.

Caddy Compson's consort, the German officer, and also her husband, Herbert Head, are associated with her fall from sexual virtue, and both of those characters illustrate hallmark traits of Gerard Badow. Caddy's "German staffgeneral" is described as "lean" (210). Badow's US passport photograph reveals that he is lean (figure 3.4). Dr. Francisco recalls that Badow was "thin."[26]

Badow's involvement with the banking industry, moreover, connects him thematically with Herbert Head, who in *The Sound and the Fury* promises Caddy's brother Jason a position with his bank (60). At the time of his immigration, Badow's US passport declares him to be a salesman,[27] but by the time of his marriage to Perle, he is associated with banking. In the passenger list for Badow and Perle's post-wedding 1927 trip return to Germany, Badow's occupation is listed as "Bankspezialist [bank specialist]."[28] The *South Reporter* states that "Mr. Badow is a trusted representative of the Collins Agency for which he has traveled for years and whose representatives stand high in all banking circles."[29] Perhaps Faulkner drew from Gerard Badow, the virtually unknown, newly arrived German, recently married to the well-known Perle Strickland, a native of the Old South and Faulkner's own home area, some of the unsavory characteristics he would lend to the out-of-state husband of his famous home-based heroine, Caddy Compson.

Caddy Compson's Three Brothers and Mammy Named Gibson—and Perle's

Perle Strickland's brothers, their group activities, and domestic servant also may have provided models for the Compson family and their mammy. Perle had three brothers: Jacob, Frank, and Claude. Caddy similarly had three brothers, all with short names: Jason, Benjy, and Quentin. Edwin Chandler, the mentally impaired son of the Chandler family in Oxford, Mississippi, whom Faulkner also visited often, has long been thought of as the model for Benjy Compson. Scholars have also believed that Faulkner's own family configuration—three brothers and one girl cousin—are a likely source for the Compson family in *The Sound and the Fury*, but none of Faulkner's brothers were "slow."

Frank Strickland, however, apparently was mentally disabled, according to Francisco III and confirmed by Hubert McAlexander.[30] Frank may be a heretofore-unrecognized model for Benjy Compson. Francisco III recalls that William Faulkner knew Frank well, and Faulkner and Edgar spent time with him: "Dad and Will spent more time observing Frank than anyone else. At least it seemed that way to me. They would retell with affectionate amusement his latest antic or saying. Perhaps that is why Frank is the only

Strickland that I personally remember Will saying that he wrote up. He said: 'Most of Frank is in Benjy, but not all of Benjy was in Frank.'"[31] Francisco III points out that although the census records sometimes list Frank as a farmer or town worker, those interested should keep in mind that "[his sister] Perle filled out the census and liked to boost him."[32]

Fire is another commonality between Benjy and Frank. Francisco III recalled:

> Frank was fascinated with the fireplace. One of his jobs was to keep coal in the grate. He would stare at the fire. Frank was very interested in fire. He would keep track of how many coal scuttles he had brought in. He would get a roaring fire. One day a coal spilled out on the rug, and they had a little fire. After that the family watched him more closely. We all sat around the fireplace in the winter when we were at Strickland Place for our elocution lessons. Perle would have to persuade Frank to move away from the fire and out of the room during the lesson. I remember running home one Saturday after lessons laughing about how upset Frank got for fear that the fire would go out if he was not watching and adding coal.[33]

Firelight calms and quiets Faulkner's Benjy Compson. His death by fire in *The Mansion* may be a dramatized and amplified fictionalizing of Frank's having started a less disastrous fire.[34]

Caddy Compson in the Swing: A Beautiful Neighbor and Possible Model

Caddy Compson in the swing is a central, highly symbolic image in *The Sound and the Fury*. Faulkner suggests Caddy's developing sexuality and maturation as she embraces her boyfriends in the swing and beyond. Later her daughter, Quentin, will behave in the same manner. The swing thus carries significant meaning for a main theme in the novel—the maturation of children into adulthood and the havoc and loss that sexuality can engender. Perle Strickland's niece in the swing at McCarroll Place, and her ensuing maturation into a beautiful woman, may have served as a model for Faulkner's portrait of the young Caddy Compson.

Perle's brother Jacob Strickland had a charming daughter—Ruth LeGrand Strickland—whose beauty is apparent in her photograph taken in the swing in the McCarroll Place side yard (figure 3.5). This memorable and inspiring

Figure 3.5 Ruth LeGrand Strickland in the swing at McCarroll Place. Photograph taken by Edgar Francisco Jr. Courtesy of Anne Weir.

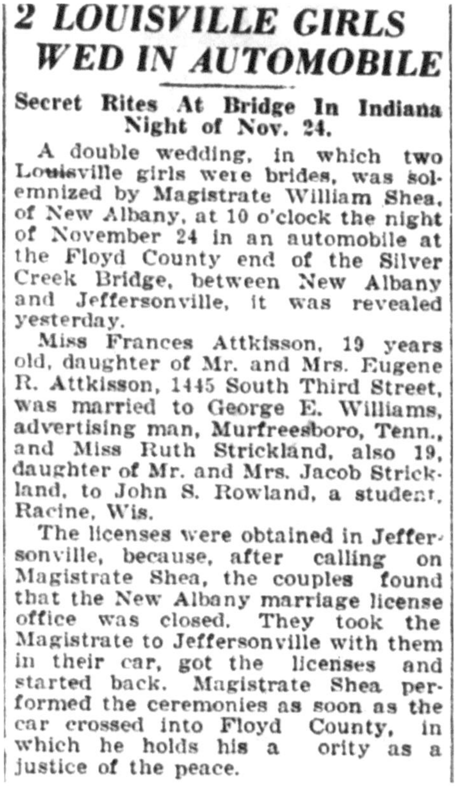

2 LOUISVILLE GIRLS WED IN AUTOMOBILE

Secret Rites At Bridge In Indiana Night of Nov. 24.

A double wedding, in which two Louisville girls were brides, was solemnized by Magistrate William Shea, of New Albany, at 10 o'clock the night of November 24 in an automobile at the Floyd County end of the Silver Creek Bridge, between New Albany and Jeffersonville, it was revealed yesterday.

Miss Frances Attkisson, 19 years old, daughter of Mr. and Mrs. Eugene R. Attkisson, 1445 South Third Street, was married to George E. Williams, advertising man, Murfreesboro, Tenn., and Miss Ruth Strickland, also 19, daughter of Mr. and Mrs. Jacob Strickland, to John S. Rowland, a student, Racine, Wis.

The licenses were obtained in Jeffersonville, because, after calling on Magistrate Shea, the couples found that the New Albany marriage license office was closed. They took the Magistrate to Jeffersonville with them in their car, got the licenses and started back. Magistrate Shea performed the ceremonies as soon as the car crossed into Floyd County, in which he holds his a ority as a justice of the peace.

Figure 3.6 Newspaper clipping describing the secret marriages of Ruth Strickland and Frances Attkisson. Source: "2 Louisville Girls Wed in Automobile: Secret Rites at Bridge in Indiana Night of Nov. 24," *Courier-Journal* (Louisville, KY), December 9, 1923, p. 3, col. 2; digital image, www.newspapers.com/image/107525961/: downloaded 5 August 2023. © The Courier-Journal—USA TODAY NETWORK.

swing was in the garden near the gate to Strickland Place and was present there when Will and Edgar were boys.[35] One section of the McCarroll Place fence extended between McCarroll Place and Strickland Place.

Caddy and Ruth: Indiana and Husbands: A Startling Parallel

The young Caddy Compson resembles Ruth LeGrand Strickland in her youthful beauty, which is apparent in the photo of Ruth in the swing in the yard at McCarroll Place, but also in the nature and location of her sexual activities and behaviors. Both were beautiful little girls who mature into sexual women with complex marital states. Ruth was the beautiful little girl next door to Will's friend Edgar. As she matured she engaged in numerous love relationships that eventuated in multiple marriages. In a startling similarity with some of Caddy Compson's behaviors in *The Sound and the Fury*, Ruth travels to Indiana for an undisclosed reason. Caddy goes to Indiana with her mother ostensibly on vacation but comes home with a husband. Ruth has a secret wedding in Indiana in a car on November 24, 1923, which was reported later in the *Courier Journal*, from her hometown of Louisville, Kentucky, December 9, 1923 (figure 3.6).[36]

Similarities between Caddy and Ruth continue. Both have multiple relationships, at least one of which for each woman takes place in Indiana. Caddy and her mother travel to French Lick, a resort town in southern Indiana, but the suggestion is that Caddy is there to seek an abortion. Quentin said Caddy "found not death at the salt lick," and he implies that she should have found death instead of embarrassing her family through her dishonorable behavior resulting in pregnancy out of wedlock (*Sound and the Fury* 61). From this trip with her mother, Caddy comes home with a new husband, but he is not the father of her unborn child (see 62, n4, and 68). Caddy "was two months pregnant with another man's child . . . when she married (1910) an extremely eligible young Indianian she and her mother had met while vacationing at French Lick the summer before. Divorced by him 1911. Married 1920 to a minor movingpicture magnate, Hollywood California. Divorced by mutual agreement, Mexico, 1925" (208).

Caddy's wedding announcement says she will reside in Indiana: "Mr and Mrs Jason Richmond Compson announce the marriage of their daughter Candace to Mr Sydney Herbert Head on the twenty-fifth of April one thousand nine hundred and ten at Jefferson Mississippi. At home after the first of August number Something Something Avenue South Bend Indiana" (59).

Ruth was married approximately six times. Her first marriage that took place in a car in Indiana did not last long, nor did Caddy's. Mrs. Anne Weir, Ruth's daughter-in-law, has no recollection of an abortion in Ruth's life.[37]

By 1925 both Ruth and Caddy are divorced, and Ruth was a student in New York at the Semple School, which was a "finishing academy for young women."[38] Her mother plans a luncheon for her: "Mrs. Jacob L. Strickland will give a buffet luncheon December 21 in honor of her daughter, Miss Ruth Strickland, who will return December 18 from Miss Semple's School in New York, to spend the holidays with her parents."[39]

Likewise, Caddy is home from school at Christmas. She says to her brother Benjy: "Did you think it would be Christmas when I came home from school. Is that what you thought. Christmas is the day after tomorrow. Santy Claus, Benjy. Santy Claus" (5). Ruth's additional marriages took place in 1926, 1938, 1942, and 1947.[40] The likeness between the real Ruth and fictional Caddy makes Ruth LeGrand Strickland a strong candidate as a role model for the young Caddy Compson.

William Faulkner knew Ruth and visited her on numerous occasions, according to Francisco III. Edgar Jr. was nine years old when "baby cousin" Ruth was born in 1907. Francisco III describes his adorable cousin Ruth LeGrand Strickland this way:

> William Faulkner certainly knew Ruth. She was the only baby at Strickland Place, and she kept coming back to visit as she grew to be an adorable little girl and a beautiful young lady. When [her father] Jacob married Ruth LeGrand Seay they [visited] Strickland Place [after their wedding], and Ruth was born in 1907. The baby was much doted on. Luella Gibson, a live-in maid, was assigned full time to Ruth. Dad was nine when she was born, his only second cousin. He grew very fond of her and called her his "baby cousin."
>
> Jacob Leonides Strickland (brother of Perle, Frank and Claude) was a first cousin of Dad's mother, Betsy, who from about age four grew up right next door to these younger cousins. Perle and Frank lived there for life. Jacob moved his family to Greenville, MS, before the 1910 census, moving on to Louisville, KY sometime later, but returning frequently to visit. When she was old enough Ruth came on her own, having grown very fond of Perle, Frank and Dad.
>
> Dad took a picture of Ruth in our swing. Also she came for his H.S. graduation in 1916 (at least he obviously enjoyed thinking that was the reason for her visit.) She came often until she married Dr. Weir, a dentist in Louisville. She returned [in what was to my knowledge]

the last time and with her grown son William Weir when Perle died in November, 1948.[41]

Since William Faulkner apparently knew the adorable Ruth LeGrand Strickland, her beauty and charm may have inspired the depiction of the young Caddy Compson, to whom Faulkner would later refer as "the beautiful one" and "my heart's darling" (*Sound and the Fury* 236). Benjy has a negative reaction to seeing his sister Caddy in the swing with a beau. Also later Benjy again is upset when he sees Caddy's daughter, Quentin, in the swing with a boy. Benjy begins to cry: "I could see the swing and I began to cry" (30). The swing is the symbol for the sexual maturation that first Caddy and then her daughter Quentin exhibit as they approach adulthood.

Ruth's daughter-in-law Anne Weir recalls that Ruth had multiple love relationships and numerous marriages and eventually left town.[42] Francisco III recalls that Ruth Weir returned at least one more time for Perle's funeral.[43] These activities also parallel Caddy Compson's. Eventually for both women, real and fictional, the vicissitudes of life swept them into departures from home. In Ruth's case that included her leaving town to attend the Semple School, a finishing school in New York for girls, and her later trip to Indiana to marry secretly. Out of all the possible states in the continental US for Caddy to go to find an abortion clinic and a husband, Faulkner chose Indiana, the same one to which Ruth traveled in real life for at least a partially similar purpose. For both women, multiple love relationships, marriages, childbearing, and divorce ultimately would take them permanently away from home. Caddy finally is so far removed that she is never seen again, except in a photograph.

During the conversation about the photos, Mrs. Weir also discussed the speculation about the rumored, alleged murder of Perle Strickland Badow by her husband, Gerard. That information bears considerably on several related topics, which received further scrutiny.[44] Francisco III remembers that:

> In November, 1948 Dad called me at college to say Perle had died and he would tell me the story at Christmas. Strickland relatives had come when Perle died. The only names I remember are Ruth LeGrand Strickland Weir and her son, William Strickland Weir. The Strickland Place was "home place" to Ruth, who lived there until age two and was most likely born there. She visited her grandmother there frequently and her Aunt Perle, whom she loved very much, and with Dad, her second cousin. Dad and Will Faulkner were fascinated by this pretty little girl who grew into a beautiful and alluring young woman.[45]

Francisco III further recalls his father's descriptions of Ruth as a young girl and woman:

> Dad's depiction of her was of a very pretty, vivacious little girl who turned into a seductively alluring young lady from about fifteen through the rest of her life. So, she turned fifteen when Faulkner was twenty-four. I imagine Faulkner did notice her with more than a little interest, but I do not recall Dad spelling that out, but then Dad would not have spelled it out. Dad spoke of her with obvious affection.[46]

Perle's Mammy Named Gibson and the Notes between the Houses

Additional connections also accrue among the real-life McCarrolls, Franciscos, and Stricklands and the fictional Compsons and Gibsons. Luella Gibson was a servant to Perle and her family, and Luella's main task was to look after Ruth. In *The Sound and the Fury*, the Compsons' principal domestic servant is Dilsey Gibson. The identical name Gibson—both for the real Luella and the fictional Dilsey—further suggests that Faulkner may have drawn on the former as one model for the latter and that he felt free to use the Gibson name without alteration. These correspondences further strengthen the argument that Faulkner drew from the Strickland and Gibson families in shaping the fictional world of *The Sound and the Fury*. Certainly, Faulkner excelled at hearing, observing, and transforming.

The street on which McCarroll Place faced for some time was named "Maury." (Later the front entrance opened onto Van Dorn Ave.) Faulkner easily would have seen the street sign with "Maury" on it when gazing out of the window of McCarroll Place. Perhaps that street name inspired the naming of the fictional character Maury, in *The Sound and the Fury*. These are significant points of contact between real and imagined events.

Perle Strickland, Germany, and Caddy's Fate

Faulkner thus seems to have drawn from the circumstances of the Strickland-Badow marriage, including courtship, wedding, and travel to Germany, for his characterizations of the older Caddy and her male companions, the lean German officer with whom she last appears and also the banker Herbert Head. Faulkner also may have viewed Perle's choice of a mate as a symbolic violation. Perle's association with a foreigner, a German national, so soon after the calamity of the First World War—that war with Germany to end all wars—may have resonated for Faulkner in various ways. He trained to participate in the war against Germany, and his brother John was injured.[47]

In *The Sound and the Fury*, Caddy and her German have a sexual alliance with politically negative overtones. Perle's boldly unapologetic actions may have fired the novelist's imagination: the older Caddy becomes a fallen woman, worthy of scorn, and doubly so because her ravisher is a Boche. When William Faulkner began work on *The Sound and the Fury* in 1927, Perle Strickland had recently departed abroad with her new German husband, for "an extended visit to the bridegroom's widowed mother in Dresden, Germany, and . . . various tours to points of interest."[48] In the appendix to *The Sound and the Fury*, Caddy is reported to have "vanished in Paris with the German occupation, 1940, still beautiful and probably still wealthy too since she did not look within fifteen years of her actual fortyeight" (208).

Two models for Caddy Compson thus emerge—Ruth LeGrand Strickland, the adorable girl in the swing, the beautiful child who grows into an attractive, sexually active young woman—and the older, risqué woman, Perle Strickland Badow, who like Caddy appears "ageless and beautiful, cold serene and damned; beside her a handsome lean man of middleage in the ribbons and tabs of a German staffgeneral" (209–10). Both Caddy Compson and Perle Strickland are "ageless and beautiful," and with their German men evoke ongoing curiosity and speculation.

Faulkner's focus on the treachery of Germany may be an adumbration of Perle's perceived betrayal of national allegiance and her flouting of traditional moral values. Faulkner's reference to a German staffgeneral suggests the looming, dark presence of political disaster and national fear. That Faulkner linked a beautiful, charming Mississippi woman with a German man may reflect Faulkner's suspiciousness toward Germans, which Francisco III notes, and it may also reflect Faulkner's resentment at having once lost Estelle, his childhood sweetheart, to a man who took her abroad for years. This emotional and psychological betrayal became in his fiction cold, hard, unpardonable treason, for which he may have found an analogue in the high-spirited nature and scandalous sexual history of an older woman in the person of Perle Strickland Badow.

POSSIBLE SOURCES FOR *THE SOUND AND THE FURY* 117

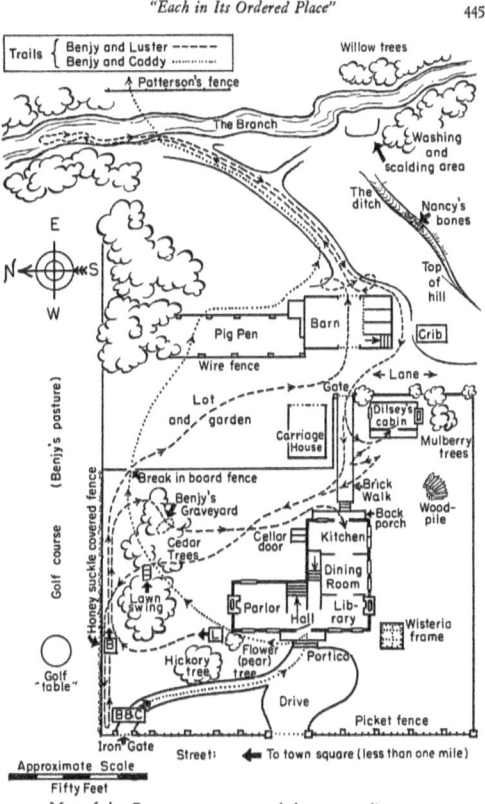

Figure 3.7 Drawing of the Compson House and grounds, in George R. Stewart and Joseph M. Backus, "'Each in Its Ordered Place': Structure and Narrative in 'Benjy's Section' of *The Sound and the Fury*," in *American Literature* 29, no. 4: 440–56. Copyright 1958, Duke University Press. All rights reserved. Republished by permission of the copyright holder, and the Publisher. www.dukeupress.edu.

McCarroll Place, Strickland Place, and the Compson House

The Compson House and grounds in *The Sound and the Fury* are remarkably like numerous features of the houses and grounds of McCarroll Place and Strickland Place. Faulkner could have noticed these details during his visits with the Francisco family in Holly Springs. Scholars previously have considered the structural composition of and sources for the Compson House. In 1958, for example, George R. Stewart and Joseph M. Backus presented a "Map of the Compson property and the surrounding area (less than one mile south of Jefferson, Mississippi)." (See figure 3.7.)

Figure 3.8 Edgar Francisco III as a child, with his mother, Ruth Bitzer Francisco, at the gate between McCarroll Place and Strickland Place. Special thanks to the late Anne Salyerds Francisco, who located this photograph and spent many hours searching for and finding McCarroll-Francisco papers, pictures, and other useful materials. Photograph taken by Edgar Francisco Jr. Photograph copy work by George Nikas, Atlanta, Georgia. Courtesy of Dr. Edgar Wiggin Francisco III.

Based on information presented in the novel, the map includes the arrangement of the rooms in the Compson House—parlor, hall, library, upstairs bedrooms, dining room, back porch featuring an entrance both to the back stairs and to the kitchen—and also specific features of the grounds.

Although other houses known to Faulkner are or also could have been sources or models for the Compson home place, some specific details of these houses and grounds resemble McCarroll Place and Strickland Place more closely even than the Thompson-Chandler house in Oxford, Mississippi, the home that people usually think of as a model for the

Compson House. According to Francisco III, a picket fence with a gate separated McCarroll Place from its neighboring Strickland Place, but the original gate was iron.[49] Children from both houses had gone through the gate to visit each other, and this traversing back and forth between the houses continued during the visits of Edgar Jr. and William Faulkner. Another fence was on the west side of the house but later was removed. (See figure 3.8.)

Francisco III recalls further details about fence, gate, honeysuckle vines, and a tennis court in the yard:

> After Badow moved in [at Strickland Place], he did not keep the path open on his side, so we had to go around to their front door. Until 1930 a fence also ran along the west side of the house, which had once been the front. A chicken-wire fence covered by honeysuckle separated McCarroll Place and Strickland Place up front where the tennis court was. Honeysuckle was so thick on this fence that it helped keep balls from going through the fence. Tennis balls that got lobbed over the fence, if not immediately spotted, were usually found under the huge magnolia whose sagging branches hid balls well.[50]

Correspondences with *The Sound and the Fury* readily emerge—even though with thick colloquial expression. The Compson children go through a gate to reach the neighbor's yard, and Benjy's caregiver Versh describes the gate as "ahun" (iron): "'I told him to keep [his hands] in his pockets,' Versh said. 'Holding on to that ahun gate'" (5). Benjy always snags his clothing on the iron fence when he and Luster or Caddy try to crawl through it. (See figure 3.9.)

Honeysuckle is a motif in *The Sound and the Fury* that evokes longing and remembrance. The scent of honeysuckle wafts symbolically through Quentin's chapter in the novel. Faulkner may have thought of the honeysuckle-covered, chicken-wire fence at McCarroll Place when he describes Benjy Compson looking through the fence and watching what is presumably a golf game: "Between the curling flower spaces, I could see them hitting" (3). Benjy's caregiver Luster looks for stray golf balls in the grass: "Luster was hunting in the grass by the flower tree. . . . 'Maybe we can find one of they balls'" (3). (Luster hopes to sell them later.) William Faulkner participated in tennis games at McCarroll Place, and Francisco III recalls that the fence was to catch straying tennis balls. This scenario may have inspired the setting in the opening pages of the novel. Faulkner, known to change details to protect or camouflage a source, simply could have changed the game from tennis to golf.

Figure 3.9 Edgar Francisco III, as a young boy, at the gate between McCarroll Place and Strickland Place. A corner of the roof of McCarroll Place is visible at left, and Strickland Place, with its chimney, appears in the right background. Photograph taken by Ruth Bitzer Francisco. Photograph copy work by George Nikas, Atlanta, Georgia. Courtesy of Dr. Edgar Wiggin Francisco III.

More parallels between the real and fictional houses are noteworthy: in both, an old servants' quarters was out back of the house, with a walkway leading there from the house. A barn, a lot and garden, a swing, an orchard behind the house, cedar trees, a cow pasture, a pigsty, a hill, brick walkways, and flowing water are common to both properties, real and fictional. In the novel the children play in the branch; a spring, now silted over, once flowed behind McCarroll Place when William Faulkner and Edgar Francisco Jr. were there. An orchard behind the house links with the orchard that has prominence in Faulkner's novel *The Unvanquished*, as well as his story "My Grandmother Millard."

The spring takes on metaphorical significance in the novel: water also marks the initiation of Caddy's sexuality, which ultimately will lead her away from her brothers. In an introduction to the novel, Faulkner recalled: "I saw that peaceful glinting of that branch was to become the dark, harsh flowing of time sweeping [Caddy] to where she could not return to comfort [Benjy], but that just separation, division, would not be enough, not far enough. It must sweep her into dishonor and shame too."[51] The flowing water metaphorically represents irrepressible time, which will sweep Caddy, as she matures into a sexual woman, into shame and dishonor.

The McCarroll grounds also had a cow pasture, barn, pig pen, slaughter area, and washing area. These landscape features are present in *The Sound and the Fury*. At McCarroll Place pigs were kept and slaughtered on the property, and this activity occurs in the novel as well. Benjy observes: "*The ground was hard. We climbed the fence, where the pigs were grunting and snuffing. I expect they're sorry because one of them got killed today, Caddy said*" (3; see also 9). Faulkner may well have been a witness to the slaughter of hogs for food at McCarroll Place during his visits there. The autobiographical impulse seems apparent here too: the emotion that Caddy expresses for the pigs' feelings may reflect William Faulkner's sympathy.

Iron gate, fence, slave cabins down a hill, and brick walkways at McCarroll Place share those same features in the novel. Benjy's fence has long been associated with the fence that once extended across the front yard of the Thompson-Chandler House in Oxford. A vestige of the old fence remained there for many years. Faulkner may well have had other models and sources in mind, however, that he may not have mentioned. Their revelation could have exposed his extensive use of the *Leak Diary* and other McCarroll Place information that he wanted people to think he had created out of whole cloth.

The McCarroll Place fence offers another plausible model for Benjy's fence and iron gate, and other features accentuate the comparison. The Chandler house was not on a hilltop, but McCarroll Place was. The Chandler House did not have a cow pasture, barn, spring, or pigsty—all of which are features in the novel—and McCarroll Place did. The house is at the top of the hill, and the servant quarters were positioned down the slope of the hill behind the house. Several old log cabins originally built for the slaves and later the homes for domestic servants were located down this hill behind the house. The Thompson-Chandler House in Oxford, by contrast, is on flat land, and a servant cabin is to the side of the house but not on a hillslope. The structures and their specific locations at McCarroll Place are credible models for Dilsey's cabin, perhaps more so than any analogous structure on the Thompson-Chandler grounds.

Not only are both the fictional Compson place and McCarroll Place located at the top of a hill, but also both have brick walkways near the house and a trail leading down to flowing water. In *The Sound and the Fury*, when Caddy and her brother Benjy go down to the branch, or creek, she helps him cross the water and go back up the hill toward the house: "She helped me across and we went up the hill" (9). Later the children play in the water. Benjy recalls that: "We were playing in the branch and Caddy squatted down and got her dress wet" (11).

The brick walkways in both real and fictional yards are similar. At McCarroll Place, according to Dr. Francisco, "All walks were brick."[52] In *The Sound and the Fury*, Versh, Caddy, and Benjy traverse a brick walk: "Versh opened the door and we went out. We went down the steps. . . . Versh put me down and Caddy took my hand and we went down the brick walk" (18). This correspondence is another important match between the two houses.

Washing and scalding also took place in both real and fictional yards. In fact, an old galvanized washtub, buried after years of use and disuse, was uncovered at McCarroll Place by a family friend who was searching the yard with a metal detector in pursuit of buried money. The legend of buried silver circulated throughout the area. Washing at the house took place by the kitchen, which is at the back of the house. In both real and fictional yards, the hill, barn with cows, branch, and washing are quite similar: "We went around the barn. The big cow and the little one were standing in the door.... We went down the hill.... They were washing down at the branch. One of them was singing" (*Sound and the Fury* 8–9). The orchard that once existed down the hill from McCarroll Place, with servants going to and from it, bears an unmistakable resemblance to the orchard and related nocturnal activities that figure hauntingly both in *The Unvanquished* and "My Grandmother Millard."

The location of the slave and later domestic servant cabins down the hill from the McCarroll Place are another important link between the real house and Faulkner's depiction. In *The Sound and the Fury*, he describes the servants as walking down a hill from the main house. His African American character T.P. says, "'We going down to our house'" (22), and Benjy recalls going "down to Versh's house" (18) or "down to T.P.'s house" (19). The children and servants first go downhill to the cabin or cabins where the Gibsons live and then walk back up to the Compson House (see, for instance, 13). These setting details compare closely with McCarroll Place and its surroundings.

The hillslope is an important place indicator again in Faulkner's novel at Caddy's wedding. Benjy has too much champagne at his sister's wedding and ultimately feels dizzy. The hill appears several times in this section of the novel, too, as the children and servants go up or down the hill: "The ground kept sloping up and the cows ran up the hill" (*Sound and the Fury* 13). T.P. says: "Me and Benjy going back to the wedding" (14). T.P. says, "Sassprilluh," implying that he is going to drink some of this sweet soft drink, like root beer, but the context suggests that he is drinking something alcoholic, such as champagne from Caddy's wedding (14).

"It was hot inside me," Benjy says, and the effects make him dizzy (14). "It was still going around, and then the shapes began. I went on with them, up the bright hill. At the top of the hill Versh put me down. 'Come on here, Quentin,' he called, looking back down the hill. Quentin was still standing there by the branch" (*Sound and the Fury* 14–15). Atop such a hill, Strickland Place, with its wedding party, family, and servants, perhaps was the setting Faulkner had in mind for Benjy's inebriation and down the hill at the wedding on the back lawn that led to a spring. The Thompson-Chandler House, most often associated with the fictional Compson House, is on flat land, with no hill in the yard, leading to no spring.

Strickland Place was a two-story structure with an exceptionally dark back staircase and two back doors. One door led outside from the hall, and the other led outside from the kitchen. Strickland Place had upstairs bedrooms accessed by a staircase at the back of the hall.[53] Faulkner describes similar features in *The Sound and the Fury*. In the novel the bedrooms are upstairs. The servants Dilsey and Versh take the children up the back staircase after supper. Dilsey says: "Versh, can you get them up the back stairs quiet. You, Jason, shut up that crying" (17). Francisco III describes a similar back staircase at Strickland Place:

> Children and adults needed a passage, sometimes when not presentable, to reach kitchen or privy, to put it indelicately. But, unique to Strickland Place was how very dark the hallways were. This was the first two story [house in town, and this dark] design [was] not copied [in later homes] maybe for that reason. [The] only light in the halls came if [the] door to a room was open. The narrow hall from front to back stairs was spooky.[54]
>
> I confessed to Dad that I was scared to look down the dark back hall, and he admitted to me that when he and Will were children they were also scared and when he mentioned this to his mother, Betsy, she agreed that it had scared her, also. That back staircase and hall were uniquely bad designs built into no other home in the area and well known to all who felt their way along them. Any time of day it was dark inside and lighter outside. Late afternoon in winter would be totally dark inside, but still some light outside.[55]

The dark hallway and back stairs at Strickland Place and the contrasting lightness outside correspond with Faulkner's description in *The Sound and the Fury*. Benjy notices the difference as he goes down the stairway into darkness and then outside into the light: "We went down stairs. The stairs went down into the dark and T. P. took my hand, and we went out the door, out of the dark" (22). The outdoors is lighter than the dark stairway in both the real and imagined stairway.

The back porch at Strickland Place also is a point of comparison with the Compson House. Francisco III recalls that from his perspective as a child, the porch appeared to him to be "wide and deep":

> The porch was wide and deep—clearly the place in the early years where most of the work got done. The porch had two back doors, heavy, old,

simple doors clearly not meant for visitor's use. The door on the left opened to the kitchen. The one on the right (east) opened to a small entry area. About six feet straight ahead was the staircase going up narrow and steep. This arrangement made it possible to go in the back door and up the stairs or down and out without being seen from the hallway. So, to enter and go down the hall you had to step left to clear the staircase and then the narrow and dark hallway came into view.[56]

Faulkner's depiction is similar. The children walk across the back porch as they come indoors for supper and then again later when they return from outdoors. As the children approach the house, the structural configuration mirrors that at Strickland Place. Benjy notes, "Father opened the door and we crossed the back porch and went in to the kitchen" (16). Later, after the children have eaten, Benjy continues: "Versh took me up and opened the door onto the back porch. We went out and Versh closed the door black" (18).

After looking at Faulkner's description, Francisco III comments on the similarity between the real and fictional:

[Faulkner describes] two entrances. Benjy goes down the steps and out the door to outside (no going through kitchen or hall). That is the door to the porch right at the stairs. Separately he says "Father opens the door," and he goes into [the] kitchen. That has to be through another door. That is exactly the way it was at Strickland Place, which is rather unusual, maybe unique. Generally, houses had one back door. With the second door right at the stairs, it was possible for children to come in and go up not only without being seen, but also without being heard, which seems to have been requested in the novel. [In the novel Father Compson wants the children to go upstairs quietly because their grandmother's funeral is taking place in the parlor.][57]

At ninety-four years old at the time of this writing, Francisco III may be one of a very few living people who remembers the two back doors at Strickland Place that were side by side but which led from two different parts of the house to the porch out back. Also he adds that not many people saw the back of Strickland Place: just the family and servants, the neighbors (Edgar Jr., Ruth, Edgar III, and Betsy Francisco)—and an occasional family visitor such as Will Faulkner. As such, Dr. Francisco's eyewitness description of the back staircase and two back doors is historically important in describing firsthand the architecture of Strickland Place.

The recollections of Francisco III also support the idea that Strickland Place may have been a model for Faulkner's depiction of the Compson House. Francisco III provides specific details—that one of the back doors leads directly from the inside stairs to the outside porch, and that the other door leads from the kitchen directly out to the porch—visually clarifies that relationship. Also his recollections speak to the uniqueness of this configuration: that the dark upper hallway was accessible by two back doors at Strickland Place. This description is helpful in establishing that this house, more so than the other antebellum houses in the Holly Springs and Oxford areas, may be a likely source for Faulkner's Compson House. These accruing parallels and details suggest that both Strickland Place and its neighboring McCarroll Place may have afforded Faulkner prototypes for the Compson House and grounds in *The Sound and the Fury*.

Faulkner had an opportunity to observe the Strickland family history, which included a dark story of deceptions, resentments, remembrance of past family affluence—and with the undergirding knowledge that the former affluence of this family was derived from the horrors of slavery—and a fall into a life of poverty, bitterness, and worse. Faulkner's fascination with the Stricklands is apparent in his inclusion of personal characteristics, actions, and motivations attributable to them. Gathering those threads into a narrative in *The Sound and the Fury* that so nearly matches their life events is noteworthy indeed.

The people and places in the McCarroll, Francisco, Leak, and Strickland families, and their location, reveal even more clearly than has previously been evident that William Faulkner wrote about what and whom he knew. In statements made at West Point and elsewhere, Faulkner makes clear that his writing experience was a product not only of what he imagined but also of what he saw, heard, and observed. These examples make a strong case that the artist's craft depended even more profoundly on the people and places of his area of the country, specifically on those longtime friends and neighbors he knew in Holly Springs, Mississippi, just thirty miles from his hometown.

Faulkner was a careful and astute listener; he took note of what he saw, heard, and remembered. He seems to have drawn the essence of some characters, including their specific names, personal traits, motivations, actions, locations, and narrative lines from his friends, their servants, and the houses of those with whom he had become familiar over time. Faulkner thereby created his own style of historical fiction, partly based on people he knew "in the country [he] was born in."[58] Examining some of these people and places as possible sources and antecedents of *The Sound and the Fury* points more clearly than ever to Faulkner's mastery in casting transitory historical truth into imperishable fiction.

Chapter Four

FAULKNER'S *ABSALOM, ABSALOM!* AND McCARROLL PLACE

Possible Antecedents

I myself would have to stop and go page by page to see just how much I drew from family annals that I had listened to from these old undefeated spinster aunts that children of my time grew up with.
—WILLIAM FAULKNER, IN FREDERICK L. GWYNN AND JOSEPH BLOTNER, EDS., *FAULKNER IN THE UNIVERSITY*, 253–54

[A writer] is completely amoral in that he will rob, borrow, beg, or steal from anybody and everybody to get the work done. . . . If a writer has to rob his mother, he will not hesitate; the "Ode on a Grecian Urn" is worth any number of old ladies.
—WILLIAM FAULKNER, IN JEAN STEIN, "THE ART OF FICTION XII"

The Plantation Desk at McCarroll Place

Faulkner appears to have drawn from McCarroll Place as a source in several other works. The people who lived at McCarroll Place, their stories of hardship and survival during and after the Civil War, the particularities of the

Figure 4.1 The McCarroll Place plantation desk. The desk exemplifies the kind of desk Faulkner describes in *Go Down, Moses*. Also, he may have modeled his description of the desk in Isaac's family home from this desk. Courtesy of Dr. Jack and Mrs. Helen Doxey Tyson.

house and grounds, the office inside the house, the plantation desk therein, and the letters on display there may have provided for Faulkner some inspiration for his novel *Absalom, Absalom!*[1]

Although other plantation desks no doubt were extant during Faulkner's lifetime, the McCarroll Place plantation desk (figure 4.1) is significant because it was among the furnishings in this house during the time of William Faulkner's likely visits. This desk calls to mind the one with similarly built-in shelves, from which the character Isaac draws down the plantation ledgers in *Go Down, Moses*: "He was sixteen then. It was . . . [not] the first time he had taken down the old ledgers familiar on their shelf above the desk ever since he could remember" (267–68).

The plantation desk evokes the image of Isaac's reaching up and retrieving the farm ledgers from the shelf in *Go Down, Moses*. The McCarroll farm ledgers were kept at McCarroll Place and were distinct from the *Leak Diary* ledgers. The family kept the McCarroll ledgers on a shelf in the plantation desk, a family heirloom from the nineteenth century. To read the McCarroll ledgers, a family member or guest would pull down a ledger from the shelf. According to Francisco III, William Faulkner was at McCarroll Place during the time in which the plantation desk was in the house, and he would have been familiar with this desk.

Unfortunately, unlike the *Leak Diary*, saved down through the generations, the McCarroll ledgers are lost. The plantation desk, however, survives and now is in the home of Helen Doxey Tyson, a first cousin to Edgar Francisco III.[2] Faulkner's evocative depiction of the ledger—and its place of safekeeping—is even more vivid with this real desk in mind. Faulkner's description of the plantation desk and shelf provides levels of perceived authenticity. A reader imagines him writing at the desk, or reading at it, or reaching up to take a book down from the shelf.

Contemporary readers gain from reading the *Leak Diary* and other similar materials alongside Faulkner's text, in knowing he might have read them, too. Knowing with certainty that he saw this desk or read the McCarroll Place documents there is not paramount; readers can gain from them without knowing the exact nature of Faulkner's relationship to them. They are authentic; they lend authenticity to our reading of his texts.

The Office in the House

The plantation desk was in the room of the house that the McCarroll/Francisco family called "the office." Amelia Leak, the great-grandmother of Edgar Francisco III, referred to a room at the back of the house as "the office," a room that vividly calls to mind the "office" in *Absalom, Absalom!* where Quentin listens, enthralled, to the account of the Sutpen family history as told by the old woman, Rosa Coldfield.[3] The McCarroll/Francisco family kept paperwork and other business-related matters in that room. Edgar Francisco III recalls that the blinds in the office were always closed because the room received direct sun and was always hot during the afternoon:

> The room called "the office" was always the southwest room, until I was old enough to have my room, and then it was my bedroom. Until then the plantation desk was there. The room got afternoon sun. The blinds were closed. Even after it was my room, the blinds were closed in the early years. I remember shafts of light through the blinds in the afternoon. That was the room Amelia liked to sit in to talk to

Dad and Will. Her chair in there was not cut down to fit her as was her chair in the parlor. She and her sister were small and short. They were small, tiny women. When I was a child, my mother would lay out the sisters' clothing on the bed in the bedroom next to the parlor during the Pilgrimage. When I saw it, I thought the clothes were for children—they were that small.

In about 1933 the desk was moved to the enclosed sun room and placed on the south wall next to Ludie's window on the west wall.[4] Then it was given to my cousin Helen Tyson. After 1958 and Dad's fiftieth anniversary in business, he understood I was not coming home to take on the insurance business, and he sold it [the business] to A. Q. Greer, he brought home his roll-top desk and swivel chair and put them back in "the office," which the room became once more.[5]

In the opening paragraph of *Absalom, Absalom!* Faulkner describes Rosa sitting in a room that eerily resembles "the office" at McCarroll Place:

From a little after two oclock until almost sundown of the long still hot weary dead September afternoon they sat in what Miss Coldfield still called the office because her father had called it that—a dim hot airless room with the blinds all closed and fastened for forty-three summers because when she was a girl someone had believed that light and moving air carried heat and that dark was always cooler, and which (as the sun shone fuller and fuller on that side of the house) became latticed with yellow slashes full of dust motes which Quentin thought of as being flecks of the dead old dried paint itself blown inward from the scaling blinds as the wind might have blown them. (*Absalom* 7)

Faulkner renders palpable the heat, the long summer day, the absence of circulation in a closed house, the intense light in the afternoon, the need for drawn blinds, and the stillness of the woman sitting in a dark, quiet room and recollecting and regretting a past that cannot be forgiven. While other southern homes also undoubtedly engaged in the drawing of blinds to counter the intense afternoon light and heat, the McCarroll Place office arguably provided Faulkner with a memory and a real model for Rosa Coldfield's room, which had been her father's office, from which vantage point she tells her tragic story to Quentin Compson, who perhaps is, in part, a fictional Faulkner, after all. Other correspondences make this one even more plausible.

Amelia's Exceptionally Short Chair --and Rosa's

Faulkner specifically describes Aunt Rosa as a short person, and Amelia and Sallie McCarroll also were diminutive in stature. Faulkner describes Rosa as "sitting so bolt upright in the straight hard chair that was so tall for her that her legs hung straight and rigid as if she had iron shinbones and ankles, clear of the floor with that air of impotent and static rage like children's feet" (*Absalom* 7). The McCarroll family had one of the chairs in the house shortened to fit Amelia, but other chairs were too tall for her. Francisco III describes his early memories of these short "sisters":

> One of my early memories is staring in disbelief at what looked like little girls' dresses on display at our house during the Pilgrimage as Mother said they belonged to Amelia, my great-grandmother and her two sisters, my great aunts when they were adults. The dresses looked too small for girls younger than me. The dresses were all black taffeta or dark blue velvet and trimmed with lace and crochet. Also, about the same time I noticed a strange chair. It wasn't a child's chair because it had a normal seat and back but had short legs. Dad told me that each of the sisters had one of these cut down chairs in their bedroom and sometimes brought them out, but sometimes just sat in the regular chairs. He especially remembered seeing two of them sitting side by side in standard-sized chairs wearing their black taffeta dresses with black stocking covered feet dangling down like little sticks swinging above the floor. He had wondered how they would get down out of the chairs.[6]

Amelia, seated uncomfortably, with pendulous legs, in a too-tall chair in the office, with its plantation desk with shelves to fit the ledgers, and treasure trove of ledgers, along with the living, eyewitness account of Dr. Edgar Francisco III, provides convincing correspondences among the Francisco/McCarroll family members and Faulkner's characters.

Absalom, Absalom! and the McCarroll Sisters

Personalities and events Faulkner depicted in *Absalom, Absalom!* also bear resemblance to the life experiences of Walter John Leak and his wife Amelia McCarroll Leak. Not every detail of their lives matches the Faulkner novel, and in some cases the particulars vary considerably. Nonetheless, numerous accruing similarities in Faulkner's work and this family suggest that they may have been models for him in various ways. Walter John Leak and Amelia Leak especially may have been sources for Faulkner's characters Ellen and Thomas Sutpen. The commonalities they share likely stem from Faulkner's familiarity with Leak family lore, their oral history, and access to documents that were in safekeeping and even sometimes on display at McCarroll Place. Sons who go to war; sisters left behind, preparing for a wedding after the sons return from war; the need for a male heir; marrying and moving to a wealthy plantation; and one sister returning home in extended grief—but who lives to tell the story—all correspond to the characteristics of and events experienced by the Sutpen and Coldfield families in *Absalom, Absalom!*[7]

Despite some differences between the real and fictional stories, the traumas suffered by Amelia and Rosa, and their grieving and repressed family trauma, parallel in important ways. Amelia's in-laws' seemingly unfair treatment of her on the financially ruined plantation after her husband's death and after the war, and Sutpen's rough treatment of Rosa when he returned from the war, as imagined by an impressionable Faulkner, exemplify parallels between the Leak/McCarrolls and Ellen and Rosa Coldfield. Faulkner apparently heard about and felt Amelia's trauma, although he did not know the cause of her distress, and so he employed his imagination to find an answer for this fictional character. Perhaps Faulkner seeks as Umberto Eco posits: a reader who can be "lured by the familiar process of narrativity; he suspends his disbeliefs and wonders about the possible course of events."[8]

Faulkner's Goodhue Coldfield is evocative of some personality traits and circumstances pertaining to John McCarroll, who was a staunch and upright member of the community. Both real and fictional men were people of integrity in town. Coldfield is a church steward known for his moral rectitude. He "was not rich and . . . not only could have done nothing under the sun to advance his fortunes or prospects but could by no stretch of the imagination even have owned anything that he would have wanted . . . who neither drank nor hunted nor gambled" (*Absalom* 20). McCarroll's son John R. McCarroll ran a mercantile store, as does Coldfield. Both McCarroll and Coldfield had marriageable daughters, each of whom left the family home to marry a wealthy planter, but in both instances, a daughter enters into a difficult marital situation and eventually returns home, aggrieved. These people and events mirror those described in the Leak/McCarroll diaries.

Key life experiences of Amelia McCarroll Leak and her spinster sister Sallie McCarroll closely resemble those of Ellen and Rosa Coldfield. Amelia died in 1909,[9] having long survived the deaths of her husband, Walter John, on October 10, 1872; her mother, Elizabeth McCarroll, May 16, 1872, and her

Figure 4.2 Betsy Leak Francisco was the grandmother of Edgar Wiggin Francisco III. Her black attire calls to mind that of Faulkner's Rosa Coldfield. Photograph copy work by George Nikas, Atlanta, Georgia. Photo courtesy of Dr. Edgar Wiggin Francisco III.

father, John R. McCarroll, on December 24, 1873. With his death, the family income diminished drastically. These losses and Amelia's relative longevity surely left her with much cause for grieving. Resonances with Faulkner's Rosa come to mind, as does Amelia's daughter, Betsy Leak Francisco (figure 4.2). Rosa was a woman who wore black for forty-three years, "whether for sister, father, or nothusband, none knew" (*Absalom* 7).[10] (See also photo of Sallie McCarroll, figure 4.3 on p. 138.)

As older women, both Amelia and Sallie carried on the vibrant oral tradition. They both told stories and seemed compelled to tell them to others, much as Rosa Coldfield does, especially about hardship surrounding the Civil War. According to Francisco III, Faulkner knew these women well, and when Faulkner was a boy and young man, along with Edgar Francisco Jr., he heard family stories directly from them. As children, the boys had listened at McCarroll Place to the family tales that the old McCarroll sisters remembered. After Amelia's death Sallie, an old spinster by then, recounted her story to William Faulkner and Edgar Francisco Jr.

Additional details correspond with Faulkner's novel. In both real and fictional accounts, one sister perishes, while the other remains alive and grows old—and lives long enough to tell her sister's dramatic story. In both accounts, the married sister who lived on the plantation dies first, and the sister at home is a spinster. During her marriage to Walter John, Amelia cared for the children from Walter John Leak's first marriage. One sister taking care of children after a family death also applies to both real and fictional accounts, as do Amelia's and Rosa's early marriages, both of which are fraught with difficulty.

Faulkner's narrative takes numerous dark turns, one of which is that the marriage of Ellen Coldfield to Thomas Sutpen does not provide an occasion for happiness, even at the wedding. Townspeople dislike and distrust Sutpen and throw tomatoes at him. Ellen weeps repeatedly at her wedding, but her tears are not signs of joy. Similarly, Walter John and Amelia married at a time when the Leak farm had been devastated by war. Money was gone. Leak borrowed a large sum of money from Amelia's mother in 1870 to keep the farm going. For Amelia, the marriage meant, according to Francisco III, "moving from one family to a family affected by war. It was a bad environment to have gone into."[11]

The absence of a male heir is an important commonality central to both real and fictional stories. Matters worsen considerably when that loss occurs. The wealthy planter Sutpen insults and offends Aunt Rosa by indicating that she must produce a male heir before he will marry her. This demand, an affront to her social, moral, and religious upbringing, appalls Rosa, and she abruptly departs for her childhood home. The absence of a male heir also figures prominently in the Leak family history. After the death of her husband and son—her two closest male relatives—Amelia McCarroll Leak abruptly left the Salem plantation for her childhood home, McCarroll Place, where she resettled with her unmarried sister, Sallie, and other family members.[12]

Without a male heir, Amelia lost financial leverage in the Leak family. Her husband, Walter John Leak, had been the main owner of the Leak property after the death of his father, Francis Terry Leak, and Walter John was the heir apparent to the Leak plantation. With Walter John's premature death, Amelia's power rested in her son, Wade. After his death, however, her financial claim diminished significantly.

Spinster Aunt Sallie perseveres through the decades and is intent on one main purpose: passing on to the next generation the broad brushstrokes—but not the excruciating details—of her sister's and her painful lives. Later the boys Will Faulkner and Edgar Francisco Jr. seem to intuit that Sallie mysteriously omitted some parts of the story and left some details ambiguous and others completely absent. In fact, she kept her dark secret from the next generation, and the secret was one that Francisco III describes as embarrassing enough to keep hidden in the family. The future generation did not receive that information. He further recalls that part of her cover-up worked very well. By the time the story of Amelia's return home reached Francisco's father's generation, the description was only that: "Things were very bad."[13]

An intriguing secret, missing information, and unanswered questions indeed provide fertile ground for the novelist. The speculations of Will Faulkner and Edgar Francisco Jr. about what Aunt Sallie omitted from her story, and why, may have informed Faulkner's development and characterization of Quentin and Shreve, as they realize that information is missing in Rosa's story and then conjecture and speculate a plausible scenario and weave their own coherent narrative:

> It was Shreve speaking, though save for the slight difference which the intervening degrees of latitude had inculcated in them (differences not in tone or pitch but of turns of phrase and usage of words), it might have been either of them and was in a sense both: both thinking as one, the voice which happened to be speaking the thought only the thinking become audible, vocal; the two of them creating between them, out of the rag-tag and bob-ends of old tales and talking. (*Absalom* 303)

With lingering questions about the fascinating story they have heard, Quentin and Shreve collaborate, embellish, extrapolate, and conjure up imagined circumstances to create from the missing details their narrative of what might have occurred, just as Faulkner and Edgar Francisco Jr. must have done at the knee of old Sallie McCarroll. Michael Millgate points to "the process by which Shreve—self-cast as confessor, psychiatrist, interlocutor, agent provocateur, Doctor Watson, academic collaborator, or what you will—assists Quentin in assessing the raw, undigested information about the past he has received from various sources and in making sense of that information, turning it into narrative. The collaboration is a brilliant quasi-authorial success."[14] Donald Kartiganer points out that Quentin "emerges in *Absalom, Absalom!* as the one who finally confers meaning on the past . . . [and] implicates him in the past. . . . [He] functions by bestowing a new intelligence on the history that has engendered him. He creates what the past *does not know about itself*, what the past has been waiting for the present to remember" (emphasis in original).[15] Kartiganer also sees Faulkner engaging in the impassioned narrative encircling a situation, a condition, a character, the factual details of which or whom not only never come clear but are fairly quickly relegated to the realm of the unknowable—almost dismissed—as if only with that candid admission can the characters and the text attend to their proper business. Something seemingly of the utmost importance is missing, and we are not going to learn—and do not need to learn—precisely what it is.[16]

Certainly the longing of Quentin and Shreve to discover the missing facts in Rosa's captivating story illustrates the importance of what is absent and why.

Documents in the Benton County courthouse indicate that a legal matter occurred that must have been difficult for the McCarrolls, and perhaps the Leaks too, and this situation no doubt brought enough stress to the McCarroll sisters to be worth hiding from the future members of the family. Amelia's circumstances may have been "very bad," but the details of that situation were left hidden, unspoken, and unrevealed. Hurt and insult of an intense and raw nature caused the McCarroll sisters to carry with them a long memory of grievances and a lifetime of bitterness.

Faulkner similarly portrays in *Absalom, Absalom!* an insult so egregious that Aunt Rosa never recovers from it emotionally, nor does she ever speak of it fully. Instead, she obfuscates and omits portions of the story that were too painful to recall or recount. She leaves her listeners, as Faulkner leaves his listening characters, to surmise, conjecture, and guess precisely what occurred.

Two lawsuits brought by the Leaks against the McCarrolls after the death of Walter John Leak are relevant to Faulkner's novel.[17] (See appendix 4-A for a timeline of these legal cases.) One was a legal guardianship suit, brought by Leak family members, against John McCarroll, Amelia's brother, who had been acting as administrator of the modest Leak estate. The Leaks won their claim for guardianship of John and Thomas Leak, Walter John's minor, male children from his first marriage, and the judge awarded the Leaks the custody of those two children. Another claim made by the Leaks, termed "exceptions to the statement accounts," accused John McCarroll of mismanaging the Leak estate funds and claimed that the Leaks were due additional money from the estate.[18]

Undoubtedly the McCarrolls regarded these legal challenges as an affront to their integrity, especially since Walter John Leak, ruined by the Civil War, had to borrow a substantial amount of money from his mother-in-law, Elizabeth McCarroll. As a result of these legal matters, Amelia lost not only some of her dower rights but also the custody of two of Walter John's children. John McCarroll eventually left Holly Springs and moved to Memphis.

The McCarrolls live in Memphis even today. Although the amount of funds awarded was not large, the judge apparently found John McCarroll's bookkeeping to be imperfect, and he was admonished. The McCarrolls surely found these court actions insulting, especially in view of the substantial financial contributions that the McCarrolls made to the Leak/McCarroll marriage. The court ultimately awarded some additional funds, after several years of proceedings, as well as custody of the two Leak boys for whom Amelia had been caring, to the Leaks. In any event, bitterness resulted from the dispute.

Clearly, the McCarroll-Leak dispute was financial in its roots but appears to have grown into long-lasting familial distress and may be a model for Rosa's tale in *Absalom, Absalom!* Amelia and Sallie remained bitter and upset. They had lost a substantial amount of savings. The sisters were agitated over this situation for years and years yet felt that they could not discuss it fully with family members. Francisco III says that "what Dad kept hearing about was how distressed Sallie was and had been distressed most of her life. They [Sallie and Amelia] were embarrassed to have nothing left for the rest of their lives. This anguish was what Dad and Will picked up. All of these bad things, plus the loss of the money."[19] This bad situation, simmering for years in the minds of the McCarroll sisters, could easily have become the genesis of a story, only partially passed down, that William Faulkner heard at McCarroll Place and wove into the fabric of Rosa's tale. According to Dr. Francisco III, his father, Edgar Jr., told him that Will Faulkner and he never knew the full truth about the case. They never figured out what was wrong. They did not know about the lawsuits. Not knowing all the facts apparently led them to fill in the blanks for themselves.[20]

Shame, scandal, and hurt are features of *Absalom, Absalom!* that Faulkner could have found at his own home. He did not absolutely need to go looking in a nearby town for shame and the scandal to use in his fiction. He had facts and lore in his family to draw upon for stories of that nature. In her memoir Dean Faulkner Wells describes reasons for omissions of information and the feeling of shame that the family incurred, especially when Faulkner's maternal grandfather, who was tax collector in Oxford, "disappeared" and "took an estimated three to five thousand dollars in embezzled city tax revenues and a beautiful octoroon, a seamstress in the Jacob Thompson household."[21] Surely this behavior and the resulting court actions brought shame and embarrassment to the family. Faulkner had information of this sort to generate material about legal, financial, and sexual shame.[22] Elisions, denials, and silences also were a part of Faulkner's family history too, and both that model and the Leaks/McCarrolls/Franciscos could have helped him to develop his characterizations and theme. Nonetheless, fascinating similarities continue to accrue with the Leak/McCarroll families, and to ignore them is to miss a possible source.

Finding hidden truth is an important theme in *Absalom, Absalom!* Speculation among multiple narrators seeking to discover truth thematically links the McCarroll/Leak history with the story of Quentin and Shreve. That Quentin is an autobiographical fictionalization of Faulkner is not a new idea. Scholars have noted the similarities between author and character.[23] Michael Millgate, for example, points out that "Quentin is in at least some texts a semi-autobiographical figure whose listening to the tales of the past had its basis in Faulkner's own experience."[24] What has been less obvious, however, is that Faulkner also may have given his childhood friend a role too. Faulkner is like Quentin: he has no choice but to sit and listen to the stories of Miss Rosa—"Aunt Rosa," as Shreve calls her—after all. Together, Quentin and Shreve, like Will Faulkner and Edgar Francisco Jr., engaged in an intense and cooperative striving toward revealing the full truth.

Amelia's destiny was to live at home, in regret, without father, mother, husband, or son. Like Rosa, "she had seen almost everything else she had learned to call stable vanish like straws in a gale" (*Absalom* 207). Even the date of Amelia's death—she died on Halloween in 1909—resonates with Rosa's, whose death is announced in a letter Quentin receives from his father in January of 1910 but arguably shifts to 1909. In their dorm room at Harvard, Shreve hands Quentin a letter from his father dated January 10, in which he reports that Miss Rosa had died the day before. (See in this endnote the relevant date revision from 1910 to 1909 of Miss Rosa's last action from the first edition of the novel to Noel Polk's corrected edition.)[25]

The McCarroll/Francisco family configuration, traits, and personal occurrences reasonably may have provided Faulkner with substantial resonances for *Absalom, Absalom!* Sallie McCarroll, who died on February 9, 1917, survived Amelia by almost ten years. Left with a legacy of hardship and tragedy, she speaks of pain and bitterness in retelling her family story.

In Sallie's family photo, carefully preserved down through the generations, she wears black attire, with lace at wrists and throat, in the form of a triangle (figure 4.3). (See also figure 4.2 of Betsy Leak Francisco on p. 132.) Sallie's spinsterhood, her black dress, and triangle of lace further align her with Rosa Coldfield, whom Faulkner describes as having "old flesh long embattled in virginity" (*Absalom* 8). Rosa appears in "eternal black" (7) with "the faint triangle of lace at wrists and throat" (8) and later with "the wan triangle of lace at wrists and throat" (11). She speaks voluminously but guardedly, concealing much, and her black attire—worn for forty-three years—is a sign of her lifetime of loss, pain, and regret.

Figure 4.3 Sallie McCarroll, a possible model for Faulkner's Rosa Coldfield. Cf. also Faulkner's description of Rosa with "lace at wrists and throat" in *Absalom, Absalom!* Photograph copy work by George Nikas, Atlanta, Georgia. Photo courtesy of Dr. Edgar Wiggin Francisco III.

Amelia McCarroll Leak and William Faulkner's Career Choice

Amelia McCarroll also may have shaped Faulkner's career choice in a more direct way. She apparently broached with him the subject of writing when she told the young William Faulkner that she admired the novel *The White Rose of Memphis*, authored by his great-grandfather, the Old Colonel. According to Francisco III, Amelia then said to the boy Faulkner: "Do you think you could ever be a writer like your great-grandfather, who wrote *The White Rose of Memphis*?"[26] Biographer Joseph Blotner notes that in the third grade Faulkner began to say: "I want to be a writer like my great-granddaddy."[27] Blotner continues that "whenever the question was posed, his answer would be the same. At the age of nine," Faulkner "had found his vocation."[28] Faulkner's brother Jack recalls that Faulkner's statement was "in accord with his character and his dreams."[29] Faulkner's imagination, Michael Millgate sums: was "fed and stirred by listening at an early age to stories told by survivors from those exciting times."[30]

Amelia McCarroll Leak was one of the survivors who may have guided the young Faulkner in multiple ways. The old woman whose story he would remember and one day eulogize may have given him his first incentive to become a writer. Amelia also is a possible role model for Granny Millard, the bossy grandmother in *The Unvanquished* and "My Grandmother Millard," who also boldly confronts Yankee soldiers who appear at her house. (See also chapter 2 on p. 83 for Francisco's account of Amelia's bossiness in confronting the Yankees who came to her door.)[31]

Faulkner seems to allude to his use of the Leak diary during his time at the University of Virginia. He was responding to a question about his sources for the character of Colonel Sartoris. Faulkner replied, "I myself would have to stop and go page by page to see just how much I drew from family annals that I had listened to from these old undefeated spinster aunts that children of my time grew up with."[32] Since most of Faulkner's aunts were married, he apparently refers in this quotation to spinster aunts unrelated to him. Perhaps he depicts the McCarroll sisters, the "old undefeated spinster aunts," and the Leaks with their "family annals," which captured his imagination in remarkable ways.

Amelia's life events render those of Faulkner's Rosa in *Absalom, Absalom!* more biographical and contextual than has previously been apparent. Sallie McCarroll, of Holly Springs, Mississippi, told a vastly and carefully truncated version of her sister Amelia's travails to William and Edgar Jr., the willing listeners. She elided the parts of the family history that were embarrassing and troubling, and the actions of others that seemed unfair and unjust.

William Faulkner, one of the willing listeners to Sallie's stories, grew into a sensitive writer who may have perceived that part of the story was missing and needed disclosing—in fiction. He drew deeply from the old tales and talking he heard around him and penned his vivid memories in *Absalom, Absalom!*, a novel of the lost plantation dream and the sad fate of the owners, told through the undefeated, but haunting, lone, haggard voice of the aged, surviving sister.

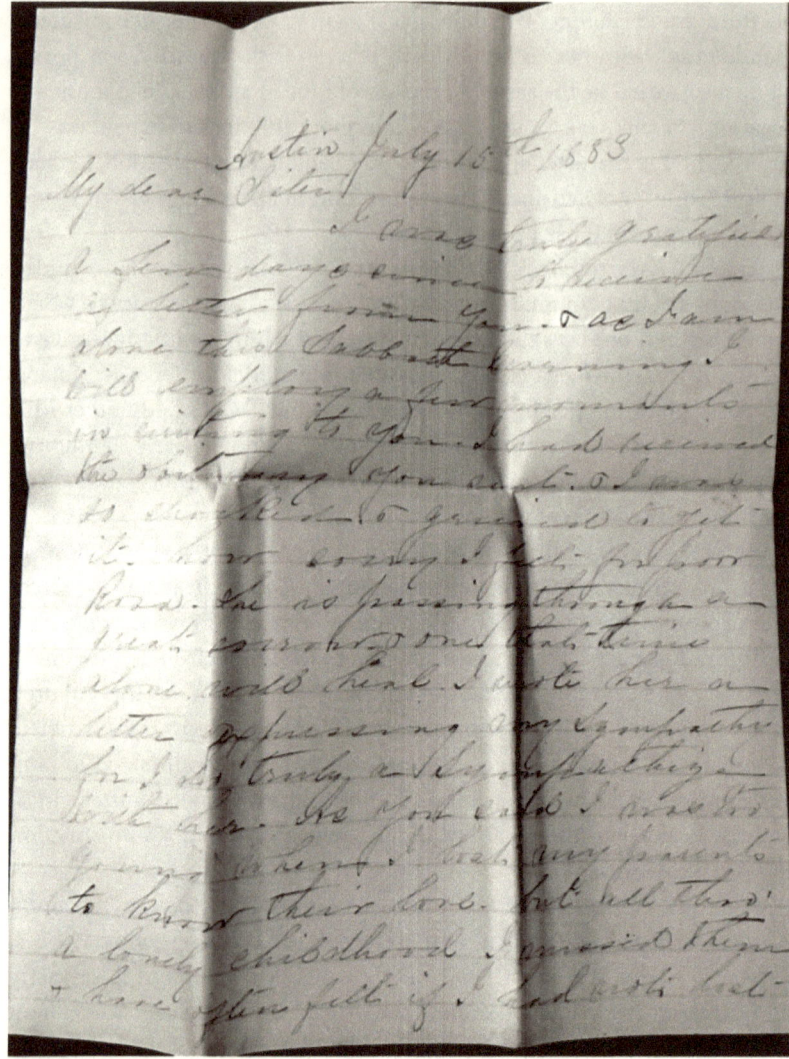

Figure 4.4 Sample from the Rosa letters, in the McCarroll Place Papers. Photography by George Nikas, Atlanta, Georgia.

Aunt Rosa and the McCarroll Place Papers

Both the McCarroll/Francisco families and their cousin, Perle Strickland Badow, as well as others in Holly Springs, liked to display old pre- and post-Civil War letters, documents, receipts, and other memorabilia during the annual Holly Springs Pilgrimage. (See pp. 90–91 for a brief history of the Holly Springs Pilgrimage.) Among the countless documents of this kind that are extant, about twenty letters—located at McCarroll Place and tied loosely with a string—are letters to, from, and/or about two women in or near Holly Springs: Rosa Clark and the widowed Rosa Tyler.

According to Dr. Francisco, these letters were on display during Pilgrimage and other times of the year at McCarroll Place, and William Faulkner had access to them. Francisco III said that the Clarks (Rosa and family) and the Franciscos were friends for many years. They are related to Kate Freeman Clark, a well-known Holly Springs artist-citizen. He recalls that the closeness between their families goes back to Amelia, who he thinks asked his family to keep Rosa's correspondence, and they saved it.[33]

The Rosa letters contain indications of Faulkner's awareness and possible use of them in the portrait of Rosa Coldfield in *Absalom, Absalom!*, at least for nomenclature. The experience of the yellow fever epidemic that they go through and their intense grieving are some examples. Several letters are addressed to or refer to "Aunt Rosa." Most of this correspondence is addressed to Mary B. Clark and refers to Rosa Clark.[34] The Francisco family and the Clark family were friends. Francisco III remembers, "We were over there a lot every month. The family did not want the letters anymore, and Dad said he'd like to have them.... We were close friends with Kate Clark, a relative of Rosa's. Amelia had been good friends with Col. Clark. The letters had been in her possession. The deaths in her family made it dramatic and historically related. Our two families had been very close going way back."[35] Francisco III remembers the Clark house in detail: "She had fancy hats on top of her floor lamps darkening the ceiling. In place of doors that could close to block the view into other rooms, she had strands of beads hanging from the top of door frames and ropes of bells, which provided privacy and an alarm system. She allowed me to walk back and forth causing the bells to twinkle, until I outgrew it."[36]

Written in the 1870s, several of the letters to or about Rosa were to express condolences for Rosa's grieving. (See figure 4.4.) One letter addressed to Rosa May Clark, Care of Col. J. W. Rutland, Cherokee, Alabama, 9/2/78, concerns the yellow fever epidemic: "My dear child,/We are all well. No new cases of Yellow Fever- Several are sick of Bilious fever & chills. Please possess your soul in patience. If anything requires you at home, you shall be notified to come. Hope you are well and not alarmed at newspaper reports. God bless you. Papa."[37]

Another letter specifically describes Rosa's grieving and readily calls to mind Faulkner's Rosa Coldfield, who grieves, indeed, but for whom no one knows. The Rosa letters describe:

> How sorry I feel for poor Rosa. She is passing through a great sorrow[,] one that time alone will heal. I wrote to her expressing my

sympathy for I do truly sympathize with her. As you said I was too young when I lost my parents to know their love but all through a lonely childhood I missed them. I have often felt that if I had not lost them how different my life would have been.[38]

An envelope is addressed to Mary Clark, Franklin College, Holly Springs, and contains a letter to "Dear Rosa" and mentions Rosa's "great sorrow." This letter makes clear that the death was Rosa's dear Papa and is dated October 18, 1878.[39] A month after he had penned his endearing and reassuring letter to Rosa, her dear Papa had died.

The Rosa correspondence makes clear that Rosa Clark lost both her father and daughter in the yellow fever epidemic that decimated the town of Holly Springs in 1878. The resonances for Rosa Coldfield seem clear. She grieves and apparently never stops, since her emotional behavior continues for forty-three summers. Like her plausible namesake, she grieved for family members, some of whom were lost to yellow fever.

Other letters include one addressed to Mrs. Mary Clark (1862 or 1882, date unclear), which mentions cousin Rosa May just married to a farmer; Mary running a school; letter to Mary B. Clark (1888 or 1885, date unclear) mentions Ellen and is signed: "Love, Sister S. Rector"; Letter to "My dear Rosa," January 14, 1885, signed by Hugh; Letter to Rosa M. Tyler (1825? date unclear): "My Dear Papa . . . [later says] Has Aunt Rosa left yet? Signed, Your loving, [signature unclear—Reisa May or more probably Rosa May]"; letter to Mary B. Clark, February 21, 1884, "Dear Sister," unsigned, mentions "Will write to Rosa Clark."[40]

Taken together, the Rosa correspondence suggests further resonances among some of the people and events of Holly Springs for Faulkner's characters and narratives. The Rosa letters, which formerly were on annual display at McCarroll Place, and thus accessible to Faulkner, detail Rosa's "great sorrow," and these personal losses for which friends and community members deeply sympathize in their letters, are possible sources for Faulkner's Rosa Coldfield, who grieves for forty-three summers, "whether for sister, father, or nothusband none knew" (*Absalom* 7).

Appendix 4-A: Timeline of the Lawsuits Brought by the Leaks against the McCarrolls

In 1870 Walter John borrowed $4,260 from his mother-in-law, Elizabeth McCarroll.

In November 1872 (after Walter John's death) W. T (?) Hamer was approved by the Court to administer the estate, which was valued at approximately $200 only.

Shortly thereafter, for reasons that are unclear, Amelia McCarroll's brother, John McCarroll, took over from Hamer as administrator of the estate. In his later testimony, John McCarroll referred to 1874 as the earliest date related to estate administration.

In April 1875 John R. McDonald petitioned the chancery court and was approved for guardianship of the two minor children, Thomas and John, who were the sons of Walter John Leak and his first wife. John R. and two others signed a $1,000 bond to ensure they would administer the guardianship faithfully.

In 1880 John McCarroll petitioned the chancery court to be discharged from his responsibility for administration of the Leak estate, and for approval of the final account he had filed. The Leak family, however, objected and excepted to the final account. One document appears to indicate that they believed $971.11 was still due to the beneficiaries of the estate. The court apparently then appointed a clerk to investigate the claims, correct any errors, and make a recommendation.

Between 1880 and 1882, testimony (including from John McCarroll and Amelia) occurred along with an extensive and complicated investigation into John McCarroll's financial handling of the estate.

A number of complicated transactions may have been perceived differently by the Leaks and McCarrolls. In her deposition Amelia received two pointed questions from the court hinting at her fault in her level of concern for her stepsons' welfare and care of her husband's gravesite.

In 1882, following the investigation, and based on the clerk's recommendation, the court ordered John McCarroll to pay $701.73 to the heirs, plus court costs.

In 1885 John R. McDonald petitioned the court to be relieved of guardianship responsibilities for Thomas and John (who were by that time adults). It appears they agreed, and no controversy was apparent, although a document with a final decree was not available.

Source: "Jno McCarroll Admin Vs. W. J. Leak, Int" [Intestate], Case File No. 84, Chancery Court, Benton County, Ashland, Mississippi.

Appendix 4-B:
A Note on the Yellow Fever Epidemic of 1878

References to yellow fever appear in Faulkner's *Absalom, Absalom!* and seem directly connected to the yellow fever epidemic that affected the Mississippi river basin and hit Holly Springs particularly hard in 1878. Molly Caldwell Crosby describes the background of yellow fever in the history of the US, the terrible 1878 US outbreak, and in particular the hardships in her home city of Memphis, Tennessee, where five thousand lives were lost to the disease.[41] Memphis became a "city of corpses."[42]

Probably transported via shipping routes, especially through New Orleans, yellow fever seemed associated with rivers, and quarantines for whole communities took place. Although people initially did not understand the exact mode of transmission of yellow fever, eventually medical scientists discovered how to curb the disease. Crosby notes the widespread reach of the epidemic stretched from Brazil to Ohio. The final toll in the Mississippi valley was twenty thousand lives and financial losses close to $200 million. Two hundred communities in eleven states experienced the fever.[43]

The 1878 scourge of yellow fever in Mississippi extended from July 1878 through November of that year. Hundreds of Holly Springs townspeople and visitors died, including several town physicians, one of whom was Dr. Charles Bonner.[44] Faulkner's characters Judith and Charles Bon die of yellow fever in *Absalom, Absalom!*[45] Both Charles Bon's name and his manner of death seem closely linked to Dr. Charles Bonner and signal Faulkner's awareness of the epidemic, which affected numerous towns in Mississippi, including Oxford.[46]

Holly Springs had a high death toll that was particularly tragic and painful because the townspeople had offered up their town to others as a safe place. Faulkner no doubt was aware that his neighboring town of Holly Springs during the epidemic had invited people to go there as a haven on high ground for those fleeing the epidemic, but visitors who went there for protection and townspeople alike suffered acutely. Winter adds, "The impact of the fever was nowhere felt more keenly than in Holly Springs."[47] With its 1,239 cases and 309 deaths, Holly Springs had one of the highest case counts and death tolls in the state. The highest was Vicksburg, with 5,000 cases and 1,149 deaths.[48]

Faulkner's hometown of Oxford participated in the quarantines. Joel Williamson notes that Oxford was affected and instituted quarantines "even to the point of allowing no trains to stop at the depot and intercepting and, prior to delivery, sanitizing the mails cast from the moving train."[49] The scourge began to recede in the fall of that year with the first frost.

Today, Holly Springs commemorates its lost citizens and visitors in several ways: the Yellow Fever Martyrs Church and Museum, open to tours, honors seven people who died while nursing other victims. The church display details the history of the disease in the area. Another commemorative location, the Yellow Fever House was, according to the yard marker, "the residence of W. J. L. Holland who gave his quarters and his life during the Yellow Fever epidemic of 1878. The benevolent Holland died while chairman of the relief committee." The Marshall County Museum has a room dedicated to remembrances of the townspeople, including artistically woven wires entwined with the hair of the victims—to recall the victims and their suffering.

The old letters recently located at McCarroll Place describe with poignancy Rosa Clark's loss of family members, including her father and daughter, in this yellow fever epidemic in Holly Springs in 1878 and express sympathy by relatives and townspeople that Rosa was undergoing a terrible tragedy. Edgar Francisco III recalls hearing that Rosa Clark had lost numerous family members in the yellow fever epidemic and that several other people lost all of their family members during this tragic time. The severity and high number of yellow fever deaths in Holly Springs link *Absalom, Absalom!* to the Mississippi scourge of 1878.

NOTES

INTRODUCTION: "I TALKED, HE LISTENED"

1. Don Doyle, *Faulkner's County: The Historical Roots of Yoknapatawpha* (University of North Carolina Press, 2001), 14.

2. Numerous Faulkner scholars supported the work. A few Faulkner enthusiasts insisted on incontrovertible documentary evidence of Francisco III's claims and mine. Dr. Don Doyle, McCausland Professor of History Emeritus at the University of South Carolina pointed out, however, "That is plausible, and you need not 'prove' it to make it plausible." The late Dr. John Lowe, Barbara Lester Methvin Distinguished Professor of English at the University of Georgia, added, "It seems apparent, after reading Dr. Wolff-King's book, much of the ledgers, and talking with Dr. Francisco, that the meditative and anguished quality of *Go Down, Moses* can largely be explained by Faulkner's agonized reading and rereading over the years of the Leak ledgers, but also by his obviously close and intellectual relationship with Dr. Francisco's father. The long series of conversations between Cass and Ike over the subject of the ledgers must have had their inspiration in the exchanges between William and Edgar." See Don H. Doyle's comment in the article Sally Wolff, "'Everybody Knew': *Ledgers of History*: Questions and Answers," *South Atlantic Review* 81, no. 4 (Winter 2016): 69, and Dr. John Lowe's comment, 68.

Scholars and others who have written about Faulkner's sources include Ward Miner, Joseph Blotner, Evans Harrington, Arthur Kinney, Don Doyle, Charles Aiken, Noel Polk, Michael Gorra, Thomas McHaney, Gabriele Gutting, and Herman E. Taylor, to name a few.

3. See Sally Wolff, *Ledgers of History: William Faulkner: An Almost Forgotten Friendship and an Antebellum Plantation Diary* (Louisiana State University Press, 2010).

4. John Faulkner varied the spelling of his last name—sometimes with the *u* and sometimes without. That variation continued onto his tombstone on which the *u* is in parentheses ("John Wesley Thompson Faulkner III," Find a Grave, www.findagrave.com/memorial/7033345/john_wesley_thompson-faulkner). Much has been written about the variation in spelling of the name Falkner and Faulkner. See, for example, Appendix A in Sally Wolff, *Talking about William Faulkner*, in which William Faulkner's nephew James M. Faulkner details the "History of the U in Faulkner" (Louisiana State University Press, 1996), 179–81.

5. Sarah Doxey Tate, "A Talk on Faulkner and the Hindman/Doxey Family," library talk at the Marshall County Library, Holly Springs, Mississippi, Fall 2003. See also the marriage certificate of John and Dolly Faulkner, figure 1.2, on p. 24.

6. W. C. Handy was a renowned blues musician and composer who for years played his music in the clubs on Beale Street in Memphis, Tennessee.

7. Carvel Collins Collection of William Faulkner Research Materials, Harry Ransom Center, The University of Texas at Austin, Box 56, Folder 5.

8. Jesse Merle "Flick" Ash Sr., telephone interview with author, November 10, 2014. Ash was from Potts Camp, MS, and served, among other roles, as the chancery clerk in Holly Springs, Mississippi, for five terms (1968–1988).

9. Carvel Collins notes that L. G. Fant Jr. (attorney at law) "sometimes played golf" with Faulkner, circa 1930. Carvel Collins Collection of William Faulkner Research Materials, Harry Ransom Center, The University of Texas at Austin, Box 56, Folder 5.

10. Helen Bell Hopkins remembers seeing William Faulkner "at a horse show in HS in about 1946 or 47" (Helen Bell Hopkins, email correspondence with author, June 9, 2014). See also Wolff, "'Everybody Knew,'" 71.

11. Joseph Blotner, *Faulkner: A Biography*, vol. 1 (Random House, 1974), 283.

12. Blotner, *Faulkner: A Biography*, vol. 1, 283, 290, 489, 551.

13. See also chapter 2 on p. 83.

14. "Garden Pilgrimage to Historical Sites," 11.

15. Hubert McAlexander, *A Southern Tapestry: Marshall County, Mississippi, 1835–2000* (Donning, 2000), 65.

16. "Historic Resources of Holly Springs," National Register of Historic Places Inventory—Nomination, United States Department of the Interior National Park Service, www.apps.mdah.ms.gov/t_nom/Historic%20Resources%20of%20Holly%20Springs.pdf, 2.

17. "Historic Resources of Holly Springs," 2.

18. Alice Long and Mark L. Ridge, *Images of America: Holly Springs* (Arcadia, 2006), 7.

19. Robert Milton Winter, *Shadow of a Mighty Rock: A Social and Cultural History of Presbyterianism in Marshall County, Mississippi* (Providence House, 1997), 98.

20. *Mississippi Encyclopedia* Staff, "Marshall County," *The Mississippi Encyclopedia*, Center for Study of Southern Culture, April 14, 2018, mississippiencyclopedia.org/entries/marshall-county.

21. "A Brief History of Holly Springs," City of Holly Springs, hollyspringsms.gov/history-of-holly-springs/.

22. Long and Ridge, *Images of America*, 7.

23. "Historic Resources of Holly Springs," 3.

24. "Historic Resources of Holly Springs," 7, 9. See figure 1.5 on p. 32 for a photo of the Smith House and figure 1.6 on p. 32 for a photo of the rose-colored windows at Grey Gables. See also the photographs of some other Holly Springs antebellum homes at educationalconsulting.services/Faulkner.

25. *Britannica*, "Holly Springs," May 29, 2020, www.britannica.com/place/Holly-Springs.

26. Long and Ridge, *Images of America*, 8.

27. *Britannica*, "Holly Springs."

28. *Mississippi Encyclopedia* Staff, "Marshall County."

29. Behind the Big House, www.behindthebighouse.org/.
30. "Programs." Behind the Big House, behindthebighouse.org/programs/behind-the-big-house-holly-springs-ms/.
31. *Britannica*, "Holly Springs."
32. *Mississippi Encyclopedia* Staff, "Marshall County."
33. "A Brief History of Holly Springs," City of Holly Springs.
34. Winter, *Shadow of a Mighty Rock*, 111.
35. "A Brief History of Holly Springs," City of Holly Springs.
36. Paraphrased from a docent lecture and tour of Walter Place, March 2019.
37. Dr. Edgar Wiggin Francisco III, telephone communication with author, August 7, 2021. Hereinafter Francisco III, correspondence or communication.
38. "Historic Resources of Holly Springs," 2.
39. Phillip Knecht, "Hill Crest Cemetery (1845)," *Hill Country History*, March 29, 2016, hillcountryhistory.org/2016/03/29/holly-springs-hill-crest-cemetery-1845/.
40. Knecht, "Hill Crest Cemetery."
41. "Hillcrest Cemetery," Wikipedia, September 20, 2023, en.wikipedia.org/wiki/Hillcrest_Cemetery.
42. *Mississippi Encyclopedia* Staff, "Marshall County."
43. Long and Ridge, *Images of America*, 47.
44. "History: Over 154 Years of Quality Education," Rust College, www.rustcollege.edu/about-rust-college/history/.
45. Long and Ridge, *Images of America*, 47.
46. *Mississippi Encyclopedia* Staff, "Marshall County."
47. *Mississippi Encyclopedia* Staff, "Marshall County."
48. Local historian Bobby Mitchell describes the following:

Franklin Female College was an educational facility for women in antebellum Holly Springs. The school was founded in 1849 by Methodist minister Stephen G. Starks, grandfather-to-be of Stark Young, noted southern writer.... By the year 1854, the enrollment of the Holly Springs campus, plus its sister campus in Byhalia, was 255 pupils. The coming of the Civil War led to the closing of the school, which was used by both armies as a hospital, and following the destruction of the Marshall County Courthouse in 1864, it was also used as the county courthouse.... The Franklin Female College was located back from College Avenue, on the northwest corner of the intersection of College Avenue and Randolph Street. The building was destroyed by fire in 1904, and was replaced with a large two-story house in which the Elliott Boone family lived.... The house was acquired by the First Baptist Church of Holly Springs about 1966 and used for classes before the church's Christian Activity Center (through the generosity of Sidney Hurdle) was constructed on the site in the 1970s.

Bobby Mitchell, "Franklin Female College," *Heritage News: A Publication of the Marshall County, Mississippi, Genealogical and Historical Society* 24, no. 1 (March 2018): 1. See also McAlexander, *Southern Tapestry*, 30.
49. *Mississippi Encyclopedia* Staff, "Marshall County."

50. Long and Ridge, *Images of America*, 46.

51. "A Brief History of Holly Springs: 1851–1860." City of Holly Springs, hollyspringsms.gov/history-of-holly-springs/.

CHAPTER ONE: SIGNS OF WILLIAM FAULKNER IN HOLLY SPRINGS

1. Joseph Blotner, *Faulkner: A Biography*, vol. 1 (Random House, 1974), 100, 166, 231, 292, 1463, 1755, 1811.

2. See the marriage certificate of John and Dolly Faulkner, figure 1.2, on p. 24.

3. For documentation and further details about the recollections of these Holly Springs interviewees, see Sally Wolff, "'Everybody Knew': *Ledgers of History*: Questions and Answers," *South Atlantic Review* 81, no. 4 (Winter 2016): 66–88.

4. See Carl Rollyson, *The Life of William Faulkner: The Past Is Never Dead, 1897–1934*, vol. 1 (University of Virginia Press, 2020), 46. See also John Faulkner's story about William Faulkner's receiving his broken nose in a football game with Holly Springs in *My Brother Bill* (Hill Street Press, 1998), 101–2.

5. Joel Williamson, *William Faulkner and Southern History* (Oxford University Press, 1993). Williamson notes that Cho Cho "was sent off to a boarding school in Holly Springs" (257).

6. Sally Wolff, *Ledgers of History: William Faulkner: An Almost Forgotten Friendship and an Antebellum Plantation Diary* (Louisiana State University Press, 2010).

7. The McCarroll Place Papers belonged to Dr. Edgar Wiggin Francisco III and his family. Upon the sale of McCarroll Place, the papers transferred to Mr. Harvey Payne, the new owner. Subsequently, Mr. Payne donated the papers to the Department of Archives & Special Collections of the University of Mississippi in 2022 and 2023. Hereinafter these papers will be referred to as the McCarroll Place Papers.

8. Jorja Lynn, telephone interview with author, May 23, 2014.

9. Jorja Lynn, email to author, May 17, 2014.

10. Robert Milton Winter, *Shadow of a Mighty Rock: A Social and Cultural History of Presbyterianism in Marshall County, Mississippi* (Providence House, 1997), 342.

11. A. I. Bezzerides, *William Faulkner, a Life on Paper* (University Press of Mississippi, 1980), 79.

12. Gwen Wyatt, telephone interview with author, July 28, 2018; see also Robert Coughlan, Faulkner's "liking for children and the outdoors combined to make him Scoutmaster of a local troop of Boy Scouts, but the Baptist minister objected to his drinking and he had to retire," in *The Private World of William Faulkner* (Harper & Brothers, 1954), 53. See also Philip Weinstein: the Faulkner boys "became scouts, and Faulkner—whose tenderness toward children was notable his entire life—later served as scoutmaster." *Becoming Faulkner* (Oxford University Press, 2010), 44. See also Blotner, *Faulkner*, vol. 1, 349.

13. Wolff, "Everybody Knew," 71.

14. Wolff, "Everybody Knew," 72.

15. Williamson, *William Faulkner and Southern History*, 39.

16. Kelly Kazek, "The Tragic Tale of William Faulkner's Forgotten Daughter, Alabama Faulkner," Alabama.com, September 25, 2015, www.al.com/entertainment/2015/09/the_tragic_tale_of_william_fau.html.

17. *The Reporter* (Holly Springs, MS), March 22, 1893.

18. *The Reporter*, January 5, 1893.

19. *The Reporter*, March 9, 1893.

20. Williamson, *William Faulkner and Southern History*, 137.

21. *The Reporter*, February 10, 1898.

22. Thomas McHaney, email to author, May 1, 2016.

23. Joseph Blotner, *Faulkner: A Biography, One-Vol. Ed.* (Random House, 1984), 4.

24. Blotner, *Faulkner*, vol. 1, see 69–72, ff.

25. Don Doyle, *Faulkner's County: The Historical Roots of Yoknapatawpha* (University of North Carolina Press, 2001), 69.

26. Faulkner, *My Brother Bill*, 11.

27. *The Reporter*, May 10, 1894.

28. *The Reporter*, March 21, 1895.

29. *The Reporter*, March 2, 1897.

30. *The Reporter*, June 22, 1899.

31. *The Reporter*, April 5, 1899.

32. *The Reporter*, April 5, 1899.

33. *The Reporter*, April 13, 1899.

34. *South Reporter* (Holly Springs, MS), March 24, 1898.

35. *South Reporter*, May 5, 1898.

36. *The Reporter*, April 29, 1897. Examples of Holly Springs citizens in Oxford, Mississippi, and Oxonians in Holly Springs, Mississippi: "The friends of Mrs. Carrie W. Smith will be glad to hear that she has returned from Oxford, where she has been teaching in Union Female College," June 2, 1898; "Hon. W. A. McDonald, of Oxford, attended Chancery Court here this week," May 12, 1898; "Misses Mattie Marshall, of Oxford, and Stella McCorkle, of Fort Smith Ark., are guests of Dr. and Mrs. Robt. K. Luckie" (*South Reporter*, February 26, 1890); "Miss Price, of Oxford, and Miss Lizzie Cayce, of Fulton, Miss., are guests of Miss Janie McWilliams this week" (*South Reporter*, June 18, 1890); "Mrs. Roberts (nee) Miss Georgie Archibald of Oxford, Miss. paid Holly Springs a visit last week the guest of Miss Mary Mosby" (*South Reporter*, July 29, 1891); "Dr. Jno. S. Burton is at Oxford this week, in attendance upon the Federal Court" (*South Reporter*, June 5, 1890); "Sam H. Pryor and daughter, Miss Lida, visited Oxford Saturday" (*The Reporter*, May 7, 1890).

37. Sarah Doxey Tate, "A Talk on Faulkner and the Hindman/Doxey Family," library talk at the Marshall County Library, Holly Springs, Mississippi, Fall 2003.

38. Francisco III, telephone communication, October 7, 2018.

39. Francisco III adds another memory: "In our teens Cousin Hindman, Jr. and I were invited to stay with the Wall Doxeys in Washington for an extended period. We ate in the dining room with senators we recognized and ran all over the place, including running up and then down the stairs of the Washington Monument. We were collared by the police. We didn't know running down the steps was illegal. Upon their discovery that we were

guests of Wall Doxey we were released into his custody and calmed down." Francisco III, letter correspondence, August 1, 2018.

40. Francisco III, telephone communication, October 7, 2018. See also Tate, "A Talk on Faulkner and the Hindman/Doxey Family."

41. See educationalconsulting.services/Faulkner for some family photos. See also, for example, the Holly Springs newspaper's articles: "Mrs. Edgar Francisco Gives Dinner Party": "Mr. and Mrs. W. T. Bitzer of Henderson, Tennessee were the guests of Mr. and Mrs. Edgar Francisco during the holidays and were entertained at dinner by Mrs. Francisco. Other guests were Mrs. Hindman Doxey, Misses Frances and Agnes Bitzer of Birmingham and Mrs. Frank Mattison" (*South Reporter*, January 5, 1939).

42. In the McCarroll Place Papers. (To see a photo of the Christmas card and other materials, please visit educationalconsulting.services/Faulkner.)

43. Francisco III, telephone communication, December 16, 2012.

44. Francisco III, email correspondence with author, June 5, 2021. See the 1921 Ole Miss yearbook page about *The Marionettes* at educationalconsulting.services/Faulkner, which lists Hindman Doxey as "Treasurer and Business Manager" of *The Marionettes*. William Faulkner's name appears on the line below Doxey's name, and Faulkner is listed as "Property Man."

45. Weinstein, *Becoming Faulkner*, 218–20.

46. Joan Williams, "Twenty Will Not Come Again." *The Atlantic*, May 1980, 58–65, www.theatlantic.com/magazine/archive/1980/05/twenty-will-not-come-again/667627/.

47. See Sally Wolff, *Talking about William Faulkner* (Louisiana State University Press, 1996), 141–44.

48. "I discovered that my own little postage stamp of native soil was worth writing about and that I would never live long enough to exhaust it," in Jean Stein, "Art of Fiction XII: William Faulkner," *Paris Review*, no. 12, Spring 1956, 52.

49. Cleanth Brooks, "History and the Sense of the Tragic," in *William Faulkner: The Yoknapatawpha Country* (Yale University Press, 1963), 309; reprinted in *William Faulkner's Absalom, Absalom!: A Casebook*, Fred Hobson, ed. (Oxford University Press, 2003), 31. See also *Absalom, Absalom!*, 188.

50. Brooks, "History and the Sense of the Tragic," 309.

51. "William Faulkner Banquet speech," NobelPrize.org, December 10, 1950, www.nobelprize.org/prizes/literature/1949/faulkner/speech/.

52. See, for example, Herman E. Taylor, *Faulkner's Oxford* (Rutledge Hill Press, 1990), 167–68. George G. Stewart also has expressed this view. See his *Yoknapatawpha, Images and Voices: A Photographic Study of Faulkner's County* (University of South Carolina Press, 2009), 50.

53. Helen Bell Hopkins, email to author, July 31, 2014.

54. Carvel Collins Collection of William Faulkner Research Materials, Harry Ransom Center, The University of Texas at Austin, Box 56, Folder 5. Thanks to library staff.

55. George M. "Minor" Buchanan, phone interview with author, August 18, 2014.

56. Alice Long and Mark L. Ridge, *Images of America: Holly Springs* (Arcadia, 2006), 24.

57. Scott Faragher, current owner of Grey Gables, communication with author, April 24, 2016.

58. 1910 US Census, Marshall County, Mississippi, with Louise Caffey Smith on line 42 (Holly Springs, ward 4, Enumeration District (ED) 41–2, sheet 11-A, p. 93 (stamped), dwelling 205, family 219, lines 40–45, imaged at Ancestry, www.ancestry.com/discoveryui-content/view/151223009:7884, citing National Archives microfilm publication T624, roll 751); 1920 US Census, Marshall County, Mississippi, Louise Caffee [sic] Smith on line 14 (Beat I, Ward 4, Enumeration District (ED) 4, sheet 6-A, p. 89; imaged at Ancestry, www.ancestry.com/discoveryui-content/view/78099363:6061, citing National Archives microfilm publication T625, roll 887).

59. Mary Wallace Crocker, *Historic Architecture in Mississippi* (University Press of Mississippi, 1973), 169–70.

60. Francisco III, correspondence, April 30, 2016, and revision by telephone, June 27, 2021.

61. Jack Baum, "Holly Springs: The Architecture of a Small Town," unpublished paper, School of Architecture, University of Tennessee, 1978, 98. Also worth noting is that the design and decoration of the Smith House came via mail order from Knoxville. That scenario may parallel the activities of Flem Snopes and Eula Varner, who furnished their mansion with mail order from Memphis. Because of their humble background, they did not know how to decorate a mansion.

62. 1910 US Census, Marshall County, Mississippi. See especially line 45 for Johnny Dancy, whose relationship to the head of the house and profession are listed as "servant." (Holly Springs, ward 4, Enumeration District (ED) 41–2, sheet 11-A, p. 93 (stamped), dwelling 205, family 219, lines 40–45, imaged at Ancestry, www.ancestry.com/discoveryui-content/view/151223012:7884, citing National Archives microfilm publication T624, roll 751.)

63. See further information about Ruth LeGrand Strickland in chapter 3: "People That I Have Known" on p. 110, ff.

64. Francisco III, telephone communication, January 18, 2013, and email correspondence with author, January 24, 2013.

65. See pp. 35–36, 103, and 105 for a description of the distrust that Francisco III said Faulkner had upon first meeting Gerard Badow. Faulkner was, apparently, suspicious of Badow's German background and motives for marrying the older woman, Perle Strickland.

66. Francisco III, correspondence, January 24, 2013.

67. Francisco III, correspondence, January 24, 2013.

68. Faulkner, "A Rose for Emily," in *Collected Stories*, 126.

69. Francisco III, correspondence, February 28, 2013.

70. Faulkner, "A Rose for Emily," in *Collected Stories*, 119.

71. Bobby Mitchell, email correspondence with author, August 19, 2015.

72. Bobby Mitchell, email correspondence with author, August 26, 2015; see also, "The 3rd U.S. Infantry (the Old Guard) is the oldest infantry unit in the Army, since 1784. It is the Army's official ceremonial unit and escort to the President. Among tasks are ceremonies at the White House, Pentagon, Tomb of Unknowns, and funeral escorts at Arlington. They are the only unit permitted to pass in review with fixed bayonets, dating from a charge against the enemy at Cerro Gordo in the Mexican War," Dan Morris, email correspondence, August 26, 2015; see also "About the Old Guard," jtfncr.mdw.army.mil/oldguard/; also, in the "Headstones Provided for Union Civil War Veterans, ca. 1879–ca. 1903" military records of the US National Archives and Records Administration, at bottom of the "receipt" for Francis

McMahon it says: "Sheldon & Sons West Rutland, Vermont, Contract date August 1888" (Margie Ann Morris, email, August 26, 2015.)

73. Bobby Mitchell, correspondence with author, August 26, 2015.

74. Bobby Mitchell, correspondence with author, August 27, 2015.

75. "Contextualization at University of Mississippi: Memorials and Contextualization," guides.lib.olemiss.edu/contextualization/memorials.

76. Dr. April Holm, associate professor of History and director of the Center for Civil War Research, the University of Mississippi, email correspondence, May 5, 2021. See also a government publication entitled *Statement of the Disposition of Some of the Bodies of Deceased Union Soldiers and Prisoners of War Whose Remains Have Been Removed to National Cemeteries in the Southern and Western States*, Quartermaster General's Office, General Orders No. 8, February 24, 1868, www.google.com/books/edition/Statement_of_the _Disposition_of_Some_of/s4xIAQAAMAAJ.

77. Bobby Mitchell, email correspondence with author, May 28, 2021, and June 5, 2021.

78. Rollyson, *Life of William Faulkner*, 48.

79. Bobby Mitchell, email correspondence with author, August 19, 2015.

80. Keith Gore Wiseman, "Down by the Station," *Invitation Oxford*, March 2018, 38.

81. Wiseman, "Down by the Station," 38.

82. Clarence Snopes and Horace Benbow, for example, disembark the train at Holly Springs en route from Oxford to Jefferson in *Sanctuary* (1st Vintage International ed., 1993), 177. Mink Snopes visits or considers visiting other depots in the novel *The Mansion* after he gets out of prison at Parchman (Random House, 1959), 288–89, 405. Ratliff describes being at the "deepo" in the novel *The Town* (Random House, 1957), 101. Chick Mallison considers killing some time at the depot but ultimately does not until Lucas Beauchamp arrives at the jail in Jefferson (*Intruder in the Dust*, Random House, 1948), 38.

83. Gwen Wyatt, telephone interview with author, July 28, 2018.

84. *South Reporter*, November 9, 1978. The article continues:

> In 1911 R. A. McDermott became manager of the dining room and hotel. His son, James, worked behind the counter in the dining room. James, later nicknamed "Tippy," could remember the jokes people used to tell about how thin his father would slice the ham: Tippy, laughing and talking at the same time, said, "Railroad men would come in and order a ham sandwich and when they got it they would tell Pop to turn off the fan so the ham wouldn't blow away."
>
> "William Faulkner even mentioned my father in his book, THE REIVERS," McDermott said. In Faulkner's story, Mr. McDermott was said to have sliced the ham so thin that he sent his entire family to Chicago on the profits of one ham.
>
> "I think that story was just a little bit stretched. Faulkner used to come to Holly Springs a lot. I can remember seeing him walk around outside. He noticed everything, but never talked to anyone. He was real quiet."

85. Gwen Wyatt, email correspondence with author, September 13, 2022, and telephone interview with author, July 28, 2018. Wyatt further recalls:

> I was a young woman when he [William Faulkner] was still alive. My father ran the Depot. He sliced ham so thin you could read the newspaper through it. Tippy said that was very true. Tippy was at the lunch counter at the Depot. He observed people. [Mr. Faulkner] talked to Tippy. Gertrude McDermott was our piano teacher. Tippy was her brother. Mr. Faulkner would come on the train [to Holly Springs], listen to the bands at the Depot, and then take the train back to Oxford. My father knew William Faulkner. My father was the health officer coroner during the time when William Faulkner died. He helped with all that. Also, Faulkner wanted to have a troop of boy scouts, and my father helped make that a reality. They made a raft and floated in it.

See also Weinstein, who states the Faulkner boys "became scouts, and Faulkner—whose tenderness toward children was notable his entire life—later served as scoutmaster," *Becoming Faulkner* (44).

86. Carvel Collins Collection of William Faulkner Research Materials, Harry Ransom Center, The University of Texas at Austin, Box 56, Folder 5. Thanks to library staff.

87. Letter from Gertrude McDermott to Carvel Collins, September 24, 1963, in the Carvel Collins Collection of William Faulkner Research Materials, Harry Ransom Center, The University of Texas at Austin, Box 57, Folder 13. With thanks to Phillip Fry and John Morris and the late Margie Ann Morris for research assistance.

88. "Garden Pilgrimage to Historical Sites," 11.

89. See "1858 Greek Revival—Holly Springs, MS," *Old House Dreams*, www.oldhousedreams.com/2016/05/13/1858-greek-revival-holly-springs-ms/, for photos of Athenia, including interior images.

90. Phillip Knecht, "Athenia (1858)," Hill Country History, October 24, 2015, hillcountryhistory.org/2015/10/24/holly-springs-athenia-1858/.

91. Stephanie McKinney of VisitHollySprings.com, telephone communication with author, April 27, 2015.

92. Francisco III, correspondence, February 26, 2022.

93. Winter, *Shadow of a Mighty Rock*, 172.

94. Quoted in Winter, *Shadow of a Mighty Rock*, 188.

95. Cf. Wolff, *Ledgers of History*, 50–51.

96. *Merriam-Webster Dictionary*, "ogre," www.merriam-webster.com/dictionary/ogre.

97. *Merriam-Webster Dictionary*, "augur," www.merriam-webster.com/dictionary/augur.

98. John Lowe, *Bridging Southern Cultures: An Interdisciplinary Approach* (Louisiana State University Press, 2005), 88.

99. Long and Ridge, *Images of America*, 47.

100. Williamson, *William Faulkner and Southern History*, 67.

101. Williamson, *William Faulkner and Southern History*, 65.

102. Melvin Backman, *Faulkner: The Major Years, A Critical Study* (Indiana University Press, 1966), 83.

103. Quoted in Backman, *Faulkner*, 83.

104. See also John Sykes, "Faulkner, Calvinism, and Religion," *Journal of Presbyterian History (1997–)* 75, no. 1 (1997): 43–53, www.jstor.org/stable/23335441.

105. In Wolff, *Talking about William Faulkner*, 80.

106. Blotner, "William Faulkner Seminar," 71. See also John Faulkner, *My Brother Bill*, xi; and also Murry C. Falkner, *Falkners of Mississippi*, 189.

107. See Wolff, *Ledgers of History*, for further details.

108. Francisco III, email correspondence to author, August 10, 2007.

109. Cf. the reference to this story in *Ledgers of History*, 69, and the rebuttals of Francisco III in this book, chapter 1, appendix 1-A.

110. Wolff, *Ledgers of History*, 85. See also see appendix 1-A on pp. 74–76 for more details of this story.

111. Francisco III, correspondence, November 17, 2022.

112. Francisco III, correspondence with author, November 11, 2022.

113. Francisco III, telephone communication, June 8, 2019.

114. Francisco III, telephone communication, June 8. 2019.

115. Hubert H. McAlexander notes: "Holly Springs long remembered the source of Herman Wohlleben's wealth, and William Faulkner found fictional uses for both that one incident and the larger drama of the Van Dorn raid, most notably in *Light in August*, where the raid provides a central image" (*Southern Tapestry* 67). Nathan Bedford Forrest's raid across West Tennessee in winter 1862–63 also cut Grant's supply chain, and this reference could allude to that raid. Faulkner may have learned of the Van Dorn connection in school or elsewhere, instead of in Holly Springs proper, but he clearly knew the details of the raid in Holly Springs.

116. Ron Chernow, *Grant* (Penguin Books, 2017), 239.

117. Chernow, *Grant*, 239.

118. Shelby Foote, *The Civil War: A Narrative: Fredericksburg to Meridian*. Vol. 2 (Random House, 1963), 70–71.

119. Foote, *Civil War*, 2:71.

120. Matt Atkinson, "Van Dorn's Raid," 1281.

121. "Shelby Foote on Faulkner," C-SPAN, May 10, 2002, www.c-span.org/video/?170042 -1/shelby-foote-faulkner.

122. Ed Phillips, "Delta Writers Featured in TV Program," *Clarksdale Press Register* (Clarksdale, MS), November 8–9, 1975, 5A.

123. Carl McIntire, "Mount Holly History," *Clarion-Ledger* (Jackson, MS), January 14, 1973, F3.

124. "Mount Holly Burns," The Lakeport Plantation, Arkansas State University, June 17, 2015, lakeport.astate.edu/2015/06/17/mount-holly-burns/.

125. McIntire, "Mount Holly History." See Taylor, *Faulkner's Oxford*, for a photo of Ammadele, 168.

126. McIntire, "Mount Holly History."

127. Phillips, "Delta Writers Featured in TV Program."

128. Anne Firor Scott, *Making the Invisible Woman Visible* (University of Illinois Press, 1984), 39.

129. Williamson, *William Faulkner and Southern History*, 172, 135.

130. Ralph Lyon, "The Early Years of the Livingston Female Academy," *Alabama Historical Quarterly* 37, no. 3 [June 1975]: 192. Lyon cites Edgar Knight, adding that the roots of these institutions were English, and those in America also show the influence of

Benjamin Franklin (Edgar W. Knight, *Public Education in the South*, Boston, 1922, cited in Lyon, 192). The goal of such academies was the serious religious and moral refinement of women (Edgar W. Knight, *The Academy Movement in the South*, 1920), cited in Lyon, 193). The curriculum, for example, at the Livingston Female Academy in Alabama, in 1852, "compared favorably with that of other academies in the South" (Knight, *Academy Movement*, cited in Lyon, "Early Years," 201). An article in the *Sumter Democrat* from August 21, 1852, describes three years of study: "algebra, geometry, ancient and modern history, astronomy, natural philosophy, chemistry, rhetoric, logic, elocution, metaphysics, ethics, classical literature, and French and Latin. Music and art were special subjects that required extra charges" (*Sumter Democrat*, August 21, 1852, quoted in Lyon, "Early Years," 201).

131. Lyon, "Early Years," 204.

132. Lyon, "Early Years," 205. Hubert H. McAlexander also records that the history of a female institute in Holly Springs was "founded before the plat of a town had ever been drawn," and that the building which had housed the institute "was burned after being used as a Civil War hospital for infectious diseases" (*Southern Tapestry*, 21).

133. Blotner, *Faulkner*, vol. 1, 827.

134. Bobby Mitchell, "Mississippi Synodical College," *Heritage News: A Publication of the Marshall County, Mississippi, Genealogical and Historical Society* 22, no. 1 (March 2016): 6.

135. Wolff, *Talking about William Faulkner*, 72.

136. Interview with John Brown, former mayor of Holly Springs, January 24, 2015.

137. Bobby Mitchell, email to author, May 30, 2023.

138. "Family in Same Residence for Ninety-Two Years," *South Reporter*, December 15, 1932.

139. Wolff, *Ledgers of History*, 85.

140. "Francisco-Bitzer Surprise Marriage," *South Reporter*, August 29, 1929.

CHAPTER TWO: "THE FRAGILE AND INDELIBLE SIGNATURE OF HER MEDITATION": LUDIE'S WINDOW AS A SOURCE FOR FAULKNER'S *INTRUDER IN THE DUST* AND *REQUIEM FOR A NUN*

1. See, for example, E. O. Hawkins Jr., "Jane Cook and Cecilia Farmer"; Noel Polk, "Faulkner's 'The Jail' and the Meaning of Cecilia Farmer"; and Jayne Isbell Haynes, "Another Source for Faulkner's Inscribed Window Panes."

2. See Sally Wolff, *Ledgers of History: William Faulkner: An Almost Forgotten Friendship and an Antebellum Plantation Diary* (Louisiana State University Press, 2010), 81–82.

3. As the result of meticulous care on the part of the family, Ludie's etching on the glass at McCarroll Place remained intact in the window on which she inscribed it since the Civil War. Because of home break-ins at McCarroll Place, and the absence of the Francisco family now, the etched window has been placed in a secure location, and an exact replica of Ludie's etching is now installed at the home. Also, an identical replica is on display at the Marshall County Museum in Holly Springs.

4. J. B. Carothers and K. J. Sheldon, "Comprehending Faulkner's Humor," *Mississippi Quarterly* 60, no. 3 (2007): 438.

5. Wolff, *Ledgers of History*, 82.

6. "In Memoriam," *Memphis Daily Appeal*, January 24, 1869, 2. Also a copy is in the personal papers of Dr. Edgar Wiggin Francisco III.

7. "Mary L. Booth, Obituary," *Memphis Daily Appeal*, January 12, 1869; death notice of Mary L. Booth, *Memphis Daily Appeal*, January 18, 1869: "M L Booth, 26 years, female white, acute gastritis."

8. Francisco III, correspondence, February 24, 2017.

9. Similar favorable sentiments about the Yankee colonel occur in Faulkner's novel *The Unvanquished*.

10. Granny Millard takes a remarkably similar stance in *The Unvanquished*.

11. See Wolff, *Ledgers of History*, 64, 80.

12. See Wolff, *Ledgers of History*, 55.

13. See especially Dean Faulkner Wells, *The Ghosts of Rowan Oak: William Faulkner's Ghost Stories for Children* (Yoknapatawpha Press, 1980).

14. Jay Parini, *One Matchless Time: A Life of William Faulkner* (HarperCollins, 2004), 12.

15. I extended my heartfelt gratitude to Ms. Haynes prior to her death and do so again here, for her guidance and assistance in preparing this book.

16. Jayne Isbell Haynes, "Another Source for Faulkner's Inscribed Window Panes," *Mississippi Quarterly* 39, no. 3 (Summer 1986): 366.

17. Haynes, "Another Source," 366.

18. Faulkner, *Intruder in the Dust*, 50, quoted in Haynes, "Another Source," 366.

19. Jack Elliott posted his findings on the William Faulkner Society, Email Discussion Group, September 9, 2013.

20. Porch. The gallery along the east side of McCarroll Place was accessible from both inside and outside the house. Although during Faulkner's day Ludie's window was visible from the outside, looking in, the gallery since then has been enclosed as a sunroom, and that change obscures what previously was her view of the street.

21. Wolff, *Ledgers*, 82.

22. Francisco III, correspondence, October 2013.

23. See also Noel Polk, "Faulkner's 'The Jail' and the Meaning of Cecilia Farmer," *Mississippi Quarterly* 25, no. 3 (Summer 1972): 316.

24. John Keats, "Ode on a Grecian Urn," www.poetryfoundation.org/poems/44477/ode-on-a-grecian-urn.

25. Jean Stein, "The Art of Fiction XII: William Faulkner," *Paris Review*, no. 12, Spring 1956, 49–50.

26. "During the planning for 1936 [the Pilgrimage] was called Centennial, since there was no plan for an annual Pilgrimage. 1937 was skipped for a reason I am not sure I remember—possibly streets or roads were under construction. So, in 1938 they called 1936 the 1st and 1938 the 2nd." Francisco III, email correspondence with author, September 19, 2023. See also George M. Moreland, "Holly Springs to Turn Back Hands of the Clock at Centennial Celebration," *Commercial Appeal* (Memphis, TN), October 4. 1936, III-3.

27. Bobby Mitchell, "Some Early History of Marshall County," The MSGenWeb Project, www.msgw.org/marshall/locales/mchist.php.

28. Francisco III, email correspondence with author, September 23, 2023.

29. Rita Cochran, "First Pilgrimage—a Big Success," *Pilgrimage Edition*, special issue of the *South Reporter* (Holly Springs, MS), October 22, 1936, 8–9. Article courtesy of Dr. Edgar Wiggin Francisco III. "The South Reporter published a Pilgrimage Special Edition after that 1st Pilgrimage. It was acclaimed to be the largest edition ever. It contained pictures and write-ups of all the homes on the tours. The edition was at least partially paid for with merchant and individual ads expressing congratulations." Francisco III, email correspondence with author, September 19, 2023. See also Winter, *Shadow of a Mighty Rock*, 389–95.

30. Cochran, "First Pilgrimage," 9.

31. Cochran, "First Pilgrimage," 9.

32. Lillian Mirando, "State's 50th Pilgrimage Season Offers More than Ever," *Clarion-Ledger, Jackson Daily News*, Saturday, March 6, 1982, 14A.

33. Noel Polk, "Faulkner's 'The Jail,'" 305–25.

34. See Sally Wolff, "'Everybody Knew': *Ledgers of History*: Questions and Answers," *South Atlantic Review* 81, no. 4 (Winter 2016): 66–88.

35. Frank Hurdle, weblog comment, April 29, 2014, on Maria Bustillos, "The Faulkner Truthers," *The Awl*, April 22, 2014, www.theawl.com/2014/04/the-faulkner-truthers/.

36. Frank Hurdle, correspondence with author, May 3, 2014. Also, Mr. Hurdle added further detail about his experience as a guide, and that of others, at Pilgrimage:

> Just to explain how it would work, there were about 100 teen-age girls who would serve in Pilgrimage in various houses. Many were from Holly Springs but others might be cousins from other towns. Grown women also served. They would wear hoop skirts and just stand in a room until visitors arrived, and then give a quick spiel about the furniture and so forth. Guides, always boys, would be hired at the picture show and ride with the guests to help them find the houses. It was actually quite nice, because we knew the home owners and would introduce them. I served as a guide for Johnny Newman, who was a professional basketball player for a short time, and apparently for an airline pilot who had been highjacked to Cuba, although I didn't know about that until I was told later. Mr. Cuba Man actually called and arranged for me to guide him a second year, which was flattering.
>
> ANYWAY, Some guides would walk through the houses with their guests. I usually would, and would make sure they were getting the full story. I usually did so, and that's why I remember the thing about the etched glass. (Frank Hurdle, correspondence with author, May 1, 2014)

Mr. Hurdle continued that

> My recollection is that I was a guide from age 12 or 13 to age 16, so roughly from 1973–76. I think I went to the Holly Theatre twice when it served as the Pilgrimage Ticket headquarters, and that is where about a dozen to 20 guides would be. We would wear a regular sportscoat and tie, if you can call any sports coat from the 1970s "regular." My recollection is that the Holly Theatre burned in the fall of 1974, so I'm more or less basing my dates on this. . . . I served as a guide. . . . I'm sure at least three, but maybe four [years].

Just a little note about how students "served" in the Pilgrimage. Generally starting at about age 5 or 6 they would be invited to serve at a home of a friend or relation, both boys and girls. The boys would, as I recall, wear bow ties and perhaps a black jacket to lend an "old-fashioned" look, but would not be in period costume. It was quite common for the girls to wear small hoop or other period garb, which would be loaned back and forth between families. The children were supposed to play in the front yard, mill about, and say hello. We tended to congregate in the Coke and cookie room. Many of the girls continue to serve until they die of old age, but the boys generally would quit at age 10 or 11. A few would become Pilgrimage guides for a few years. When the girls hit their later teens they might be asked to serve in a room in a house, where they would describe the furniture and history of the house or room. . . .

After serving at a "morning" house many of the kids would walk around and visit their friends at some of the afternoon houses; however the McCarroll Place was not a house that many people would go to see their friends. Montrose was open all day and was Pilgrimage Central, so people would drop by there. Mrs. Moss' house on Salem was an afternoon house with lots of kids, so it was a popular stop. Back then there were 11 houses on the tour, five morning, five afternoon, and Montrose all day. (Frank Hurdle, correspondence with author, May 3, 2014)

37. Correspondence with Bobby Mitchell, March 8, 2015.
38. Interview with Scarlett Hurdle, May 21, 2014.
39. Interview with Jane Callicutt, May 28, 2014.
40. E. O. Hawkins Jr., "Jane Cook and Cecilia Farmer," *Mississippi Quarterly* 18, no. 4 (Fall 1965): 249.
41. Hawkins, "Jane Cook," 249. See also further discussion of this point in Wolff, *Ledgers of History*, 53ff.
42. Hawkins, "Jane Cook," 249.
43. Polk, *Faulkner's Requiem for a Nun*, 264–65.
44. Michael Millgate, *Faulkner's Place* (University of Georgia Press, 2008), 11.
45. Jay Watson, *Forensic Fictions: The Lawyer Figure in Faulkner* (University of Georgia Press, 1995), 206–7.
46. Catalina Montes, "'Listen, Stranger: This Was Myself; This Was I': *Requiem for a Nun*," in *Faulkner and History*, ed. Javier Coy and Michel Gresset (Salamanca, 1986), 197–212. See also Polk, "Faulkner's 'The Jail,'" 324–25.
47. Montes, "Listen, Stranger," 197, 198.
48. See Wolff, *Ledgers of History*, 86–88.
49. Francisco III, telephone communication. Also see Wolff, *Ledgers of History*, 87–88.
50. See "William Faulkner to Harrison Smith" [probably February 1934], in William Faulkner, *Selected Letters*, ed. Joseph Blotner (Vintage Books, a Division of Random House, 1978), 79.
51. Joel Williamson, *William Faulkner and Southern History* (Oxford University Press, 1993), 244.

CHAPTER THREE: "PEOPLE THAT I HAVE KNOWN": WILLIAM FAULKNER, A FAMILY WHO INFLUENCED HIM, AND POSSIBLE SOURCES FOR *THE SOUND AND THE FURY*

1. Sally Wolff, *Ledgers of History: William Faulkner, an Almost Forgotten Friendship, and an Antebellum Plantation Diary* (Louisiana State University Press, 2010).

2. Dr. Francisco III, ninety-four at this writing, recalls his father's accounts of having visited the Stricklands with Will Faulkner, both as adults and children, and having gone back and forth through the gate that connected the adjoining properties. Edgar and Will were well aware of the personalities and activities of Edgar's Strickland cousins. In the previous generation, Edgar's mother, Betsy, had also gone back and forth through this gate to visit her cousins (Francisco III, correspondence, February 13, 2013).

3. Perle was the daughter of William Strickland and Jane E. (Janie) Leak Strickland, who was the daughter of Francis Terry Leak. Betsy was the daughter of Amelia McCarroll and Walter John Leak, a son of Francis Terry Leak. Matrimony joined Francis Terry Leak's son, Walter John Leak, and Amelia McCarroll in 1866.

4. Francisco III explains the following:

William Strickland and John R. McCarroll had a long friendship prior to the time the two families were related through marriages to these two children of Frances Terry Leak. Mildred Thompson married William Strickland. Mildred's father, Dr. James Thompson, built what would become known as the Strickland Place right next door to McCarroll Place, in 1838, two years after McCarroll moved the home he had built a few hundred feet down the hill at the spring up to the corner of Depot and Maury Streets. In an extant letter, Mildred Strickland praises the manners of Union General Alexander Hamilton, who occupied lodgings in her home and established his military headquarters at McCarroll Place next door. [In *The Unvanquished*, the Yankee colonel is similarly well mannered.] In 1867, several years after Mildred died, Amelia McCarroll claims to have arranged the marriage of [Francis Terry Leak's daughter] Jane E. (Janie) Leak to William Strickland [Strickland was Amelia's next-door neighbor in Holly Springs. Janie moved to Holly Springs to Strickland Place and brought two of her younger sisters with her.] In only a few years the daughters would be living next door to each other, visiting back and forth through the gate connecting the properties. [Janie gave birth to Perle in 1869, and Amelia had given birth to Betsy in 1868. Amelia and Betsy apparently moved home from the plantation to McCarroll Place after Walter's death, and the two first cousins grew up next door to each other and spent their entire lives as neighbors—with a gate between the houses.] These events illustrate the close interconnectedness of the two families across several generations. (Francisco III, correspondence, August 12, 2011)

5. According to Joseph Blotner, one of Faulkner's friends said that in 1925 Faulkner let him read a story about a girl and her brothers that "became *The Sound and the Fury*." See Blotner, *Faulkner: A Biography, One-Vol. Ed.* (Random House, 1984), 209. Blotner

speculates that Faulkner could have been working on the story earlier than 1928, since Faulkner mentioned to Liveright in a February 1927 letter that he was working on "short stories of my townspeople" (206). Nonetheless Blotner settles on "late winter or early spring of 1928" as the probable date for the beginning of writing "Twilight" (209).

6. Francisco III, telephone communication, February 18, 2018.

7. Francisco III, telephone communication, July 11, 2011. See figure 3.3 on p. 104. Quoted with permission of The South Reporter, Inc. The wedding of Perle to Gerard took place on November 30, 1926.

8. Pauline Stevenson grew up across the street from Edgar Jr. and continued to live there after she married Barney Hammond and raised their children. Edgar and Pauline were lifelong friends, as were their mothers.

9. Francisco III, correspondence, July 11, 2011.

10. Francisco III, telephone communication, December 16, 2012. Chesley Thorne Smith recalls in her memoir that fellow Holly Springs citizen Harris Gholson nicknamed Mr. Badow "Bad Dough." See Chesley Thorne Smith, *Childhood in Holly Springs: A Memoir* (Thomas-Berryhill Press, 1996), 85.

11. *South Reporter* (Holly Springs, MS), November 18, 1926, 3.

12. Mrs. Lucius (Nell) Dancy, "Miss Perle Strickland Becomes Bride of Gerard Badow," *South Reporter*, December 2, 1926, 1.

13. Dancy, "Miss Perle Strickland Becomes Bride," 1.

14. Hubert H. McAlexander, *A Southern Tapestry: Marshall County, Mississippi 1835–2000* (Donning, 2000), 138.

15. Robert Milton Winter, *Civil War Women: The Diaries of Belle Strickland and Cora Harris Watson: Holly Springs, Mississippi July 25, 1864–June 22, 1868* (Thomas-Berryhill Press, 2001), photo section between 142–43.

16. Dancy, "Miss Perle Strickland Becomes Bride," 1. Also, Hindman Doxey Sr. had acted in one of Faulkner's plays at the University of Mississippi (Francisco III, correspondence, December 16, 2012). See pp. 26–27 for additional discussion of Doxey's role in Faulkner's theater group.

17. Dancy, "Miss Perle Strickland Becomes Bride," 4.

18. Sarah Doxey Tate, "A Talk on Faulkner and the Hindman/Doxey Family," library talk at the Marshall County Library, Holly Springs, Mississippi, Fall 2003.

19. Mary Bitzer and Ruth Bitzer were sisters who moved to Holly Springs with their parents when their father, Dr. George Bitzer, became pastor of the First Presbyterian Church in 1926. Hindman Doxey, born 1899, married Mary Bitzer in June of 1929. Edgar Francisco Jr., born 1898, married Ruth Bitzer in August of 1929 (Francisco III, correspondence, July 4, 2011). Will Faulkner, born September 25, 1897, also married in 1929, in June.

20. William Faulkner, *The Sound and the Fury: An Authoritative Text, Backgrounds and Contexts, Criticism*, 2nd ed., ed. David Minter (Norton, 1994), 210. Subsequent references to this edition will appear parenthetically in the text.

21. Dancy, "Miss Perle Strickland Becomes Bride," 1.

22. For further discussion of Estelle's wedding as an antecedent of Caddy's, see Sally Wolff, Marie Nitschke, and Robert J. Roberts, "'The Voice That Breathed o'er Eden': William

Faulkner's Unsung Wedding Hymn," *Mississippi Quarterly* 58, no. 3-4 (Summer–Fall 2005): 595-610, www.jstor.org/stable/26476610.

23. Dancy, "Miss Perle Strickland Becomes Bride," 4.

24. 1870 US Federal Census (Population Schedule), Holly Springs, Ward 4, Marshall, Mississippi, National Archives and Records Administration Microfilm Publication 593, Roll 40, accessed on Ancestry Library database June 2011; 1880 US Federal Census (Population Schedule), Holly Springs, Marshall, Mississippi, National Archives and Records Administration Microfilm Publication T9, Roll 657, accessed on Ancestry Library database June 2011.

25. 1930 US Federal Census (Population Schedule), Holly Springs, Marshall, Mississippi, National Archives and Records Administration Microfilm Publication T626, Roll 1158, accessed on Ancestry Library database June 2011.

26. Francisco III, telephone communication, December 16, 2012.

27. "U.S., Passport Applications, 1795-1925," database, *Ancestry* (ancestry.com), entry for Gerard Martin Johannes Badow, citing National Archives and Records Administration (NARA); *Passport Applications, January 2, 1906—March 31, 1925*; Roll #: *1767*; Volume #: *Roll 1767—Certificates: 94126-94499, 28 Oct 1921-31 Oct 1921*.

28. "Hamburg Passenger Lists, 1850-1934," database, *Ancestry* (ancestry.com), entries for Gerard and Perle Badow (lines 128 and 129), aboard *Cleveland* (Hamburg to Boulogne; Cobh; New York; Boston), leaving 3 March 1927; citing Bestand [inventory] no. 373-7I, VIII, A1 (Auswanderungsamt I [Emigration List—Indirect]), Band [vol.] 343; Staatsarchiv Hamburg microfilm series K 1701–K 2008, S 17363–S 17383, 13116–13183.

29. Dancy, "Miss Perle Strickland Becomes Bride," 1.

30. Hubert H. McAlexander, comp. and ed., *From the Chickasaw Cession to Yoknapatawpha: Historical and Literary Essays on North Mississippi* (Nautilus, 2017), 283.

31. Francisco III, telephone communication, January 18, 2013.

32. Francisco III, email correspondence, January 15, 2018.

33. "Later, when retelling the story to Faulkner," Dr. Francisco III recalls, "I had my lesson composition book with me. He asked to see it and he read a couple of the poems and stories to which Perle would attach a gold star when I learned to recite them. He looked at Dad and said: 'Damn it, Edgar, nobody ever gives me a gold star.'" Francisco III, correspondence, January 23, 2013.

34. See William Faulkner, *The Mansion* (Random House, 1959), 322.

35. Dr. Francisco III points out that eventually the rope that held the swing broke and was replaced with a chain. "Probably more than one rope broke, but I recall much fretting over the swing rope breaking when I was very young. Someone else was in the swing at the time. The rope was replaced with the chain (as shown in pictures from then on) and the seat was replaced also at that time by family carpenter, Arthur Marsh. (Also, he is the carpenter who replaced the fence)." Francisco III, correspondence, January 24, 2013, and February 9, 2013.

36. "2 Louisville Girls Wed in Automobile: Secret Rites at Bridge in Indiana Night of Nov. 24," *Courier-Journal* (Louisville, KY), December 9, 1923, 3, col. 2; digital image, www.newspapers.com/image/107525961/.

37. Mrs. Anne Weir, text correspondence with author, August 15, 2024.

38. "The Personal Side," *Courier-Journal* (Louisville, KY), October 20, 1925, 7, col. 1; digital image, www.newspapers.com/image/107530708/; Lily Koppel, "An Opulent Home, a Rich Past," *New York Times*, April 3, 2007, www.nytimes.com/2007/04/03/nyregion/03mansion.html.

39. "The Personal Side," *Courier-Journal* (Louisville, KY), December 7, 1925, 5, col. 1; digital image, www.newspapers.com/image/107606426/.

40. 1926: "The Personal Side: Strickland—Weir," *Courier-Journal* (Louisville, KY), October 18, 1926, 5, col. 3; digital image, www.newspapers.com/image/107542089/.

1938: "Marriage Licenses," *Courier-Journal* (Louisville, KY), June 16. 1938, 24, col. 4; digital image, www.newspapers.com/image/107733756/.

1942: "The Social Side: Weir—Martin," *Courier-Journal* (Louisville, KY), November 17, 1942, 17, col. 3; digital image, www.newspapers.com/image/108378784/.

1947: "Indiana, U.S., Marriages, 1810–2001," database, Ancestry (www.ancestry.com), entry for Ruth S Weir [Ruth S Strickland], spouse James Frankum, November 14, 1947, citing "Indiana, Marriages, 1810–2001. Salt Lake City, Utah: FamilySearch, 2013."

Ruth apparently married and divorced an additional time before she died because she was listed as "Mrs. J. C. Rice III" in a marriage announcement for her son ("St. John—Weir," *Courier-Journal* (Louisville, KY), June 5, 1954, 10, col. 6; digital image, www.newspapers.com/image/107756165). At the time of her death in 1971, however, her obituary lists her as "Ruth S. Weir" ("WEIR, Ruth S.," *Courier-Journal* (Louisville, KY), April 10, 1971, B-11, col. 2; digital image, www.newspapers.com/image/109785480/).

41. Francisco III, correspondence, January 22, 2013, and February 28, 2013. Upon further questioning, Dr. Francisco III clarifies, "I know several pictures were taken at the time of the graduation, and I saw them in an album which is missing. This picture is not dated, so while most likely it was taken then, this picture could be one taken a year or two before, but it is definitely the same swing."

42. Mrs. Anne Weir, correspondence, January 18, 2013.

43. Francisco email correspondence with author, January 15, 2013. Correspondence with Mrs. Anne Weir, January 28, 2013. Mrs. Weir also remembers a photo of Ruth and Rube Weir in which "they are seated on the back fender of a car.... She is behind him. On the back of the photo it says 'Rube and me~just married. April 24, 1927.'" Mrs. Weir is the widow of Dr. William Weir, Jacob Strickland's grandson. William Weir attended Perle's funeral with his mother, Ruth. Local Memphis historian Melissa McCoy-Bell contacted Will Weir, who led her to Anne Weir, who generously shared photographs of Perle Strickland Badow, Ruth LeGrand Strickland Weir, and Rube Weir. Go to educationalconsulting.services/Faulkner to see the photos.

44. See also Sally Wolff, "'Everybody Knew': *Ledgers of History*: Questions and Answers," *South Atlantic Review* 81, no. 4 (Winter 2016): 66–88.

45. Francisco III, email correspondence with author, January 24, 2013.

46. Francisco III, correspondence, February 19, 2013.

47. Joseph Blotner, *Faulkner: A Biography*, vol. 1 (Random House, 1974), 1196.

48. Dancy, "Miss Perle Strickland Becomes Bride," 4.

49. Francisco III, correspondence, January 24, 2013.

50. Francisco III, correspondence, October 6, 2011. See also email August 7, 2023.

51. William Faulkner, "An Introduction to *The Sound and the Fury*" (1973), in Faulkner, *Sound and the Fury*, 230.

52. Francisco III, correspondence, January 24, 2013.

53. Francisco III, correspondence, February 24, 2013.

54. Francisco III, correspondence, February 19, 2013.

55. Francisco III, correspondence, February 24, 2013.

56. Francisco III, correspondence, February 24, 2013.

57. Francisco III, correspondence, February 15, 2013. See also further descriptions of the two back doors at Strickland Place in Francisco III, email correspondence, September 19, 2016, September 20, 2016, and September 21, 2016.

58. Fant and Ashley, eds., *Faulkner at West Point*, 96.

CHAPTER FOUR: FAULKNER'S *ABSALOM, ABSALOM!* AND McCARROLL PLACE: POSSIBLE ANTECEDENTS

1. See Sally Wolff, *Ledgers of History: William Faulkner, an Almost Forgotten Friendship, and an Antebellum Plantation Diary* (Louisiana State University Press, 2010) for discussion of McCarroll Place and furnishings.

2. Ruth Bitzer Francisco, the mother of Dr. Edgar Wiggin Francisco III, gave the plantation desk to Helen Doxey at the time of her marriage to Dr. Jack Tyson in 1958.

3. Amelia McCarroll Leak, wife of Walter John Leak, who was the son of the wealthy planter Francis Terry Leak. Amelia was also the great-grandmother of Dr. Edgar Wiggin Francisco III.

4. Ludie's Window refers to the etching on the glass windowpane at McCarroll Place that Mary Louisa Baugh (Ludie) placed there. For a full explanation, see Wolff, *Ledgers of History*, and chapter 2 of this text.

5. Various in-person conversations with Francisco III, one of which occurred on August 7, 2021.

6. Francisco III, correspondence, September 16, 2023.

7. Walter John Leak's brother, Frank Leak, fought in the Civil War. Walter John was a private in the CSA army, Company G, Third Mississippi Cavalry.

8. Quoted in Gary Gravely, "A Multiverse of Narratives: Possible Worlds Theory and Authorship from the Lone Artist to Corporate Authors," PhD diss., Middle Tennessee State University, August 2015, 51.

9. In *Absalom, Absalom!* even Amelia McCarroll Leak's date of death—1909—resonates with Quentin's hearing Rosa's story: "this September afternoon in 1909" (11). In their dorm room at Harvard, Shreve hands Quentin a letter from his father dated January 10, 1910, in which he reported that Miss Rosa had died the day before. Amelia McCarroll Leak died on Halloween 1909. The end of October 1909 is not far from January 1910, and it may have taken a while for Quentin's father to write to him at Harvard. That Rosa's death date is so similar to Amelia's deserves consideration as a source link. (See endnote 25 for explanation

of the date revision from 1910 to 1909 of Miss Rosa's last action from the first edition of the novel to Noel Polk's corrected edition. See photo of Sallie McCarroll's will at educational-consulting.services/Faulkner.)

10. The timing of Amelia's return home is somewhat uncertain, but she returned home from the plantation after the deaths of both her husband and mother in 1872 and the death of her son in March 1873, and before the death of her father in December of that year. McCarroll family lore emphasizes that Amelia came home with only her daughter, Betsy, which suggests that at the time of her decision to return home, both her husband and son were deceased. Francisco III recalls the family understanding that his grandmother Betsy was four years old when she and Amelia returned to Holly Springs. (Francisco III, correspondence, December 13, 2018.)

11. Francisco III, telephone communication, December 16, 2019.

12. Francisco III recalls hearing from his father that when Amelia returned home with only her girl child, Betsy, and the plantation ledger books known as the *Leak Diary*, Amelia thought these farm ledgers would provide documentary evidence of what assets belonged to Walter John, and as the widow of Walter John Leak, some of that money was due her. Adequate funds, however, were not forthcoming, and after the war, to help ends meet, she became a seamstress (Wolff, *Ledgers of History*, 140). Francisco III provides additional details in section IV of "Ludie's Story," on pp. 84–85.

13. Wolff, *Ledgers of History*, 110.

14. Michael Millgate, *Faulkner's Place* (University of Georgia Press, 2008), 6.

15. Donald Kartiganer, "Quentin Compson and Faulkner's Drama of the Generations," in *Critical Essays on William Faulkner: The Compson Family*, ed. Arthur Kinney (G. K. Hall, 1982), 399.

16. Kartiganer, "Modernism as Gesture: Faulkner's Missing Facts, Culture, Theory, and Critique," *Renaissance and Modern Studies, Faulkner and Modernism* 41 (1998): 15.

17. Upon conferring with a colleague about what Faulkner could have heard about this family that would constitute an insult, Dr. Marie Nitschke, retired librarian, Robert W. Woodruff Library, Emory University, said, "Maybe it was a lawsuit." She was correct. See appendix 4-A for a timeline regarding these legal cases.

18. "Jno McCarroll Admin Vs. W. J. Leak, Int" [Intestate], Case File No. 84, Chancery Court, Benton County, Ashland, Mississippi.

19. Francisco III, telephone communication, December 7, 2018.

20. Francisco III, telephone communication, August 4, 2024.

21. Dean Faulkner Wells, *Every Day by the Sun: A Memoir of the Faulkners of Mississippi* (Broadway Paperbacks, 2011), 37.

22. See Susan Snell, *Phil Stone of Oxford: A Vicarious Life* (University of Georgia Press, 1991), for some examples of these entanglements, e.g., 193; see also Williamson and Wells for additional examples. Jay Watson, in *Forensic Fictions*, presents a thorough and cogent account of the numerous lawyers in Faulkner's family, familiarity with the law environment in which he grew up, and how those factors emerge in his oeuvre. Michael Millgate lists the "several lawyers in [Faulkner's] family—a great-grandfather, a grandfather, an uncle, and a first cousin," and he notes too the amount of time Faulkner spent with his

lawyer friend Phil Stone (Millgate, *Faulkner's Place*, 96). Also Millgate quotes Faulkner's advice to prospective writers: "Read a lot, and of everything—fiction, biography, history, law. I read all the law and medical books of my father and grandfather" (Millgate, *Faulkner's Place*, 16).

23. See, for example, Jackson J. Benson, "Quentin Compson: Self-Portrait of a Young Artist's Emotions," in *Twentieth-Century Literature* 17, no. 3 (July 1971): 143–59.

24. Millgate, *Faulkner's Place*, 42.

25. See dates pertaining to Rosa's last actions and death in Noel Polk's corrected text of *Absalom, Absalom!* in comparison with incongruous dates in the first edition of the novel. See p. 381 of the first edition and p. 474 of William Faulkner, *Absalom, Absalom! The Corrected Text* (Noel Polk, ed. Vintage International, Vintage Books, 1987). Although Rosa's actions in the first edition appear to be 1910, as listed in the chronology, regarding her finding Henry, a conflict in dates emerges when considering Rosa's activities in late 1910. In September 1910, Rosa and Quentin find Henry hidden in the house, and in December 1910, she goes out to "fetch Henry to town." Mr. Compson's letter to Quentin at Harvard states that Rosa "died yesterday," and the letter is dated January 1910. Rosa could not have died in January 1910, if she found Henry in the house in September of 1910 and goes to "fetch Henry to town" December 1910. Noel Polk's correction to 1909 for Rosa's actions with Henry, as listed in the chronology, accommodates for this discrepancy and is more logical, and then the letter from Mr. Compson to Quentin follows regarding the news of her death "yesterday" in January 1910 and is closer to Amelia's death date.

26. Francisco III, telephone communication, December 13, 2018.

27. Joseph Blotner, *Faulkner, One-Volume Ed.* (Random House, 1984), 23.

28. Blotner, *Faulkner, One-Volume Ed.*, 23. See also Robert Coughlan, *The Private World of William Faulkner* (Harper & Brothers, 1954), 43.

29. Quoted in Blotner, *One-Volume Ed.*, 23; original in Murry C. Falkner, *The Faulkners of Mississippi: A Memoir* (Louisiana State University Press, 1967).

30. Millgate, *Faulkner's Place*, 5.

31. See also Francisco III, correspondence, December 13, 2018. Email and in-person communication. Also telephone communication, August 7, 2010.

32. Frederick L. Gwynn and Joseph Blotner, eds., *Faulkner in the University* (University of Virginia Press, 1995), 253–54.

33. Francisco III, telephone communication, August 5, 2018.

34. US Census: Rosa Barton Tyler head of family, 67 (thus, born around 1843); Roger Barton Tyler son, age 28 (thus, born around 1882); Jane McCrosky Tyler, daughter-in-law, age 23 (thus, born around 1887). Roger Barton Tyler, father: Fisher A. Tyler born 1812, died, Holly Springs, MS, 1902; mother: Rosana Barton Tyler born July 5, 1841, MS, died May 1937 Austin, Texas. Per death certificate she is buried at Holly Springs, MS.

Source Citation: Year, 1910; Census, Place: Holly Springs, Marshall, Mississippi; Page: 9A; Enumeration District: 0042; Source Information: Ancestry.com and www.findwww.findagrave.com/memorial/69570133.

35. Francisco III, email correspondence, October 26, 2023.

36. Francisco III, email correspondence, October 26, 2023.

37. The Rosa Letters, McCarroll Place Papers.

38. "Austin, July 15, 1883," letter regarding Rosa; August 1, 1874, "My dear Papa," letter regarding Rosa in the McCarroll Place Papers.

39. The Rosa Letters, McCarroll Place Papers.

40. The Rosa Letters, McCarroll Place Papers.

41. Molly Caldwell Crosby, *The American Plague: The Untold Story of the Yellow Fever Epidemic That Shaped Our History* (Berkley Publishing Group, Penguin Group, 2006), 88.

42. Crosby, *American Plague*, 57.

43. Crosby, *American Plague*, 87.

44. Robert Milton Winter, *Shadow of a Mighty Rock: A Social and Cultural History of Presbyterianism in Marshall County, Mississippi* (Providence House, 1997), 247. See also "Dr Charles Bonner," Find a Grave, www.findagrave.com/memorial/83456949/charles-bonner.

45. NB: In the "Chronology" section in the first edition, Faulkner noted that Judith and Charles E. St. V. Bon died of smallpox (*Absalom* 381). Noel Polk's corrected edition based on the holograph and galley manuscript alters their causes of death to yellow fever (*Absalom, Absalom! The Corrected Text*, Vintage International, Vintage Books, 1987), 474.

46. See Sally Wolff, "'Everybody Knew': *Ledgers of History*: Questions and Answers," *South Atlantic Review* 81, no. 4 (Winter 2016): 81, for further analysis of Charles Bon and Dr. Charles Bonner.

47. Winter, *Shadow of a Mighty Rock*, 247.

48. "Table 2. Reported Yellow Fever Cases and Deaths in Mississippi in 1878," in Deanne Stephens Nuwer, *Plague among the Magnolias: The 1878 Yellow Fever Epidemic in Mississippi* (University of Alabama Press, 2009), 117–18.

49. Joel Williamson, *William Faulkner and Southern History* (Oxford University Press, 1993), 90. See also 134.

BIBLIOGRAPHY

"1858 Greek Revival—Holly Springs, MS." *Old House Dreams*. July 25, 2022. www.oldhousedreams.com/2016/05/13/1858-greek-revival-holly-springs-ms/.

"About the Old Guard." Joint Task Force-National Capital Region and the US Army Military District of Washington. jtfncr.mdw.army.mil/oldguard/.

Atkinson, Matt. "Van Dorn's Raid." *The Mississippi Encyclopedia*, ed. Ted Ownby, Charles Reagan Wilson, et al. University Press of Mississippi, 2017, 1280–81. Also available at *The Mississippi Encyclopedia*, Center for Study of Southern Culture, April 15, 2018, mississippiencyclopedia.org/entries/van-dorns-raid/.

Backman, Melvin. *Faulkner: The Major Years, a Critical Study*. Indiana University Press, 1966.

Baum, Jack. "Holly Springs: The Architecture of a Small Town." Unpublished paper, School of Architecture, University of Tennessee, 1978. Available at the University of Mississippi Library archives.

Behind the Big House. www.behindthebighouse.org/.

Benson, Jackson J. "Quentin Compson: Self-Portrait of a Young Artist's Emotions." *Twentieth-Century Literature* 17, no. 3 (July 1971): 143–59.

Bezzerides, A. I. *William Faulkner, a Life on Paper*. University Press of Mississippi, 1980.

Blotner, Joseph. *Faulkner: A Biography*. 2 vols. Random House, 1974.

Blotner, Joseph. *Faulkner: A Biography: One-Volume Edition*. Random House, 1984.

Blotner, Joseph. "William Faulkner Seminar." *Studies in English* 14, no. 1 (1976), egrove.olemiss.edu/ms_studies_eng/vol14/iss1/6.

"A Brief History of Holly Springs." City of Holly Springs, hollyspringsms.gov/history-of-holly-springs/.

"A Brief History of Holly Springs: 1851–1860." City of Holly Springs, hollyspringsms.gov/history-of-holly-springs/.

Britannica, Editors of Encyclopaedia. "Holly Springs." *Encyclopedia Britannica*. May 29, 2020. www.britannica.com/place/Holly-Springs.

Carothers, James B., and Kimma Jean Sheldon. "Comprehending Faulkner's Humor." *Mississippi Quarterly* 60, no. 3, Special issue on William Faulkner (Summer 2007): 437–60. www.jstor.org/stable/26467073.

Chernow, Ron. *Grant*. Penguin Books, 2017.

Cochran, Rita Binion. "First Pilgrimage—a Big Success." *Pilgrimage Edition*, special issue of *South Reporter* (Holly Springs, MS), October 22, 1936, 8–9.

"Contextualization at University of Mississippi: Memorials and Contextualization." Library Guides at University of Mississippi Libraries, guides.lib.olemiss.edu/contextualization/memorials.

Coughlan, Robert. *The Private World of William Faulkner*. Harper & Brothers, 1954.

Crocker, Mary Wallace. *Historic Architecture in Mississippi*. University Press of Mississippi, 1973.

Crosby, Molly Caldwell. *The American Plague: The Untold Story of the Yellow Fever Epidemic That Shaped Our History*. Berkley Publishing Group, Penguin Group, 2006.

Dancy, Mrs. Lucius (Nell). "Miss Perle Strickland Becomes Bride of Gerard Badow." *South Reporter* (Holly Springs, MS), December 2, 1926, 1, 4.

Doyle, Don. *Faulkner's County: The Historical Roots of Yoknapatawpha*. University of North Carolina Press, 2001.

Falkner, Murry C. *The Falkners of Mississippi*. Louisiana State University Press, March 1, 1999.

Fant, Joseph L. III, and Robert Ashley, eds. *Faulkner at West Point*. Random House, 1964.

Fargnoli, A. Nicholas, and Michael Golay. *William Faulkner A to Z: The Essential Reference to His Life and Work*. Facts on File, 2001.

Faulkner, John. *My Brother Bill*. Hill Street Press, 1998.

Faulkner, William. *Absalom, Absalom!* Random House, 1936.

Faulkner, William. *As I Lay Dying*. Jonathan Cape and Harrison Smith, 1930.

Faulkner, William. *The Collected Stories of William Faulkner*. Random House, 1950.

Faulkner, William. *Faulkner at Nagano*. Edited by Robert A. Jelliffe. Kenkyusha, 1966.

Faulkner, William. *Go Down, Moses and Other Stories*. Random House, 1942.

Faulkner, William. *Intruder in the Dust*. Random House, 1948.

Faulkner, William. *Light in August*. Harrison Smith and Robert Haas, 1932.

Faulkner, William. *The Mansion*. Random House, 1959.

Faulkner, William. *The Reivers*. Random House, 1962.

Faulkner, William. *Requiem for a Nun*. Random House, 1951.

Faulkner, William. *Sanctuary*. First Vintage International Edition, December 1993.

Faulkner, William. *Sartoris*. Harcourt Brace, 1929.

Faulkner, William. *Selected Letters*. Edited by Joseph Blotner. Vintage Books, 1978.

Faulkner, William. *The Sound and the Fury: An Authoritative Text, Backgrounds and Contexts, Criticism*. 2nd ed. Edited by David Minter. Norton, 1994.

Faulkner, William. *The Sound and the Fury: An Authoritative Text, Backgrounds and Contexts, Criticism*. 3rd ed. Edited by Michael Gorra. Norton, 2014.

Faulkner, William. *The Town*. Random House, 1957.

Find a Grave, database and images, www.findagrave.com.

Foote, Shelby. *The Civil War: A Narrative: Fredericksburg to Meridian*. Vol. 2. Random House, 1963.

"Garden Pilgrimage to Historical Sites." Holly Springs Garden Club. April 22–26, 1939. Brochure. digitalcommons.memphis.edu/speccoll-pub-us/11.

Gravely, Gary. *A Multiverse of Narratives: Possible Worlds Theory and Authorship from the Lone Artist to Corporate Authors*. PhD diss., Middle Tennessee State University, August 2015.

Gwynn, Frederick L., and Joseph Blotner, eds. *Faulkner in the University*. University of Virginia Press, 1995.

Hawkins, E. O. Jr. "Jane Cook and Cecilia Farmer." *Mississippi Quarterly* 18, no. 4 (Fall 1965): 248–51.
Haynes, Jayne Isbell. "Another Source for Faulkner's Inscribed Window Panes." *Mississippi Quarterly* 39, no. 3 (Summer 1986): 365–67, www.jstor.org/stable/26474977.
"Hillcrest Cemetery." Wikipedia, Wikimedia Foundation. September 20, 2023. en.wikipedia.org/wiki/Hillcrest_Cemetery.
Hines, Thomas S. W. *William Faulkner and the Tangible Past: The Architecture of Yoknapatawpha*. University of California Press, 1977.
"Historic Resources of Holly Springs." National Register of Historic Places Inventory— Nomination, United States Department of the Interior National Park Service. www.apps.mdah.ms.gov/t_nom/Historic%20Resources%20of%20Holly%20Springs.pdf.
"History: Over 154 Years of Quality Education." Rust College. www.rustcollege.edu/about-rust-college/history/.
Howell, Elmo. "A Note on Faulkner's Presbyterian Novel." *Papers on Language and Literature* 2, no. 2 (Spring 1966): 182–87.
Johnson, Robert L. "William Faulkner, Calvinism and the Presbyterians." *Journal of Presbyterian History (1962–1985)* 57, no. 1 (Spring 1979): 66–81. www.jstor.org/stable/23327941.
Kartiganer, Donald. "Faulkner's Missing Facts." *Renaissance and Modern Studies: Faulkner and Modernism* 41 (1998): 13–28.
Kartiganer, Donald. *The Fragile Thread: The Meaning of Form in Faulkner's Novels*. University of Massachusetts Press, 1979.
Kartiganer, Donald. "Quentin Compson and Faulkner's Drama of the Generations. In *Critical Essays on William Faulkner: The Compson Family*, ed. Arthur Kinney, 381–401. G. K. Hall, 1982.
Kazek, Kelly. "The Tragic Tale of William Faulkner's Forgotten Daughter, Alabama Faulkner." Alabama.com. September 25, 2015. www.al.com/entertainment/2015/09/the_tragic_tale_of_william_fau.html.
Knecht, Phillip. "Athenia (1858)." Hill Country History. October 24, 2015. hillcountryhistory.org/2015/10/24/holly-springs-athenia-1858/.
Knecht, Phillip. "Hill Crest Cemetery (1845)." Hill Country History. March 29, 2016. hillcountryhistory.org/2016/03/29/holly-springs-hill-crest-cemetery-1845/.
Long, Alice, and Mark L. Ridge. *Images of America: Holly Springs*. Arcadia, 2006.
Lowe, John. *Bridging Southern Cultures: An Interdisciplinary Approach*. Louisiana State University Press, 2005.
Lyon, Ralph. "The Early Years of the Livingston Female Academy." *Alabama Historical Quarterly* 37, no. 3 June (1975): 195–205.
McAlexander, Hubert, ed. *From the Chickasaw Cession to Yoknapatawpha: Historical and Literary Essays on North Mississippi*. Nautilus, 2017.
McAlexander, Hubert. *A Southern Tapestry: Marshall County, Mississippi, 1835–2000*. Donning, 2000.
McIntire, Carl. "Mount Holly History." *Clarion-Ledger* (Jackson, MS), January 14, 1973, F3.
Millgate, Michael. *Faulkner's Place*. University of Georgia Press, 2008.
Mirando, Lillian. "State's 50th Pilgrimage Season Offers More than Ever," *Clarion-Ledger, Jackson Daily News*, March 6, 1982, 14A.

Mississippi Encyclopedia Staff. "Marshall County." *The Mississippi Encyclopedia*, edited by Ted Ownby and Charles Reagan Wilson, et al. University Press of Mississippi, 2017, 772–74. Also available at *Mississippi Encyclopedia*, Center for Study of Southern Culture, April 14, 2018, mississippiencyclopedia.org/entries/marshall-county/.

Mitchell, Bobby. "Franklin Female College." *Heritage News: A Publication of the Marshall County, Mississippi, Genealogical and Historical Society* 24, no. 1 (March 2018): 2–3.

Mitchell, Bobby. "Mississippi Synodical College." *Heritage News: A Publication of the Marshall County, Mississippi, Genealogical and Historical Society* 22, no. 1 (March 2016): 6–7.

Mitchell, Bobby. "Some Early History of Marshall County." The MSGenWeb Project. www.msgw.org/marshall/locales/mchist.php.

Montes, Catalina. "'Listen, Stranger: This Was Myself; This Was I': *Requiem for a Nun*." In *Faulkner and History*, ed. Javier Coy and Michel Gresset, 197–212. Ediciones Universidad de Salamanca, 1986.

Moreland, George M. "Holly Springs to Turn Back Hands of the Clock at Centennial Celebration." *Commercial Appeal* (Memphis, TN), October 4, 1936, III-3.

"Mount Holly Burns." The Lakeport Plantation. Arkansas State University. June 17, 2015. lakeport.astate.edu/2015/06/17/mount-holly-burns/.

Nuwer, Deanne Stephens. *Plague among the Magnolias: The 1878 Yellow Fever Epidemic in Mississippi*. University of Alabama Press, 2009.

Parini, Jay. *One Matchless Time: A Life of William Faulkner*. HarperCollins, 2004.

Phillips, Ed. "Delta Writers Featured in TV Program." *Clarksdale Press Register* (Clarksdale, MS), Nov. 8–9, 1975, 5A.

Polk, Noel. *Faulkner's Requiem for a Nun: A Critical Study*. Indiana University Press, 1981.

Polk, Noel. "Faulkner's 'The Jail' and the Meaning of Cecilia Farmer." *Mississippi Quarterly* 25, no. 3 (Summer 1972): 305–25.

Polk, Noel, ed. *Absalom, Absalom! The Corrected Text*. Vintage International, Vintage Books, a Division of Random House, 1987.

Polk, Noel, ed. *New Essays on The Sound and the Fury* Cambridge: Cambridge University Press), 1993.

"Programs." Behind the Big House. www.behindthebighouse.org/programs/behind-the-big-house-holly-springs-ms/.

Pruitt, Olga Reed. *It Happened Here: True Stories of Holly Springs*. South Reporter Printing Company, 1950.

Rollyson, Carl. *The Life of William Faulkner: The Past Is Never Dead, 1897–1934*. Vol. I. University of Virginia Press, 2020.

Runyan, Harry. *A Faulkner Glossary*. Citadel Press, 1964.

Scott, Anne Firor. *Making the Invisible Woman Visible*. University of Illinois Press, 1984.

"Shelby Foote on Faulkner." C-SPAN. May 10, 2002. www.c-span.org/video/?170042-1/shelby-foote-faulkner.

Smith, Chesley Thorne. *Childhood in Holly Springs: A Memoir*. Thomas-Berryhill Press, 1996.

Snell, Susan. *Phil Stone of Oxford: A Vicarious Life*. University of Georgia Press, 1991.

Statement of the Disposition of Some of the Bodies of Deceased Union Soldiers and Prisoners of War Whose Remains Have Been Removed to National Cemeteries in the Southern and

Western States. United States: U.S. Government Printing Office, 1868. www.google.com/books/edition/Statement_of_the_Disposition_of_Some_of/s4xIAQAAMAAJ.

Stein, Jean. "The Art of Fiction XII: William Faulkner." *Paris Review*, no. 12 (Spring 1956): 28–52.

Stewart, George G. *Yoknapatawpha, Images and Voices: A Photographic Study of Faulkner's County.* University of South Carolina Press, 2009.

Sundquist, Eric. *Faulkner: The House Divided.* Johns Hopkins University Press, 1983; reprint 1985.

Sykes, John. "Faulkner, Calvinism, and Religion." *Journal of Presbyterian History (1997–)* 75, no. 1 (1997): 43–53. www.jstor.org/stable/23335441.

Tate, Sarah Doxey. "A Talk on Faulkner and the Hindman/Doxey Family." Library talk at the Marshall County Library, Holly Springs, Mississippi, Fall 2003.

Taylor, Herman E. *Faulkner's Oxford.* Rutledge Hill Press, 1990.

US Federal Census, National Archives and Records Administration, accessed on Ancestry Library database.

Watson, Jay. *Forensic Fictions: The Lawyer Figure in Faulkner.* University of Georgia Press, 1995.

Weinstein, Philip. *Becoming Faulkner.* Oxford University Press, 2010.

Wells, Dean Faulkner. *Every Day by the Sun: A Memoir of the Faulkners of Mississippi.* Broadway Paperbacks, 2011.

Wells, Dean Faulkner. *The Ghosts of Rowan Oak: William Faulkner's Ghost Stories for Children.* Yoknapatawpha Press, 1980.

"William Faulkner Banquet Speech." NobelPrize.org, December 10, 1950. www.nobelprize.org/prizes/literature/1949/faulkner/speech/.

Williams, Joan. "Twenty Will Not Come Again." *The Atlantic*, May 1980, 58–65. www.theatlantic.com/magazine/archive/1980/05/twenty-will-not-come-again/667627/.

Williamson, Joel. *William Faulkner and Southern History.* Oxford University Press, 1993.

Winter, Rev. Robert Milton. *Civil War Women: The Diaries of Belle Strickland and Cora Harris Watson: Holly Springs, Mississippi July 25, 1864–June 22, 1868.* Thomas-Berryhill Press, 2001.

Winter, Rev. Robert Milton. *Shadow of a Mighty Rock: A Social and Cultural History of Presbyterianism in Marshall County, Mississippi.* Providence House, 1997.

Wiseman, Keith Gore. "Down by the Station." *Invitation Oxford*, March 2018, 36–38. issuu.com/invoxford/docs/invox_mar2018_final.

Wolff, Sally. "'Everybody Knew': *Ledgers of History*: Questions and Answers." *South Atlantic Review* 81, no. 4 (Winter 2016): 66–88.

Wolff, Sally. *Ledgers of History: William Faulkner: An Almost Forgotten Friendship and an Antebellum Plantation Diary.* Louisiana State University Press, 2010.

Wolff, Sally. *Talking about William Faulkner.* Louisiana State University Press, 1996.

INDEX

Page numbers in *italics* indicate figures and tables.

abomination, 52–55
Absalom, Absalom! (Faulkner), 7, 41–45, 60, 62, 98, 100, 127, 165n9, 167n25; features of, in Faulkner's own home, 136; hidden truth as theme in, 137; McCarroll sisters and, 130–38, *138*; office in, 128–29
Airliewood, also known as Coxe Place and Coxe-Dean Place (Holly Springs, MS), 11, 42, 91
Altman, Robert, 11
Ammadele (Oxford, MS), 57
arsenic, 34–36, 67
As I Lay Dying (Faulkner), 49, 52, *61*, 62
Athenia, also known as Oakleigh and Clapp-West-Fant House (Holly Springs, MS), 42. *See also* Oakleigh
Attkisson, Frances, 111
augur/ogre, 43–44
Autry, Micajah, 14

back porches, *117*, 118, 123–25
back staircase, 118, 123–25
Backman, Melvin, 46
Backus, Joseph M., *117*. *See also* Stewart, George R.
Badow, Gerard, 34–36, 59, 66–68, 102–9, *104*, *108*, 114–16, 119
Badow, Perle Strickland, 7, 23, 29, 34–36, 66–68, 100–110, *101*, *102*, 113–16, 140
balancing the books, metaphor of, 45
Barber & Kluttz (Knoxville, TN), 33

Baugh, Emily, 81, 84
Baugh, Ludie. *See* Booth, Mary Louisa Baugh (Ludie)
Baugh, Richard, 79, 80, 81–84
Baum, Jack, 33
"Bear, The" (Faulkner), 49
"Bear Hunt, A" (Faulkner), *61*
"Behind the Big House," 11–12, 91
Benton, Samuel, 13
"Beyond" (Faulkner), *62*
Birdsong, Aaron, 59
Bitzer (Reverend George) Papers, 48, 51
Bitzer, George L., 20, 26, 47–52, 55, 106
Bitzer, Mary (Mary Bitzer Doxey, wife of Hindman Doxey Sr.), 25, 152n41, 162n19
Bitzer, Mrs. George (Mamie Rolston), 26
Bitzer, Ruth. *See* Francisco, Ruth Bitzer
blasphemy, 50, 52, 68–69
Blotner, Joseph, 4, 6, 17, 22–23, 49, 126, 138–39, 161n5
Boling, Spires, 14, 33
Bonner, Charles, *60*, 144
Bonner, Sherwood. *See* McDowell, Katharine Sherwood Bonner
Bonner-Belk House, also known as Cedarhurst (Holly Springs, MS), 91
Booth, John (Henry), 79–80, 82, 83, 8, 85, 89
Booth, Mary Louisa Baugh (Ludie), 7, 29, 73–74, 78–89, 92–96, 98–99
bootleggers, 5–6, 17, 27–28, 56
Box Hill (Holly Springs, MS), 91

brick walkways, 117, 120–21
Brooks, Cleanth, 28
Brown, Margaret, 20
Buchanan, Minor, 30–31
Buchanan, Mrs. George, 90–91
Burton, Mary Malvina Shields, 46
Burton family, 45–46, 59
Burton Place, also known as Fleur de Lys (Holly Springs, MS), 11, 46
Bussey, Miss, 24
Butler (Falkner), Maud. *See* Falkner, Maud (Butler)

Callicutt, Jane, 94, 95
Carothers, J. B., 79
Caruthers, Joseph, 60
Carter, Chelius, 11–12
Cary, Nell, 24
Cather, Willa, 19
"Centaur in Brass" (Faulkner), 60
Chandler, Edwin, 109
Chandler House. *See* Thompson-Chandler House
Chernow, Ron, 55–56
Chickasaw Bluffs, 10
Chickasaw people, 10, 70, 72–73
Cho Cho (Victoria Franklin Fielden, stepdaughter of William Faulkner), 6, 17, 58
Civil War soldiers, buried together, 36–39
Civil War Women (Winter), 106
Clapp, Jeremiah Watkins, 7, 41–42, 60
Clapp-West-Fant House, also known as Athenia and Oakleigh (Holly Springs, MS), 42. *See also* Oakleigh
Clark, Col., 141
Clark, Kate Freeman, 11, 13–14, 141
Clark, Mary B., 141–42
Clark, Rosa, 140–42, 145
Clark family, 141
Cochran, Dave, 18
Cochran, Rita, wife of Vadah Cochran, 90, 91
Cochran, Vadah, 19
Cochran House (Holly Springs, MS), 91
Colhoun, Garrie, 20

Collins, Carvel, 6, 31, 41, 148n9
Compson House and grounds, similarity of, to McCarroll Place and Strickland Place, 117–25
Confederate Cemetery (University of Mississippi, Oxford, MS), 38
Cook, Jane T., 86–87, 98
Cookie's Fortune (dir. Altman), 11
Cook-Tate House (Oxford, MS), 87
Corinth National Cemetery (Corinth, MS), 38
"Courtship, A" (Faulkner), 60
Coxe-Dean Place. *See* Airliewood
Craft, Nina, 90–91
"Crevasse" (Faulkner), 62
Crocker, Mary Wallace, 33
Crosby, John W., 37
Crosby, Molly Caldwell, 144
Crump Place (Holly Springs, MS), 91
Crusade for Justice (Wells), 14

Daniel, Motee, 28
Diehl, Charles Edward, 51
Depot, the (Holly Springs, MS), 7, 8, 39–41; Café, 6, 17, 40; Hotel, 39–40, 41; Ludie watching soldiers march to, 73, 79, 82; Union supplies at, 12, 56; Van Dorn's raid, 7–8, 12, 55–56
devil imagery, 52–55
Diary of Francis Terry Leak (Leak Diary), 3–4, 18, 45, 64–70, 84, 103, 106, 121, 127–28, 130, 131, 139, 147n2, 166n12
Dos Passos, John, 19
Doxey, Helen. *See* Tyson, Helen Doxey
Doxey, Hindman, Jr., 5, 25–26, 27
Doxey, Hindman, Sr., 5, 24–25, 26–27, 106
Doxey, Natalie, 14, 91
Doxey, Sarah. *See* Tate, Sarah Doxey
Doxey, Wall, 13–14, 25, 60. *See also* Wall Doxey State Park
Doyle, Don, 3, 23, 147n2
"Dry September" (Faulkner), 61
Dunlap, Thornwell, 23

Eco, Umberto, 131

Eddins, Mary, 81
Eggleston, Jenifer, 11–12
Elliott, Jack D., Jr., 64, 70–71, 72, 73, 75–77, 158n19

Fable, A (Faulkner), 60
Falconer, Kinloch, 13
Falkner, Alabama (Alabama Leroy Falkner McLean; Aunt Bama), 5, 21–22, *21*
Falkner, Emeline, 46
Falkner, Fannie, 46
Falkner, Holland Pearce, 22
Falkner, John Wesley Thompson, 5, 23–24
Falkner, Maud (Butler), 5–6, 22, 23, 57
Falkner, William Clark (the Old Colonel), 20–21, 46, 138
Falkner family, visiting Holly Springs, 5–6, 17, 20–24
Fant, L. G., Jr., 6
Fant, Nettie. *See* Thompson, Nettie Fant
Faragher, Scott, 32
Fargnoli, Nicholas, 59
Faulkner, Alabama (infant), 21
Faulkner, James M. (Jimmy), 5, 21, 49, 58–59
Faulkner, Lucille (Dolly) Ramey, 5, 17, *24*, 25
Faulkner, Estelle Oldham, 18–19, 21, 57, 106–7, 116
Faulkner, Murry Charles (Jack), 49, 139
Faulkner, John, 5, 17, 23, 24, 25, 106, 116, 147n4
Faulkner, John Wesley Thompson, 22
Faulkner, William: animosity toward Badow, 35, 36, 103, 105; on an artist fixing motion, 78, 89–90; blasphemy of, 50, 68–69; Boy Scout troop and, 6, 17, 19, 41; career choice of, and Amelia McCarroll Leak, 138–39; Christian faith of, 49; churchgoing by, 49; creating own style of historical fiction, 125; disappearing from Oxford, 6; dominating southern literary tradition, 4; final trip of, to Byhalia, MS, 28; Francisco family, Faulkner visiting, 20–22, 43, 50, 55, 69, 76, 112, 113, 114, 117, 119, 120–21, 123, 124, 127–28; *Hamlet*, Faulkner's possible allusion to, 44; host and stranger, Faulkner's depiction of, 29, 92–96, 99; and McCarroll sisters' stories, 130–37; past and present intermingling in works of, 85, 92–93; on period costumers at Pilgrimage, 91, 96–98; Presbyterianism, Faulkner's negative view of, 46–55; Royal Canadian Air Force (RCAF), officer in, 41; seeking to know the past, 28; self-portrait (autobiographical), 8, 29, 43–44, 78, 87–90, 92–93, 99, 121, 129, 137; sense of self-disgust, 44; sourcing real-life people for characters' names, 29, 30, 37–38, 40, 42, 45–46, 58–63, 115, 140–42; suspiciousness toward Germans, 105, 115–16; on time as boundless continuum, 93; University of Mississippi, with Hindman Doxey Sr. together at, 26–27; reading the Leak ledgers, 45, 65–66, 139 (see also *Diary of Francis Terry Leak*); viewing Ludie's window, 73–74, 85–88, 93–95, 99. *See also* titles of individual works
Faulkner at Nagano (ed. Jelliffe), 30
Faulkner family: changing name spelling from Falkner, 21, 147n4; visiting Holly Springs (*see* Falkner family, visiting Holly Springs)
Faulkner Glossary, A (Runyan), 59
Fearn, Anne Walter, 18–19
Featherston, Elise, 23
Featherston, Winfield S., 13
Featherston Place (Holly Springs, MS), 91
female academies, 57, 156n130; Franklin Female College (Holly Springs, MS), 15, 149n48; Holly Springs Female Collegiate Institute, 15; Industrial Institute and College for the Education of White Girls of Mississippi (Mississippi University for Women), 57; Livingston Female Academy, 57, 157n130; Mary Baldwin College (Staunton, VA), 57; Mississippi Synodical College (Holly Springs, MS), 6, 15, 17, 41, 58; Semple School, 113, 114

Fenelon Hall (Holly Springs, MS). *See* Mississippi Synodical College
Finley, Augusta, 23
fire, as commonality between character and real-life model, 110
First Presbyterian Church of Holly Springs, 47, 162n19
Fleur de Lys (Holly Springs, MS), 46. *See also* Burton Place
Foote, Shelby, 56–57
Fort-Daniels House, also known as Craft House (Holly Springs, MS), 11
Francisco, Anne Salyerds, 69, 118
Francisco, Betsy Leak, 22, 65, 66, 84, 101, 113, 123, 124, 132, 137, 161nn2–4, 166n10, 166n12
Francisco, Edgar Wiggin, Jr., 5–6, 8, 18, 29, 35, 43, 48, 49, 51, 64, 72–73, 74–76, 80, 81, 84, 86, 87, 90, 94, 102, 103, 106, 109, 112, 119, 120, 124, 129, 130; Faulkner's relationship with, 24–27, 50, 85, 94, 123; as host at Pilgrimage, 29, 92–96, 99; and McCarroll sisters' stories, 132–37; photograph taken by, 97, 111, 118; secret of, 65–70; stories about Ruth LeGrand Strickland Weir, 113–15 (see also *Sound and the Fury, The*: real-life antecedents for characters in)
Francisco, Edgar Wiggin, Sr., 4, 55, 75–76
Francisco, Edgar Wiggin, III, 3, 5, 12, 18, 22, 24–26, 27, 33, 34–36, 43, 44, 47, 48, 50, 51, 55, 63, 80, 87, 90, 94, 95, 97, 101–3, 109–10, 113–5, 116, *118*, 119, *120*, 121, 123–25, 130, 132, 133, 134, 136, 138, 141, 145; on the McCarroll Place office, 128–29; rebutting Elliott's "Confabulations of History," 64–77; retelling Ludie's story, 80–85; stories about Ruth LeGrand Strickland Weir, 113–15 (see also *Sound and the Fury, The*: real-life antecedents for characters in)
Francisco, Ruth Bitzer (Mrs. Edgar Jr.), 47, 55, 48, 66, 72–73, 76, 90–91, 97, *118*, 124, 129, 130; and dislike of Faulkner, 20, 49–50, 51, 64–65, 68–69, 74; first meeting with Faulkner, 74–75; on period costumers at Pilgrimage, 96–98; photograph taken by, 26, 102, 120; secret of, 68–70
Francisco family, 21, 24–26, 56, 88, 100, 125, 140, 141; Faulkner visiting, 20–22, 43, 50, 55, 69, 76, 112, 113, 114, 117, 119, 120–21, 124, 127–28; secrets of, 64–70
Franklin, Cornell, 107
Franklin Female College (Holly Springs, MS), 15, 149n48
Freedmen's Aid Society of the Northern Methodist Episcopal Church, 14, 45–46
Freeman Place (Holly Springs, MS), 91
From the Chickasaw Cession to Yoknapatawpha (McAlexander), 109, 163n30

Gable, Clark, 19
Germans, Faulkner's suspiciousness toward, 105, 115–16
Gholson, Miss, 5, 21–22
Gholson, Mrs. S. C., Jr., 21
Gholson family, 21–22
Gibson, as common southern name, 29
Gibson, Luella, 29, 101, 109, 113, 115
Go Down, Moses (Faulkner), 4, 45, 59, *60*, 61, 69, 100, 127, 147n2
Golay, Michael, 59
Govan, Daniel, 13
Grant, Mrs. Ulysses S., 12–13, 18
Grant, Ulysses S., 7, 12, 18, 55–56, 63, 83
Greer, A. Q., 129
Grey Gables (Holly Springs, MS), 7, 11, 31–34, *32*, 91

"Hair" (Faulkner), *61*, 62
Hale, Dr., 33
ham, thinly sliced, 39–41
Hamer, W. T., 143
Hamlet, The (Faulkner), *61*
Handy, W. C., 6
Harris, Gladys, 90–91
Harrison, James L., 63
Hawkins, E. O., 95
Hawks, Howard, 19

Hawthorne, Nathaniel, 53
Haynes, Jane Isbell, 86–87, 158n15
Hemingway, Ernest, 19
hidden truth, finding of, as theme in *Absalom, Absalom!*, 137
Hightower, Lynwood, 59
Hill, Byrd, 70–71, 72, 81
Hill, Louisa Eddins, 70, 81
Hill Crest Cemetery (Holly Springs, MS), 13–14, 36–39, 59, 61, 62, 91
Hines, Thomas S., 32
Hinton, Lt., 23
Historic Architecture in Mississippi (Crocker), 33
Holland, W. J. L., 13, 145
Holly Springs, MS: African American presence in, 14, 45–46, 59, 91; Civil War history of, 12–13, 63–64; Falkner family visiting, 5–6, 17, 20–24; geography of, 9–10; grand ball in, 22; history of, 10–12, 63–64; importance of, to Faulkner, 3, 28, 63–64; liquor available in, 27–28; names in, and Faulkner's places and characters, 29, 30, 37–38, 39–40, 42, 45–46, 56–63; names from, and fictional counterparts, 59–63; newspaper reporting travels in and through, 23–24; oral tradition in, 11, 15, 31, 34, 36, 39, 63–64, 77, 79, 96, 102, 131, 132; Oxford, travel to and from, 40–41; Oxford's proximity to, 5–6, 9–10, 20, 22–24, 63; present-day, 10–11; railroad in, 5, 12, 22–23, 42, 82, 154n84; slavery in (*see* slavery); social crowd of, 23–24; townspeople's views of Faulkner, 3–4, 18, 25, 63; train travel and, 5, 6, 17, 22–23, 40–41 (*see also* Holly Springs, MS: railroad in); yellow fever epidemic in, 13, 15, 37, 141–42, 144–45
"Holly Springs: Architecture of a Small Town" (Baum), 33
Holly Springs Courthouse, 6, 12, 13. *See also* Marshall County Courthouse
Holly Springs Depot, 7, 8, 39–41
Holly Springs Female Collegiate Institute, 15

Holly Springs Garden Club, 7, 11, 41–42, 90–91, 97
Holly Springs National Forest, 11
Holly Springs Pilgrimage, 7, 11–12, 18–19, 29, 30–31, 41, 71, 73, 86–87, 90–99, 129, 130, 140–41; clothing worn during, 96–98; first, 90–91; host tags for, 93, 94–95
Holm, April, 38
honeysuckle motif, in *Sound and the Fury*, 119
"Honor" (Faulkner), 62
hoop skirts, 97–98
Hopkins, Helen Bell, 30–31, 148n10
host and stranger, Faulkner's depiction of, 29, 92–96, 98–99
House, James J., 33
Howell, Elmo, 46
Hurdle, Frank, 94–95
Hurdle, Scarlett, 94, 95

I. C. Hotel (Holly Springs, MS), 22
Indian Removal Act of 1830, 10
Industrial Institute and College for the Education of White Girls of Mississippi (Mississippi University for Women), 57
Ingram, Ben, 60
Intruder in the Dust (Faulkner), 56, 57, 59–62, 154n82; windowpane inscriptions in, 7, 29, 78, 86–88, 98, 99
Invitation Oxford, 39
It Happened Here (Pruitt), 35

Johnson, Irene Walter, 19
Johnson, Robert L., 46
Jones, Egbert, 90–91
"Justice, A" (Faulkner), 60

Kartiganer, Donald, 134–35
Keats, John, 89
Kiefer, Charles A., 37
Knecht, Phillip, 13, 42
Knight's Gambit (Faulkner), 57, 61, 62
Kruse, Beth, 38
Kyle, Mrs., 24
Kyle and Mitchel, 70

Lafayette County, MS, 27, 28
Laurance, Evelyn, 24
Leak, Amelia McCarroll, 7, 65, 73, 80–85, 97, 128–39, 140–41, 143, 161n3, 161n4; stood up to Union military, 83
Leak, Betsy. *See* Francisco, Betsy Leak
Leak, Francis Terry, 100, 101, 133, 165n3. *See also Diary of Francis Terry Leak*
Leak, Janie, 103
Leak, John (son of Walter John Leak), 133, 135, 143, 144
Leak, Thomas (son of Walter John Leak), 133, 135, 143, 144
Leak, Wade, 133
Leak, Walter John, 84, 130–32, 133, 135, 143–44, 161n3, 165n3
Leak Diary. *See Diary of Francis Terry Leak*
Leak family: bringing lawsuits against the McCarrolls, 135–36, 143–44; plantation ledgers of (*see Diary of Francis Terry Leak*)
Leak/McCarroll/Francisco family, informing Faulkner's novels, 100–142
ledger imagery in *Absalom, Absalom!*, 45
Ledgers of History (Wolff), 3, 4, 18, 24–25, 45, 64, 68–70, 74, 94, 100
Lewellen and Alderson, 70
Light in August (Faulkner), 7, 8, 14, 45–55, 56, 59, 60, 98; abomination in, 52–55; religious fanaticism in, 52–55; sin in, 52–55
Like unto Like (Bonner), 11
Livingston Female Academy, 57, 157n130
Long, Alice, 10, 14, 15
Lowe, John, 44, 147n2
Luckett, Jean, 57
Ludie's story, 80–85. *See also* Booth, Mary Louisa Baugh (Ludie)
Ludie's window, 73–74, 78–89, 86, 92–95, 98–99, 129
Lynn, Jorja, 18–19, 93
Lyon, Ralph, 57

Mackie's Café (Holly Springs, MS), 6, 17
Mansion, The (Faulkner), 60, 61, 110, 154n82
Mann, Thomas, 19
Maplewood (Holly Springs, MS), 91
Marionettes, The (Faulkner), 26–27
Marshall County, MS, 10, 14–15, 90; African American presence in, 14, 45–46, 59, 91
Marshall County Courthouse, 5, 13, 149n48. *See also* Holly Springs Courthouse
Marshall County Museum, 145, 157n3
Mary Baldwin College (Staunton, VA), 57
Mattison, Katherine (Mrs. Frank), 90–91, 152n41
Mattison, Lewis, 23
Maury Institute (Holly Springs, MS). *See* Mississippi Synodical College
McAlexander, Hubert H., 8, 59, 60, 61, 62, 105–6, 109, 156n115, 157n132
McCarroll, Amelia. *See* Leak, Amelia McCarroll
McCarroll, Elizabeth Eddins, 70, 72–73, 81, 82–83, 84, 131–32, 133, 135, 143
McCarroll, John R., 70–73, 81, 82, 83–85, 90, 131–32, 161n4
McCarroll, John R. (son of John R. and Elizabeth Eddins McCarroll), 131, 135–36, 143–44
McCarroll, Sallie, 7, 81, 84, 97, 128–39, *138*
McCarroll farm ledgers, 127–28
McCarroll Place (Holly Springs, MS), 4, 7, 8, 9, 11, 18, 20, 21–22, 29, 43, 51, 55, 56, 61, 63, 69, 91, 97, 115, 136; Amelia returns to, 84, 133; deed for, 70–71; Faulkner views inscribed windowpane at, 73–74, 85–88, 93–95, 99; fence separating McCarroll Place and Strickland Place, 112, 119–21; gate between McCarroll Place and Strickland Place, *118, 120*; history of, 71–73; inscribed windowpane at, 73–74, 78–89, 86, 92–95, 98–99; Ludie Baugh sent to stay at, 79, 82; Ludie Baugh's spirit resides at, 74, 85; occupied by the Union military, 83; office in, 128–29; papers from (*see* McCarroll Place Papers); plantation desk at, 126–28, *127*; resident curse at, 65–68; and Strickland Place and the Compson House, 117–25; swing in side yard of, 110, *111*, 112, 113, 120

McCarroll Place Papers, 18, 29, *48*, 55, 118, 131, 140–42, 145, 150n7
McCarroll sisters, 45, 128–39. *See also* Leak, Amelia McCarroll; McCarroll, Sallie
McCarroll-Leak dispute, 135–36, 143–44
McClain, Mrs. G. W., 22
McCrosky, Levi, 90
McCrosky, Marjorie, 90–91
McDermott, Gertrude, 41
McDermott, James (Tippy), 40, 41
McDermott, Robert, 40, 41, 59, *61*
McDonald, John R., 143–44
McDonald, W. A., 24, 151n36
McDowell, Katharine Sherwood Bonner, 11
McDowell, Mary Bonner, 24
McGowan, Robert, *61*
McHaney, Thomas, 22, 147n2
McIntire, Carl, 57
McKie, Fannie, 23
McKie, Mary, 23
McMahon, Francis, 37, 38
Memphis, TN, 5, 6, 9–10, 12, 19, 22, 27, 28, 29, 40, 41, 72, 79–84, 91–93, 135–36, 144, 153n61, 164n43
Millgate, Michael, 96, 134, 137, 139, 166n22
miscegenation, 53–54
Mississippi Encyclopedia, 10, 12, 14, 56
Mississippi Industrial College (Holly Springs, MS), 14
Mississippi State Normal School (Holly Springs, MS), 14
Mississippi Synodical College (Holly Springs, MS), 6, 15, 17, 41, 58; Fenelon Hall, founded as, 15; Maury Institute, formerly known as, 15; North Mississippi Presbyterian College, formerly known as, 15, 58
Mitchell, Bobby, 36–37, 39, 71, 94–95
Mitchell, C. B., 24
Montes, Catalina, 96
Montrose (Holly Springs, MS), 11, 160n36
Moore, Delilah Love, 70
Moore, John B., 70
Mosby, Ray, 24
Mosquitoes (Faulkner), 62

Mount Holly (Foote, MS), 56–57
Murphy, R. C., 56
Murry family, 22, 23
My Brother Bill (J. Faulkner), 23, 150n4
My Days of Strength (Fearn), 19
"My Grandmother Millard" (Faulkner), 7, 79–80, 88–89, 120, 122, 139
Myers, Absalom, 62

Nabers, Benjamin D., 13–14
Neilson house (Oxford, MS), 7, 30
Nelson, James Henry, 33
Nelson, Maria Goodrich, 33
Nelson, Mr., 42
North Mississippi Presbyterian College. *See* Mississippi Synodical College

Oakleigh (Holly Springs, MS), 33, 42. *See also* Athenia
Oberti, Anacletus, 13
"Ode on a Grecian Urn" (Keats), 89, 126
ogre/augur, 43–44
Oldham, Estelle. *See* Faulkner, Estelle Oldham
Oxford, MS, 28, 30, 46, 136; dances in, 23–24; Holly Springs, travel to and from, 15, 40–41; Holly Springs' proximity to, 5–6, 9–10, 20, 22–24; impression of, made on Faulkner, 23; yellow fever quarantines in, 145

Palmer, Miss, 24
Parini, Jay, 85
Payne, Harvey, *48*, 150n7
Phi Sigma society, 23
Pilgrimage. *See* Holly Springs Pilgrimage
Pines, The (Holly Springs, MS), 91
Polk, Noel, 95–96, 137, 147n2, 168n45
Polk Place (Holly Springs, MS), 91
Pontotoc Creek, Treaty of, 10
Pontotoc Ridge, 9–10
Presbyterianism, Faulkner's negative view of, 46–55
Preserve Marshall County and Holly Springs, Inc., 11

Pruitt, Olga Reed, 35, 36
Pryor, Misses, 24
pure of heart, rewarding of, 52
Pylon (Faulkner), 62

Quiggins, Kinloch, 23

Ramey, Lucille (Dolly). *See* Faulkner, Lucille (Dolly) Ramey
Ramsey, Hyson, 37
Randolph, William, 10
Rapid Ramblings in Europe (Falkner), 21
Reivers, The (Faulkner), 7, 39–41, 60, 61, 62
religious fanaticism, 47, 50, 52–55
Reporter, The, 151n36
Requiem for a Nun (Faulkner), 7, 29, 57, 62; Holly Springs Pilgrimage and, 90–99; windowpane inscriptions in, 78, 88–99
Revels, Hiram Rhodes, 13–14
Ridge, Mark, 10, 14, 15
Rittelmeyer (the name), 6, 59, 62
Rollyson, Carl, 39
Rosa letters, *140*, 141–42
"Rose for Emily, A" (Faulkner), 7, 30–31, 32, *61*; arsenic in, 34–36; Confederate and Northern soldiers buried together in, 36–39; rose motif in, 7, 30–34; rose-tinted window in relation to, 31, 34. *See also* Grey Gables
Royal Canadian Air Force (RCAF), 41
Runyan, Harry, 59
Rust, Richard S., 14
Rust College A Cappella Choir, 14. *See also* Rust College Singers
Rust College (University; Shaw University; Shaw School), 14, 45–46
Rust College Singers, 91. *See also* Rust College A Cappella Choir
Rutland, J. W., 141

salvation, 46, 49, 52, 54–55
Sanctuary (Faulkner), 23, 62, 63, 154n84
Sartoris (Faulkner), 55, *59*, 60, *61*
Scott, Anne Firor, 57

Seay, Ruth LeGrand. *See* Strickland, Ruth LeGrand Seay
self-portrait, Faulkner's (autobiographical), 8, 29, 43–44, 78, 87–90, 92–93, 99, 121, 129, 137
Semple School, 113, 114
"Shall Not Perish" (Faulkner), *61*
Shaw, S. O., 14
Shaw University, 14, 45–46
Sheldon, K. J., 79
Sheldon and Sons (West Rutledge, VT), 36–37
Shipman, Rev. Mr., 22
Shipp, Lois Swaney, 33
Simmons, Lowry, 6
sin, 52–55, 68
slavery, 10, 11–12, 14, 18, 65, 82, 91, 96, 125; restitution and, 45; slave and servant cabins, 120–22. *See also* "Behind the Big House"
Smith, Carrie, 24, 151n36
Smith, Chesley Thorne, 58, 162n10
Smith, Harrison, 98
Smith, L. A., 33
Smith, Louise Caffey (Mrs. Leonard Marbury), 6, 7, 30, 31, 33–34
Smith, Mrs. L. A., 33
Smith House (Holly Springs, MS), 7, 11, 30–34, *32*
Soldiers' Pay (Faulkner), 38, 59, *61*, 62
Sound and the Fury, The (Faulkner), 7, 29, *59*, 60, 62; real-life antecedents for characters in, 100–116, 125; real-life antecedents for locations in, 117–25; swing image in, 101, 110–12, *111*, 114
Southern Horrors (Wells), 14
Southern Tapestry, A (McAlexander), 59, 60, *61*, 62, 156n115, 157n132
South Reporter (Holly Springs, MS), 71–72, 104, 105, 109, 151n36, 152n41, 154n84, 159n29
spirit world, Faulkner's belief in, 74, 85
spring/water, significance of, in *Sound and the Fury*, 120–21

INDEX

Stein, Jean, 78, 89–90, 92, 126, 152n48
Stewart, George G., 152n52
Stewart, George R., 117. *See also* Backus, Joseph M.
Strickland, Claude, 109, 113
Strickland, Frank, 34, 105, 109–10, 113
Strickland, Jacob Leonides, 34, 105, 107, 109, 110, 113, 164n43
Strickland, Mildred (Thompson), 83, 161n4
Strickland, Perle. *See* Badow, Perle Strickland
Strickland, Ruth LeGrand. *See* Weir, Ruth LeGrand Strickland
Strickland, Ruth LeGrand Seay (Mrs. Jacob Leonides), 107, 113
Strickland, William, 34, 103
Strickland Place (Holly Springs, MS), 34–35, 67, 82, 83, 101, *102*, 105, 106, 110, 112, 113, 114, *120*; and McCarroll Place and the Compson House, 117–25
Strickland-Badow marriage, 102–9, 115–16
Summer Trees (Holly Springs, MS), 91

Talking about William Faulkner (Wolff), 21, 147n4
Tampico, MS, 55
Tate, Sarah Doxey, 5, 24–25, 27, 106
Thompson, Jacob, 136
Thompson, Nettie Fant, 9
Thompson-Chandler House (Oxford, MS), 118–19, 121, 122–23
Tournament (Foote), 57
Town, The (Faulkner), 60, 61, 154n82
train travel, 5, 6, 17, 22–23, 40–41. *See also* Depot, the (Holly Springs, MS)
Treaty of Pontotoc Creek, 10
Trilogy, The (Snopes trilogy), 60, 61
Trotter, James F., 13–14
Tucker, Mrs. Jim, 90–91
"Two Dollar Wife" (Faulkner), 61
"Two Soldiers" (Faulkner), 61
Tyler, Rosa, 141, 142
Tyson, Helen Doxey, 127, 128, 129, 165n2
Tyson, Jack, 127, 165n2

University of Mississippi, Faulkner and Hindman Doxey Sr. together at, 26–27

Unvanquished, The (Faulkner), 7, 12–13, 23, 55, 60, 61, 78, 86, 87, 120, 122, 139, 158n9, 161n4

Van Dorn, Earl, 7–8, 12, 55–56
Van Dorn Avenue (Holly Springs, MS), 4, 8, 41, 56, 70, 82, 115
Van Dorn's raid, 7–8, 12, 55–56
Vicksburg, MS, 12, 29, 55, 83, 145

Wall Doxey State Park (near Holly Springs, MS), 11
Walter family, 18–19. *See also* Fearn, Anne Walter; Johnson, Irene Walter
Walter Place (Holly Springs, MS), 11, 12, 18, 19, 91, 93; Grant's takeover of the top floor, 83
Walthall, Edward, 13
Wasson, Ben, 39
Watson, Annie, 24
Watson, Jay, 96, 166n22
Watson, Jean, 24
Weir, Anne, 35, 36, 101, 111, 113, 114, 164n43
Weir, Ruby, 113, 164n43
Weir, Ruth LeGrand Strickland, 34, 35, 36, 100, 110–16, 164n43
Weir, William Strickland, 34–35, 113–14, 164n40, 164n43
Wells (Ida B.) Museum (Holly Springs, MS), 14
Wells, Dean Faulkner, 136
Wells, Ida B., 14
West, Absolom Madden, 13, 42, 62
White Rose of Memphis, The (W. C. Falkner), 138
Wild Palms, The (Faulkner), 6, 62
Wilkins, J. P., 22
William Faulkner A to Z (Fargnoli and Golay), 59
Williams, Joan, 6, 27
Williamson, Joel, 20–21, 22, 46, 57, 98, 145, 150n5, 166n22
window etchings: in Faulkner's novels, 7, 29, 78, 86–99; in Oxford and environs, 87
Winter, Robert Milton, 12, 19, 42, 47, 106, 145
Wittjen, Mrs. Jack, 91

Wolff, Sally, 21, 64–65, 67, 68–70, 74, 75, 80, 84, 147n2
Word, Thomas Jefferson, 20–21
workless/worklessness, 88–90, 94, 98–99
Wyatt, Gwen, 19, 40–41

yellow fever epidemic (1878), 13, 15, 141–42, 144–45
Yellow Fever House (Holly Springs, MS), 145
Yellow Fever Martyrs Church and Museum (Holly Springs, MS), 145
"Young Goodman Brown" (Hawthorne), 53

ABOUT THE AUTHOR

Sally Wolff earned her bachelor's degree at Vanderbilt University and her master's and PhD degrees in English from the Laney Graduate School at Emory University. She previously has published four books about Southern literature and three books about Emory history, with the latest book published in fall 2023.

Her previous work on William Faulkner includes *Ledgers of History: William Faulkner, an Almost Forgotten Friendship, and an Antebellum Diary* (LSU Press, 2010), which has been called "one of the most exciting literary finds in recent history" and "a major discovery in Faulkner scholarship." Her twenty-one invited speaking engagements around the country about this book included lectures at the Library of Congress in Washington, DC, and the William J. Clinton Presidential Center.

Wolff is also the author of *Talking about William Faulkner* (1996), coeditor of *Southern Mothers: Fact and Fiction in Southern Women's Writing* (1999), both with LSU Press, and *A Dark Rose: Love in Eudora Welty's Stories and Novels* (LSU Press, 2015). She teaches "Literature and Medicine" at Emory and writes and lectures about Southern writers, including Eudora Welty, with whom she shared an eighteen-year literary friendship.

With Emory University Vice President Gary S. Hauk, she coedited an Emory history book, titled *Where Courageous Inquiry Leads: The Emerging Life of Emory University* (Hauk and King, Bookhouse Group, 2010). Other publications on Emory history include *To the Ultimate Good: A History of the Emory Clinic*, Sally Wolff King, ed. (Bookhouse Group, 2019), *The Enduring Legacy of James Edgar Paullin, MD*, by Carter Smith Jr., Sally Wolff King and Sylvia Wrobel, eds. (Bookhouse Group, 2021), and a new book, *The Smartest and Most Promising: A History of the Emory University School of Medicine*, Armand Hendee and Juha Kokko, with Gary S. Hauk, Sally Wolff King, and Sylvia Wrobel, eds., was published by Bookhouse Group in September 2023.

Wolff served for twenty years as assistant and associate dean in the College of Arts and Sciences at Emory and as assistant vice president in the Emory University Office of the President. She taught in the Department of English for thirty years and currently is the historian emerita of the Robert W. Woodruff Health Sciences Center.

For more information about her work, visit www.educationalconsulting.services and www.med.emory.edu/directory/profile/?u=SWOLFF.

www.ingramcontent.com/pod-product-compliance
Lightning Source LLC
Chambersburg PA
CBHW030236240426
43663CB00037B/1170